A Failure of Nerve

EDWIN H. FRIEDMAN

A

FAILURE

OF

NERVE

Leadership
in the Age of the
Quick Fix

Editors
Margaret M. Treadwell
Edward W. Beal

Seabury Books
NEW YORK

Library of Congress Cataloging-in-Publication Data
Friedman, Edwin H.
  A failure of nerve : leadership in the age of the quick fix / Edwin H. Friedman ; editors, Margaret M. Treadwell, Edward W. Beal. -- [New ed.].
      p. cm.
  Includes index.
  ISBN-13: 978-1-59627-042-8 (pbk.)
  I. Leadership. I. Treadwell, Margaret M. II. Beal, Edward W. III. Title.

BF637.L4F75 2007
158'.4--dc22

2006033685

Cover design: Stefan Killen

Printed in the United States of America.

Church Publishing, Inc.
445 Fifth Avenue
New York, NY 10016
www.churchpublishing.org

◆CONTENTS

◆ ACKNOWLEDGMENTS

Colleagues and friends often asked my father how he found time to be so prolific. Resting his mouth left of center while the corners flirted with a smile, he'd say in his best Murray Bowen Tennessee accent, "Because I have to." Like a shark that must keep moving to survive, this is how my father saw writing.

My father considered *A Failure of Nerve: Leadership in the Age of the Quick Fix* the summation of all his ideas. His untimely death threatened to prevent its completion. My mother, Carlyn Friedman, refused to let his legacy die with him. With the help of Ted Beal, Peggy Treadwell, my brother Ari Friedman, and the faculty members at the Center for Family Process, my mother brought my father's manuscript to the public in what she deemed a labor of love.

Edward M. (Ted) Beal's leadership, professional knowledge, editing judgment, and connections were crucial to my father's original manuscript and to this current edition. Of equal importance were his friendship, spirit, and perfectly anointed humor.

Margaret (Peggy) Treadwell's special interest in the connection between emotional process and spirituality bridged my father's coupling of the religious sector with family therapy in both editions. Her introduction of *A Failure of Nerve* to Cynthia Shattuck made this new revised edition of the 1999 private publication possible. Their close collaboration and boundless optimism also kept the project thriving.

Susan Luff, Myrna Carpenter, Mickie Crimone, and Gary Emanuel at the Center for Family Process were and continue to be integral in spreading "the word of Ed," as my mother affectionately called it. Their judicious consultation and unwavering dedication have allowed my father's ideas to proliferate a decade later.

I would especially like to thank Cynthia Shattuck for her vision, enthusiasm, and clear grasp of my father's work. Her brilliant editing, creativity, and playfulness brought new vitality and excitement to this edition.

Special thanks are due also to Susan Kanaan, Jubran Kanaan, Elizatheth Geitz, and Susan Kilborn.

A Failure of Nerve: Leadership in the Age of the Quick Fix could not exist without my mother's commitment and unique insight into my father's thinking. It is to her memory this book is dedicated.

SHIRA FRIEDMAN BOGART

◆ EDITORS' PREFACE

T he premature death of our colleague and friend Edwin H. Friedman on October 31, 1996 illustrates the moral of his fable *The Bridge:* "When things start going really well, watch out." Internationally known as a lecturer and author, Ed's sense of paradox, humor, and particular brand of storytelling were the trademark of his teaching style:

- ◆ "Playfulness can get you out of a rut more successfully than seriousness."
- ◆ "Triangles are the plaque in the arteries of communication and stress is the effect of our position in the triangle of our families."
- ◆ "If you are a leader, expect sabotage."
- ◆ "The colossal misunderstanding of our time is the assumption that insight will work with people who are unmotivated to change. If you want your child, spouse, client, or boss to shape up, stay connected while changing yourself rather than trying to fix them."

Ed's immediate draw was his paradoxical wit and playfulness, which he always attributed to his mother—"the quickest one-liner I ever met." His ability to capture ambiguities and paradox with a turn of phrase energized and delighted audiences. Those of us who worked with him were challenged in a way that brought hope and courage in defining ourselves, or as Ed entitled his ideas in one sold-out conference, "charting your course in a changing world." When we thanked him, he usually responded, "I'm just the coach: you're the athlete."

Generation to Generation was published in 1985 and provided a new way of thinking about emotional process at home and at work in religious, educational, therapeutic, and business systems. *Friedman's Fables* came out in 1990. By then Ed was deeply engaged with his work on what would become *A Failure of Nerve*, testing it out with students and faculty and incorporating changes raised by questions about leadership as a function of emotional systems. His sudden death was a shock to everyone close to him: many of us had believed that the publication of *A Failure of Nerve* would be the crowning achievement of a remarkable mind and career.

Ed died before completing the second half of his work, in which he planned to challenge the seldom questioned assumption that human beings function solely according to their nature, gender, or background. Rather, he believed they function according to the position they occupy within the emotional processes of their relationship system, whether family, church, or business. Ed asserted that from the perspective of the emotional process view of reality, the way most leadership programs understand the human phenomenon is tantamount to still assuming that the world is flat.

Ed's widow, Carlyn Friedman, believed *A Failure of Nerve*, even in its unfinished form, was an important part of her husband's legacy and she was committed to bringing it to the public. She therefore invited us to be the book's principal editors and to make it ready for publication through the Edwin Friedman Trust. As a colleague of Ed's, Ted had already been asked to read the manuscript and offer comments at many points; likewise, as Ed's adjunct faculty member, Peggy knew drafts of various chapters. Yet reading the manuscript in its entirety was particularly exciting because it gave us the opportunity to observe Ed Friedman's mind at work—like seeing an artist's sketch embedded in a partially finished painting. Even though what he envisioned and described was not fully realized, we believed that many readers would appreciate *A Failure of Nerve* as an impetus to free the imagination and stimulate new ways of thinking. Furthermore, the task of actually completing the manuscript became less important to us as we realized, in consultation with Ed's faculty, that while we could edit the syntax, spelling, punctuation, and organization of the text, we could not improve on the original thinking. If we tried to fill in the missing pieces, it would not be Ed's book.

The book was privately published in 1999 under the auspices of the Trust and went into a second printing in 2003. In 2004, while keynoting a conference on congregational leadership in San Diego, Peggy met Cynthia Shattuck, now editorial director at Church Publishing. Cynthia, who was intrigued with the book's story and especially its healthy "underground life," expressed interest in bringing it to a wider audience. Ed's children, Shira Bogart and Ari Friedman, were enthusiastic and we all agreed that Cynthia's understanding of our vision made her the best possible editor.

Ed was always aware that the original manuscript, even in its unfinished state, needed more work: cutting and polishing, reorganizing, checking historical references, taking out redundancies and duplications, rethinking some shifts and emphases. Throughout the editing process we have stayed faithful to these principles. Readers of this new edition for a larger trade and professional audience will also see that the design is more consistent and, we hope, clearer and more inviting to those previously unacquainted with Friedman's work. The original publication consisted of ten chapters written in two parts, but since the final chapters were unfinished, we decided to eliminate this division. The second half of the book is now three chapters in length with a short epilogue, and we have added to them material from the "unfinished chapter notes" originally situated at the end of each chapter. Finally, the copies of ancient maps originally in the first chapter have been removed and we have slightly edited the text to make sure Ed's points are still clear.

As in the original version, even though what he envisioned and described is not fully realized, we believe that "the big picture" does emerge. Ed Friedman's character and wit shine through these pages, continuing to bring his original ideas, fresh insights, and new strategies to light. It has been an honor and privilege to work with Carlyn, Shira, and Ari Friedman so that this important piece of Ed's lifework can reach a larger public on the tenth anniversary of his death.

EDWARD W. (TED) BEAL, M.D.
MARGARET M. (PEGGY) TREADWELL, L.I.C.S.W.
OCTOBER 31, 2006

*Those who wish to disrupt leadership will always
frame the problem in terms of liberty and order,
while those in positions of leadership will always
see the problem as one of order and chaos.*

Introduction

◆ THE PROBLEM
WITH LEADERSHIP

In *Five Stages of Greek Religion,* Gilbert Murray suggested that after
Socrates had "dis-illusioned" his society, Greek civilization was
around the corner from the Renaissance. But, he said, they
seemed to panic at the prospect and, instead, bought into new myths.
In a chapter entitled "A Failure of Nerve," he wrote:

> The great thing to remember is that the mind of man cannot be
> enlightened permanently by merely teaching him to reject some
> particular set of superstitions. There is an infinite supply of other
> superstitions always at hand; and the mind that desires such things,
> that is, the mind that has not trained itself to the hard discipline of
> reasonableness and honesty, will, as soon as its devils are cast out,
> proceed to fill itself with their relations.

In this book on leadership, I will describe a similar "failure of nerve"
affecting American civilization today. But, I will add, when anxiety
reaches certain thresholds, "reasonableness and honesty" no longer
defend against illusion, and then even the most learned ideas can
begin to function as superstitions.

I believe there exists throughout America today a rampant sabo-taging of leaders who try to stand tall amid the raging anxiety-storms of our time. It is a highly reactive atmosphere pervading all the institutions of our society—a regressive mood that contaminates the decision-making processes of government and corporations at the highest level, and, on the local level, seeps down into the delib-erations of neighborhood church, synagogue, hospital, library, and school boards. It is "something in the air" that affects the most ordi-nary family no matter what its ethnic background. And its frus-trating effect on leaders is the same no matter what their gender, race, or age.

It is my perception that this leadership-toxic climate runs the danger of squandering a natural resource far more vital to the continued evolution of our civilization than any part of the environ-ment. We are polluting our own species. The more immediate threat to the regeneration, and perhaps even the survival, of American civi-lization is internal, not external. It is our tendency to adapt to its immaturity. To come full circle, this kind of emotional climate can only be dissipated by clear, decisive, well-defined leadership. For whenever a "family" is driven by anxiety, what will also always be present is a failure of nerve among its leaders.

This book is for parents and presidents. It is also for CEOs and educators, prioresses and coaches, healers and generals, managers and clergy. It is about leadership in the land of the quick fix, about lead-ership in a society so reactive that it cannot choose leaders who might calm its anxiety. It is about the need for clarity and decisive-ness in a civilization that inhibits the development of leaders with clarity and decisiveness. It is for leaders who have questioned the widespread triumphing of data over maturity, technique over stamina, and empathy over personal responsibility. And it is for anyone at all who has become suspicious of the illusions of change—suspicious of the modern fashion wherein solutions, as well as symptoms, burst upon us in every field of endeavor (manage-ment, healing, education, parenting) and then disappear as unexpect-edly as they had first appeared, only to be supplanted by the fad of another "issue" or cure, sending everyone back to square one.

The emphasis here will be on strength, not pathology; on chal-lenge, not comfort; on self-differentiation, not herding for togetherness. This is a difficult perspective to maintain in a "seatbelt society" more oriented toward safety than adventure. This book is not, therefore, for those who prefer peace to progress. It is not for those who mistake another's well-defined stand for coercion. It is not for those who fail to see how in any family or institution a perpetual concern for consensus leverages power to the extremists. And it is not for those who lack the nerve to venture out of the calm eye of good feelings and togetherness and weather the storm of protest that inevitably surrounds a leader's self-definition. For, whether we are considering a family, a work system, or an entire nation, the resistance that sabotages a leader's initiative usually has less to do with the "issue" that ensues than with the fact that the leader took initiative.

It will be the thesis of this work that leadership in America is stuck in the rut of trying harder and harder without obtaining significantly new results. The rut runs deep, affecting all the institutions of our society irrespective of size or purpose. It even affects those institutions that try to tackle the problem: universities, think-tanks, and consultants. These institutions are "stuck," and there exists a connection between the paralysis that leaders experience and the paralysis in the thinking processes of those who would get them unstuck.

In the pages that follow I will show that America's leadership rut has both a conceptual and an emotional dimension that reinforce one another. The conceptual dimension is the inadequacy of what I shall refer to as *the social science construction of reality.* This construction fails to explain these emotional processes, much less to offer leaders a way of gaining some separation from their regressive influence. The emotional dimension is the chronic anxiety that currently ricochets from sea to shining sea. However, the word *emotional* as used throughout this work is not to be equated with feelings, which are a later evolutionary development. While it includes feelings, the word refers primarily to the instinctual side of our species that we share in common with all other forms of life.

By *the social science construction of reality* I mean a worldview that focuses on classifications such as the psychological diagnosis of individuals or their "personality profiles" and sociological or anthropological niche (categorized according to culture, gender, class, race, age, and so on) rather than on what will be emphasized in this work: the emotional processes that transcend those categories and that all forms of "colonized protoplasm" share in common, irrespective of those differences. This applies in particular to the tension between the forces for self and togetherness; the reciprocal, adaptive, compensatory functioning by the partners to any relationship; and the evolutionary consequences of self-differentiation for both that individual and other members of his or her community.

These two dimensions of America's leadership rut, the conceptual and the emotional, are inextricably linked. The emotional climate of a society affects not only the models it conceives and clings to; it also influences what information we consider important and which issues attract our attention.

In neither case, therefore, can the way out be obtained simply by developing some new method for "tinkering with the mechanics," or by redoubling our efforts to try harder. The way out, rather, requires shifting our orientation to the way we think about relationships, from one that focuses on techniques that motivate others to one that focuses on the leader's own presence and being.

In the first part of this book, I will describe the emotional processes in society that I see affecting the functioning of "parents and presidents." And I will show how our denial of those processes in both families and in society at large (1) erodes and devalues the individuation necessary for effective leadership; and (2) influences the very way we conceptualize leadership problems to begin with. Then, in the second part of this book, I will present new ways of understanding leadership that are applicable to all families and institutions, taking those emotional processes into account and emphasizing the importance of the leader's own self-differentiation.

These views on leadership and American society did not burst upon me in some "Eureka" moment of insight. They evolved gradually during forty years of teaching and practicing in a spectrum of fields that included various branches of the helping professions, the military, management, business, and government. This pool of experience has afforded both a long-range and a broad-based perspective, with nodal moments of awareness. Therefore I will describe in these introductory pages how my experience increasingly raised doubts in my mind about the usefulness for leaders of the social science construction of reality; how those doubts eventually led me to reorient my views on leadership; and some of the radically new perspectives for leadership training that came out of that reorientation to reality.

◆ HOW I CAME TO THIS STUDY

I have lived and worked in the Washington, D. C., metropolitan area for almost four decades. During this period I have watched families and institutions recycle their problems for several generations, despite enormous efforts to be innovative. The opportunity to observe this firsthand was provided by my involvement in the major institutions designed by our civilization to foster change: religion, education, psychotherapy, and politics (I have been here since Eisenhower). That experience included twenty years as a pulpit rabbi, an overlapping twenty-five years as an organizational consultant and family therapist with a broadly ecumenical practice, and several years of service as a community relations specialist for the Johnson White House helping metropolitan areas throughout the United States to voluntarily desegregate housing, before Congress passed appropriate civil rights legislation.

Eventually, the accumulation of this experience began to show me how similar all of our "systems of salvation" are in their structure, the way they formulate problems, the range of their approaches, and their rationalizations for their failures. It was, indeed, the basic similarity in their *thinking processes,* despite their different sociological classifications, that first led me to consider the possibility that our constant failure to change families and institutions fundamentally has less to do with finding the right methods than with misleading emotional and conceptual factors that reside within society itself.

For example, having been in the rare position of working in the fields of both healing and management, I could not help notice that the batting average in the war on cancer and the batting average in the struggle to heal chronically troubled institutions is remarkably similar, with cancer perhaps a little ahead. I have been struck by how families, corporations, and other kinds of institutions are constantly trying to cure their own chronic ills through amputations, "strong medicine," transfusions, and other forms of surgery, only to find that, even when successful for the moment, the excised tumor returns several years later in "cells" that never knew the "cells" that left.

"New blood" rarely thwarts malignant processes, anywhere. Indeed, with both cancer and institutions, malignant cells that appear to be dead can often revive if they receive new nourishment. Or, to put the problem another way, when we say something has gone into remission, where do we think it has gone?

I came to see that malignancy is rarely only a physical state; it is almost always the perversion of a basic life principle. Ignoring the emotional processes connected to systemic disease process, either in an organism or an organization and whether one is an oncologist or a business consultant, will rarely produce a lasting cure. In both medicine and management, administrative, managerial, and technical solutions seldom alter emotional processes fundamentally. Furthermore, focus on psychology is not focus on emotional processes, and focus on emotional processes cannot be reduced to psychology. It raises the question of whether or not psychology as a cultural phenomenon is a force for denial rather than a force for insight.

Another experience that contributed to my doubts about the adequacy of our society's traditional models for helping leaders was that although I was quite knowledgeable about what conventional social science theories have to say about marriage and child development, over the long run I was constantly fooled in my expectations of how children would grow up, how marriages would turn out, and what organizational ventures would succeed. In addition, I was continually bewildered by the fact that the same values that motivated people to do good work in society often did not seem to operate in their closest personal relationships. It was, in fact, the consistency of my inability to predict the future course of relationships in families and institutions over the course of several decades that first led me to question the adequacy of the social science construction of reality and eventually led me to wonder if an intended source of enlightenment had become, in fact, a force for denial.

What other crucial variables, I began to ask, had conventional models in the field failed to take into account? For example, if one serves a congregation in Bethesda, Maryland—the site of the National Institutes of Health and the Bethesda Naval Hospital, a hub for think-tanks of every imaginable stripe, and the bedroom community for thousands of lawyers, administrators, physicians, and other scientists—then there is a good chance that most of your congregation are either therapists or in therapy. Over the years, I often witnessed successful results from the various forms of counseling individuals experienced, either in symptom relief or an increased capacity to function better. But I also saw from my three-generation perspective that these various forms of therapy generally did not succeed in preventing family emotional processes from passing the problems of one generation on to the next.

This has remained constant, from my perspective, no matter what new form of therapy became fashionable, what symptom became faddish, or how any traditional counseling approach was reinvented. It was almost as though all forms of therapy succeeded only in helping people acquire new characteristics; and, as is well known, acquired characteristics are never inherited by the next generation unless they enter an organism's germ plasm. What did it take, I began to ask myself, to get into the "germ plasm" of family or organizational emotional processes?

A third observation that contributed to my questioning traditional social science models was my experience with families from many different cultures. As Washington is a mecca for people from all over the world, sooner or later I came into contact with families from a very broad spectrum of backgrounds that included every habitable continent on the planet—literally, the "four corners of the earth." Although the social science construction of reality tends to emphasize how families differ from one another, I began to see that knowledge of what they have in common could be more important, as a basis both for promoting change and for enabling leaders and consultants to recognize the universal elements of emotional processes found in all institutions as well as in all families.

Rather than assuming that a family's cultural background determined its emotional processes, I found it far more useful to see culture as the medium through which a family's own unique multi-generational emotional process worked its art. I began to see that stripping families of their cultural camouflage forced family members to be more accountable for their actions and their responses to one another. I also saw that once one focused on how families were similar rather than on how they differed, it was possible to see universal "laws" of emotional process that were obscured by becoming absorbed in the myriad data on family differences. And later I found that this principle applied to other kinds of institutions as well.

For example, as I began to focus on emotional process rather than cultural background, it eventually became obvious to me that whatever the nature of a family's customs and ceremonies, the universal problem for all partnerships, marital or otherwise, was not getting closer; it was preserving self in a close relationship, something that no one made of flesh and blood seems to do well. (I eventually came to define my marriage counseling, no matter what the cultural mix, as trying to help people separate so that they would not have to "separate.")

Another universal principle of family life transcending cultural or ethnic differences seemed to be that whatever their affliction, individuals who are cut off from their families generally do not heal until they have been reconnected.

Similarly, there seemed to be three universal laws regarding the children of all families that transcended their cultural and sociological characteristics.

◆ The children who work through the natural problems of maturing with the least amount of emotional or physical residue are those whose parents have made them *least* important to their own salvation. (Throughout this work, *maturity* will be defined as *the willingness to take responsibility for one's own emotional being and destiny.*)

◆ Children rarely succeed in rising above the maturity level of their parents, and this principle applies to all mentoring, healing, or administrative relationships.

◆ Parents cannot produce change in a troubling child, no matter how caring, savvy, or intelligent they may be, until they become completely and totally fed up with their child's behavior.

Soon I began to realize that cultural camouflage also obscured the universality of emotional process in institutions. For example, frequently, the leaders of a church would come to me seeking techniques for dealing with a member of the staff or a member of the congregation who was acting obstreperously, who was ornery, and who intimidated everyone with his gruffness. I might say to them, "This is not a matter of technique; it's a matter of taking a stand, telling this person he has to shape up or he cannot continue to remain a member of the community." And the church leaders would respond, "But that's not the Christian thing to do." (Synagogue leaders also tolerate abusers for the same reason.) Overall, this long-range perspective brought me to the point of wondering if there were not some unwitting conspiracy within society itself to avoid recognizing the emotional variables that, for all their lack of concreteness, are far more influential in their effects on institutions than the more obvious data that society loves to measure. Perhaps data collection serves as a way of avoiding the emotional variables.

After all, the denial of emotional process is evident in society at large. If, for example, we succeed in reducing the number of cigarettes smoked by our nation's youth but do nothing to reduce the level of chronic anxiety throughout the nation, then the addiction will just take another form, and the same children who were vulnerable to one kind of addiction will become easy prey for the as-yet unimagined new temptation.

It may be in the ubiquitous phenomenon of terrorism that one can most easily see how universal emotional processes transcend the conventional categories of the social science construction of reality. According to the latter, families are different from nations, profit-making corporations are different from nonprofit corporations, medical institutions are different from school systems, one nation's infrastructure is different from another's, and so on. Yet whether we are considering any family, any institution, or any nation, for terrorism to hold sway the same three *emotional* prerequisites must always persist in that relationship system.

◆ There must be a sense that no one is in charge—in other words, the overall emotional atmosphere must convey that there is no leader with "nerve."

◆ The system must be vulnerable to a hostage situation. That is, its leaders must be hamstrung by a vulnerability of their own, a vulnerability to which the terrorist—whether a bomber, a client, an employee, or a child—is always exquisitely sensitive.

◆ There must be among both the leaders and those they lead an unreasonable faith in "being reasonable."

From an emotional process view of leadership, whether we are talking about families or the family of nations, these three emotional characteristics of a system are the differences that count.

◆ LEADERSHIP AS EMOTIONAL PROCESS

Since the publication of my first thoughts on the subject in 1985 in *Generation to Generation,* I have had the opportunity to present my evolving concepts of leadership and the emotional processes in institutions and society both in workshops and as a consultant in forty states. At the beginning, I worked with leaders in almost every branch of the helping professions and their various divisions (healers, teachers, attorneys, educators, clergy). Eventually, my work came to include as diverse a range as religious communities, state governors and their staffs, managers from various segments of business and industry, and the General Staff of the United States Army in Europe. It was then, after my presentations to thirty-two generals, that I first began to see how similar the approach to leadership problems was throughout our civilization. After two days of presentations, a three-star general, the commander of an entire Army corps—two panzer divisions—stood up and said to me, "You know, one of our problems is that the sergeant-majors coddle the new recruits, and we keep telling them that such helpfulness will not make them very good soldiers in the field." And then he turned to his fellow officers and said, "But from what Ed has been saying here the past two days, we're not going to have any more luck changing the sergeant-majors than they are having trying to change the new recruits."

Now this man had three stars on his shoulder; how much more authority would you want? He commanded more weapons of destruction than exploded in all of World War II; how much more power do you need? Yet neither his authority nor his power were enough to ensure a "command presence." And I began to think about similar frustrations reported to me by imaginative psychiatrists who were frustrated by head nurses, creative clergy who were stymied by church treasurers, aggressive CEOs who were hindered by division chiefs, mothers who wished to take more responsible stands with their children but who were blindsided by their chronically passive husbands, not to mention my experience of watching nine eager Presidents sabotaged by a chronically recalcitrant Congress.

Eventually I came to see that this "resistance," as it is usually called, is more than a reaction to novelty; it is part and parcel of the systemic process of leadership. Sabotage is not merely something to be avoided or wished away; instead, it comes with the territory of leading, whether the "territory" is a family or an organization. And a leader's capacity to recognize sabotage for what it is—that is, a systemic phenomenon connected to the shifting balances in the emotional processes of a relationship system and *not* to the institution's specific issues, makeup, or goals—is the key to the kingdom.

My experience with the superiors of religious orders also helped me see the similarity of all leadership problems, irrespective of the culture of the institution. After two days of intense and varied discussions of the problems of being a leader in a monastery— problems one could just as easily find in a corporation or a street gang, such as cliques, backbiting, withdrawal, polarizations, subversion—one superior rose and said, "We know that while we entered the monastery in order to leave the world, we also brought that world with us." But what he did not understand was that these issues stemmed not from what they had "learned" outside and brought in, but from the basic nature of life.

My travels affected my thinking in two ways. One result was that every concept and perspective in this work has been put to the challenge of other leaders' responses and constantly refined and modified through such dialogue. Second, during this feedback process, several factors began to emerge so consistently that I began to see a pattern. While each branch of American society thought its troubles were due to something within its own discipline (religion, therapy, medicine, education, government, business) or were peculiar to its own region ("Here in the South," the Midwest, the Far West, the Northeast), the problems were, as I had already begun to suspect, nationwide.

The more my perspective broadened, the more confirmed I became in my view that contemporary leadership dilemmas have less to do with the specificity of given problems, the nature of a particular technique, or the makeup of a given group than with the way everyone is framing the issues. In addition, I began to realize that this similarity in thinking processes had to do with regressive (in the sense of counter-evolutionary) emotional processes that could be found everywhere. Nor did gender, race, or ethnicity seem to make a difference in the strength or the effects of these processes.

Here are four major similarities in the thinking and functioning of America's families and institutions that I have observed everywhere, and which I believe are at the heart of the problem of contemporary America's orientation toward leadership:

◆ *A regressive, counter-evolutionary trend* in which the most dependent members of any organization set the agendas and where adaptation is constantly toward weakness rather than strength, thus leveraging power to the recalcitrant, the passive-aggressive, and the most anxious members of an institution rather than toward the energetic, the visionary, the imaginative, and the motivated.

◆ *A devaluation of the process of individuation* so that leaders tend to rely more on expertise than on their own capacity to be decisive. Consultants (to both families and organizations) contribute further to this denial of individuation by offering solutions instead of promoting their clients' capacity to define themselves more clearly.

◆ *An obsession with data and technique* that has become a form of addiction and turns professionals into data-junkies and their information into data junkyards. As a result, decision-makers avoid or deny the very emotional processes within their families, their institutions, and within society itself that might contribute to their institution's "persistence of form." (This phrase is borrowed from biology, which tries to understand the uncanny self-organizing ability of some embryos that duplicate themselves even after some of their parts have been rearranged or cut away.)

◆ *A widespread misunderstanding about the relational nature of destructive processes in families and institutions* that leads leaders to assume that toxic forces can be regulated through reasonableness, love, insight, role-modeling, inculcation of values, and striving for consensus. It prevents them from taking the kind of stands that set limits to the invasiveness of those who lack self-regulation.

This book will develop an approach to leadership that goes in a different direction. It will encourage leaders to focus first on their own integrity and on the nature of their own presence rather than through techniques for manipulating or motivating others. I will suggest that the importance of leaders being well-informed is over-rated, and that the focus on the intellect outside of an emotional context is actually anti-intellectual. It will show leaders how not to be victimized nor held hostage by victims, and offer empowering models of leadership and relationship systems based on the natural thinking systems found in contemporary biology and physics, rather than on "psychological" and other abstract social science models that, despite the accuracy of their data, tend to view life in the para-digm of nineteenth-century mechanics.

My own understanding of the fact that leadership is essentially an *emotional* process rather than a *cognitive* phenomenon, and my aware-ness of the vital importance of well-differentiated leadership for the functioning and survival of institutions, came to me in the following manner. I had been coaching members of various professions concerning either the relational problems experienced by their clients or those that were occurring in their own work systems. As I listened to everyone describe their bonds and their binds, the following universal law of leadership began to formulate itself—one that I regard as the bottom-line concept of this entire work:

In any type of institution whatsoever, when a self-directed, imag-inative, energetic, or creative member is being consistently frustrated and sabotaged rather than encouraged and supported, what will turn out to be true one hundred percent of the time, regardless of whether the disrupters are supervisors, subordinates, or peers, is that the person at the very top of that institution is a peace-monger. By that I mean a highly anxious risk-avoider, someone who is more concerned with good feelings than with progress, someone whose life revolves around the axis of consensus, a "middler," someone who is so incapable of taking well-defined stands that his "disability" seems to be genetic, someone who functions as if she had been filleted of her backbone, someone who treats conflict or anxiety like mustard gas—one whiff, on goes the emotional gas mask, and he flits. Such leaders are often "nice," if not charming.

This principle of organizational life is so universal it may be rooted in protoplasm itself. It will operate to the same extent regardless of the sociological or psychological profiles of the individuals involved, and it is equally applicable to a family or a nation—that is, to a parent or a president.

While I first saw this leadership principle at work when consulting with various types of organizations, the more I thought about its systemic character, the more I came to realize that what I had been observing with regard to families for more than a quarter of a century was identical. I began to see that if I were to consider, with a two- or three-generation perspective, the thousands of families I had observed go into crisis (whether the crisis was due to sudden loss, acting-out children, severe illness, intense polarized marital conflict, financial problems, or other external impacts), without question the single variable that most distinguished the families that survived and flourished from those that disintegrated was the presence of what I shall refer to throughout this work as *a well-differentiated leader.*

I want to stress that by *well-differentiated leader* I do not mean an autocrat who tells others what to do or orders them around, although any leader who defines himself or herself clearly may be perceived that way by those who are not taking responsibility for their own emotional being and destiny. Rather, I mean someone who has clarity about his or her own life goals, and, therefore, someone who is less likely to become lost in the anxious emotional processes swirling about. I mean someone who can be separate while still remaining connected, and therefore can maintain a modifying, non-anxious, and sometimes challenging presence. I mean someone who can manage his or her own reactivity to the automatic reactivity of others, and therefore be able to take stands at the risk of displeasing. It is not as though some leaders can do this and some cannot. No one does this easily, and most leaders, I have learned, can improve their capacity.

Eventually, I found this correlation between self-differentiation in the leader and the nature of the emotional processes of any human institution to be so universal that I was often able to make predictions about how the leader was functioning within minutes of hearing someone talk about the nature of their institution's (or family's) problems. The fact that I found the principle to hold true for both families and organizations, and for leaders of both genders and any racial or ethnic background, again forced me to question the value for leadership of the social science construction of reality. I knew that its categories have often been accurately described and are useful in social planning, but I began to wonder if these were the differences that really mattered when it came to the problems of leadership.

◆ THE SYSTEMIC POWER OF LEADERSHIP

I also saw something else regarding leadership and systemic emotional process that ultimately revolutionized my approach to leadership training. When creative, imaginative, and self-starting members of any organization are being sabotaged rather than supported, the poorly differentiated person "at the top" does not have to be in direct contact with the person being undercut. In fact, neither even has to know that the other exists. What I began to appreciate from that moment on was the wide-ranging *systemic power* of leadership—specifically, that the functioning of leaders somehow affected the institution they lead on a far more fundamental level than could be accounted for by traditional psychological concepts that focus on the brain, such as role-modeling, emulation, identification, or personality profiles. Institutions, I was coming to see, could be conceptualized as emotional fields—environments of force that, for all their influence over people's thinking processes, were, like magnetic fields or gravitational fields, largely invisible to the naked eye.

What made these systemic processes invisible was the fact that they could not be explained by the usual mechanistic models that emphasize flow charts, trickle-down concepts, and motivational techniques. It was not that such models were wrong, but rather that they were inadequate for understanding the organic nature of human colonization. Explaining families and institutions in terms of the nature of their parts, I began to think, was like trying to reduce chemistry to physics. Other forces come into play when one studies "molecules" rather than "atoms," even though molecules consist of atoms. Relational processes in an institution, I concluded, cannot be reduced to psychodynamic or personality factors in the individuals of which they consist. A different level of inquiry was required than one that tries merely to understand "the minds" or personalities of the individuals involved.

What was needed to account for the connection between leader and follower, I was beginning to realize, was an approach that did not separate them into neat categories nor polarize them into oppo-site forces, nor even see them as completely discrete entities. Rather, what was needed to explain an emotional process orientation to lead-ership was a concept that was less moored to linear cause-and-effect thinking. It had to be one that conceptualized the connection between leader and follower as reciprocal and as part of larger natural processes, many of which, I came to realize, were intergener-ational. Leadership in both families and organizations, I was begin-ning to see, was rooted in processes that could be found in all colonized life. After all, had not Nature seen to its being built into pods, prides, swarms, schools, flocks, and herds?

While our species is fond of emphasizing the distinctions between humans and animal life, this focus on the intellect can also be a distraction. While the intellect gives us an advantage over other species, it is only an advantage when we are able to deal adequately with what we have in common with other forms of life—in partic-ular, the instinctual side of ourselves as manifest in the anxiety (reac-tivity) that automatically responds to change and the tension in any community between self and togetherness.

Eventually, I found an uncanny parallel that enabled me to put leader and follower together conceptually in a systemic way. The parallel lies between the latest understanding of the connection between the brain and the body in a human organism, on the one hand, and the effects of a "head's" functioning on a "body politic" in a human organization, on the other. For in any age, concepts of leadership must square with the latest understanding of the relation-ship between brain and body. Recent findings about the brain-body connection have the potential to revolutionize our concept of hier-archy. For they suggest that to a large extent we have a liquid nervous system. The brain turns out to function like a gland. It is the largest organ of secretion, communicating simultaneously with various parts of the body, both near and far, through the reciprocal transmission of substances known as neurotransmitters. In other words, the head is *present* in the body!

So, too, the connection between a "head" and its body in any family or institution is not necessarily a function of proximity. The functioning of a "head" can systemically influence all parts of a body simultaneously, and totally bypass linear, "head-bone-connected-to-the-neck-bone" thinking. What counts is the leader's presence and being, not technique and know-how. It is precisely these systemic aspects of an institution's emotional processes that explain why a leader does not have to know personally those who are being sabotaged or those who are the saboteurs in order for the leader's own functioning to contribute to that nefarious process.

We can see this in the natural systems process in society, both in the actions of today's government leaders and in new understandings of the functioning of past ones. For example, the systemic effects of a well-defined leadership presence can be seen by observing what happens in a community after major catastrophes such as tornadoes, hurricanes, earthquakes, and assassinations. One can observe an inverse correlation between the speed with which the top political officer in a community defines a presence and the amount of disintegration or looting that occurs. It is not merely the presence of the National Guard that dissuades looters—leaders function as the immune systems of their institutions. When they are well defined, the resulting systemic effects on a society inhibit the probability that the opportunistic infections we call looters are likely to form. In other words, the crucial issue of leadership in democratic societies may not be how much power they exercise but how well their *presence* is able to preserve that society's integrity.

Viewing the Civil War through this principle of leadership, it is possible to see that the war was no more "caused" by the issue of slavery than a divorce results from the perceived differences between spouses. In either case, the "cause" had more to do with the ways in which family emotional processes turned those differences into divisive factors. From this perspective, "the great American divorce" was ultimately the result of the failure of the five Presidents before Lincoln (particularly Fillmore, Pierce, and Buchanan, but also to some extent Polk and Taylor) to function in a differentiated manner.

The way in which these glad-handing, conflict-avoiding, compromising "commanders-in-chief" avoided taking charge of our growing internal crisis when they occupied the position "at the top" is exactly the same way I have seen today's leaders function before their organizations (or families) "split."

◈ A REVOLUTION IN LEADERSHIP TRAINING

My growing awareness of the universality of these systemic principles of leadership raised fundamental questions in my mind about the nature of most leadership training (including courses on parenting) that puts primary emphasis on others (children or employees) as objects to be motivated rather than on the systemic effects of the presence, or self, of the leader. I began to see that the same emotional processes that produced dysfunction in an institution when the leader was anxiously reactive or absent could work in reverse. These emotional processes could be salutary rather than destructive. If the leader did not have to be in direct contact with every member in order to influence them, then it should follow that if a leader could learn to be a well-differentiated presence, by the very nature of his or her being he or she could promote differentiation and support creative imagination throughout the system. This would be the case not by focusing on techniques for moving *others*, but by focusing on the nature of his or her own being and presence.

Such a reorientation to the leader is a true paradigm shift rather than a technical innovation, for it changes the criteria for what information is important. Rather than being concerned with the size of an organization or its product, or the latest fad for reorganization, those criteria have to do with a leader's capacity to avoid being regulated by an institution's emotional processes as they are transmitted and reinforced from generation to generation. A leader must separate his or her own emotional being from that of his or her followers while still remaining connected. Vision is basically an emotional rather than a cerebral phenomenon, depending more on a leader's capacity to deal with anxiety than his or her professional training or degree. A leader needs the capacity not only to accept the solitariness that comes with the territory, but also to come to love it. These criteria are based on the recognition that "no good deed goes unpunished"; chronic criticism is, if anything, often a sign that the leader is functioning better! Vision is not enough.

These insights led to a major shift in my mode of consultation with regard to both families and work systems. With families, I stopped creating encyclopedias of data about all their issues and began to search instead for the member with the greatest capacity to be a leader as I have defined it. That person generally turned out to be the one who could express himself or herself with the least amount of blaming and the one who had the greatest capacity to take responsibility for his or her own emotional being and destiny. I began to coach the "leader" alone, letting the rest of the family drop out and stay home. I stopped trying to get people to "communicate" or find better ways of managing their issues. Instead, I began to concentrate on helping the leader to become better defined and to learn how to deal adroitly with the sabotage that almost invariably followed any success in this endeavor. Soon I found that the rest of the family was "in therapy" whether or not they came into my office. For it is the integrity of the leader that promotes the integrity or prevents the "dis-integr-ation" of the system he or she is leading.

I then started to function in the same way with organizations, regardless of their nature, their purpose, or their size. I stopped collecting mounds of data, trying to foster team-building, focusing on the difficult people. I stopped polling the workers or going around to the different divisions. Instead, I concentrated on working with only one or two leaders at the top. Soon I found that for organizations, too, by focusing on and supporting the strengths in the system rather than letting the pathology or the pathogens (read *troublemakers*) determine my focus, the rest of the network was "in therapy" whether or not they came into my office and whether or not I joined them on a retreat.

Next, I began to establish leadership seminars emphasizing the self-differentiation of the leader rather than focusing on method and technique. The subject matter of the programs, instead, was directed toward an understanding of how an institution's emotional processes took shape and persisted; how the emotional processes of leaders' and followers' own families interlocked with the emotional processes of the institution in which they worked; and how the emotional processes in society at large also merged with those streams so that problems in any of these systems could produce symptoms in others. In order to enable participants to increase their capacity to recognize and deal adroitly with these binds, an integral part of the seminar had each leader-in-training make an effort to understand how multi-generational factors in his or her family of origin shaped his or her emotional being. It was then only a small step to ask how that emotional field might still be continuing to regulate their functioning (even at a distance), thus inhibiting their ability to observe and avoid being led by the chronic anxiety and other multigenerational forces in their institutions.

What stood out from the very beginning is that to the extent leaders are successful in their differentiating efforts in their own family of origin, there is immediate carry-over to their functioning in the organizations (or families) which they lead. What has also been striking is the universality of the process, no matter what the profession. The reciprocity between leaders' ability to be less avoidant of emotional factors in their family of origin and their ability to function likewise within the emotional system where they worked was exactly the same for managers, clergy, therapists, physicians, or parents.

But this type of focus on self-differentiation, I also learned, is not easy to foster, especially when society's own emotional processes are in a state of regression (as I shall describe in chapter 2). For the endeavor to gain more regulation over one's own reactive mechanisms requires commitment to the lifetime project of being willing to be continually transformed by one's experience. Frankly, it is easier to focus on data and technique. Yet, at this point, I am convinced that to the extent leaders of any family or institution are willing to make a lifetime commitment to their own continual self-regulated growth, they can make any leadership theory or technique look brilliant. And conversely, to the extent they avoid that commitment, no theory or technique is likely to succeed for very long. As long as new innovations are focused on method and technique rather than on the elements of emotional process, all changes are doomed to recycle.

The following two vignettes will capture the difference between reactive leadership and self-differentiated leadership.

After *Generation to Generation* was first published, I began to receive calls from leaders in various parts of the country. At first I listened to the details of their experience, trying to learn more about my own theories. Then one day I realized that almost everyone who called was functioning in a reactive, defensive way and failing to define his or her own position clearly. They had become so focused on the aches and pains (the pathology) in the system that they had been thrown off course by the complaints. They had stopped supplying vision, or had burned out fighting the resistance; they had ceased to be the strength in the system. In short, they had forgotten to lead. I therefore stopped listening to the content of everyone's complaints and, irrespective of the location of their problem or the nature of their institution, began saying the exact same thing to everyone: "You have to get up before your people and give an 'I Have a Dream' speech."

The outcome was dramatic! Most of those who followed through with what I had suggested found that the chaos in their group soon waned. There was, however, another group of "leaders" who were absolutely desperate to stay in their position. They might have been at an age where it would be difficult to find another job, or their spouse had finally found the position of a lifetime, or their kids had just one more year to finish high school. As they put it, "to have to leave right now would be a family tragedy." Yet, when they heard my advice—that the way out of their dilemma was not some quick-fix technique to apply to others but rather a matter of developing their own self-differentiation—their nerve failed them, and they quit their position rather than having to grow.

It was at this point that I began to realize that before any technique or data could be effective, leaders had to be willing to face their own selves. Otherwise the effect of technique was like trying to build up energy in a spring where the initial twists store up more potential and then suddenly, with one twist too many, the entire spring unwinds. If this sounds similar to the recovery problems of alcoholics, there may be more to the association than we would care to admit. As I shall describe in chapter 3, the chronic anxiety in American society has made the imbibing of data and technique addictive precisely because it enables leaders not to have to face their selves.

But there is another kind of potential leader, as illustrated by this second tale. One evening I boarded a flight in Dallas headed for

New York. At least twenty minutes went by past take-off time, and the doors still had not been closed. When I asked the chief flight attendant what the problem was she replied that the smoke detector in one of the lavatories was broken and they were waiting for someone to fix it. Appalled at how many people-hours were being wasted, I asked, "Why don't you just rip it out or seal it off?" "Oh sir," she responded, "you can't do that." When I went back to my seat, my neighbor and I began to commiserate. He was a liquor distributor and several of his young-adult children worked for him. The conversation got around to women in the marketplace, and I asked if he planned to bring his daughter into what was traditionally a man's world. He answered, "I had been hesitant, even though she's probably the most competent and responsible member of the litter. But after a recent experience, I have changed my mind."

He told me this story. His daughter had been working for an ad agency that had a deadline for a multimillion-dollar proposal. Everyone went home, leaving her in charge of making sure that the proposal made the last plane out. But someone goofed and they missed the overnight mail deadline. So on her own, she called the airport, found out the cost of a private jet, and decided that as extravagant as the cost might be, it was a small price to pay to ensure the contract. When her immediate superiors came in the next morning and found out what she had done on her own responsibility, they were furious at her—but, said her father, "That's when I decided to take her into my business."

◆ THE PURPOSE, SUMMARY, AND
CONTENTS OF THIS BOOK

A Failure of Nerve was born out of readers' responses to my earlier book, *Generation to Generation,* and results from my dialogue over the past decade with those who have written to me, consulted with me, or been present at my presentations in various parts of America. In the final analysis it has been the response of others to my original concepts that has induced me to go further with my ideas. Let me assure those readers, therefore, that while here and there some ideas from *Generation to Generation* (or from my *Fables*) have needed to be included, *A Failure of Nerve* is not a repeat of the former but its logical continuation.

If the ideas in this work are often unconventional, so was the process of putting it together. This may mean that the reader cannot read it in a conventional way. Because of the interrelatedness of all the concepts, it was impossible to write this book one chapter at a time. I constantly found that I could not finish, or sometime even totally outline, one chapter until I had written the next. Thus, a kind of parallel processing occurred in which all the chapters in this book were actually written simultaneously. Ultimately, that process occurred between the two major sections, as well. The construction of this work, therefore, wound up being isomorphic to its content, as perhaps any book will that emphasizes a process view of reality rather than linear formulations of life.

Since the same may be true for the reader, I have created short synopses of each chapter. While it naturally follows that later material in any book is often dependent on concepts described in earlier chapters, readers also will find that sometimes material in an earlier chapter will make the most sense if they already know what is coming next.

First I will illustrate what I perceive to be the major emotional and conceptual barriers to the development and expression of well-defined leadership in America's families and institutions today. I will begin by comparing the emotional processes of medieval Europe before the Renaissance with the regression that I perceive to be afflicting contemporary American society. The exact same kind of adventurous leadership that enabled the Old World to pull out of its doldrums five hundred years ago is what is needed if the New World is also to have a renaissance, now.

Chapter I is in the form of an extended metaphor. By describing some of the earliest maps depicting Europe's gradual unveiling of the New World, I will show that it is indeed possible for an entire civilization to be stuck in its orientation and that the type of leadership that was required for the Old World to go in new directions is the exactly the same kind that is necessary for reorienting any relationship system in any age and enabling it to "go the other way." This chapter also emphasizes the inhibiting effect on adventure and imagination of the "equator" (understood as the mythical, anxiety-provoking end of the world), so that in later chapters parallels can be drawn to similar contemporary emotional barriers with the same limiting effect on leaders' (and researchers') horizons today.

In chapter 2, I describe how contemporary American civilization, despite its high level of technical achievement, is in the midst of a regression rather than a renaissance. Our orientation toward relationships today is as stuck as medieval Europe's orientation toward the major parameters of its world, partly because of the high level of chronic anxiety that has been steadily increasing over the past quarter-century. Five interlocking comparisons are made between highly anxious, regressed families with acting-out children, on the one hand, and the functioning of contemporary American society, on the other. The five aspects of chronic anxiety are reactivity, herding, blaming, a quick-fix mentality, and lack of leadership—the last not only a fifth characteristic of societal regression but one that stems from and contributes to the other four. Each of these perverts natural principles of evolution, namely, self-regulation, adaptation to strength, the response to challenge, and allowing time for processes to mature.

Chapters 3 to 5 describe the imagination-limiting "equators" of our time that are symptomatic of our society's regression; they also describe how the devaluing of self inhibits an adventurous spirit. These myths are: (1) an orientation toward *data* rather than the capacity to be decisive, together with the illusion that "if only we knew enough we could do (or fix) anything," and its obverse, "we failed because we did not use the right technique"; and (2) an orientation toward *empathy* rather than responsibility, with a focus on weakness rather than strength and on ways to avoid personal responsibility.

However lofty the original concept of empathy (a word that only came into the English language in 1922), societal regression has distorted it to the point at which it has become a power tool in the hands of the weak to sabotage the strong. It also serves as a rationalization for the inability of those in helping positions to develop self-control and not enable or interfere, a disguise for unacknowledged anxiety that desires a quick fix, and an indulgence for those who are not in a position where they have to make tough decisions. But the most deleterious effect on leaders is that empathy misleads them as to the factors that go into growth and survival and the nature of what is toxic to life itself.

By showing that what all destructive forces share in common is unregulated invasiveness—a characteristic that is totally unresponsive to empathy—I describe in chapter 4 how the focus on empathy rather than responsibility lessens the potential for survival of both leaders and followers. Leaders are victimized by victimization. In contrast, a leader's self-definition is equivalent to an immune response, and it often forces the invasive organism to "mutate," that is, change.

The third equator-like barrier to imaginative thinking and an adventurous spirit today is the confusion of self with selfishness. The tension between self and togetherness is universal. It appears in areas as diverse as biology, marriage, and politics. There is a tilt toward the togetherness end of the scale, however, when a relationship system becomes emotionally regressed. Then, self becomes threatening to the togetherness needs of the group and is perceived as cruel, cold, and selfish.

The way out of this dilemma is not by finding the proper balance of self and togetherness, but by reorienting one's understanding of togetherness and self so that they are made continuous rather than polarized. In chapter 5, therefore, I draw distinctions between the narcissistic self, which is unconnected, and the well-differentiated self, which is the key to integrity. Continuing the theme of immunology, this chapter shows that the latest understanding of the immune response views it less as a force to ward off enemies and more as a force for coherence of the organism. Five comparisons are drawn between the natural processes of immunity as it has evolved in life on this planet and the need for a similar process of integration in each human being's own evolution. Thus self-differentiation is shown to be a force that is not anti-togetherness; on the contrary, it is a force that modifies the emotional processes within any group's togetherness so that a leader actually promotes community through the emerging self-differentiation (autonomy, independence, individuality) of the other members.

In the second half of the book* I will employ the new orientation toward relational processes introduced earlier as the basis for what I call "leadership through self-differentiation." This focuses

* *Edwin Friedman was working on these later chapters at the time of his death in 1996, and they are incomplete.*

leaders (parents or presidents) on themselves rather than on their followers, and on the nature of their presence rather than on their technique and "know-how." An underlying theme will be that in families and other institutions, emotional processes are always more powerful than ideas. Thus the aims of these chapters are:

◆ to show how power lies in presence rather than method;
◆ to enable leaders to avoid trying to instill insight into the unmotivated;
◆ to help leaders see that concepts such as "role modeling," "emulation," and "identification" are illusions that unnecessarily stress leaders, placing too much emphasis on the brain (or at least the cortex) and tending to work only with those who are not the problem in the first place;
◆ to show how the self-differentiation of leaders and parents can make the dependency of the unimaginative and the recalcitrant work for instead of against them.

Chapter 6 is the keystone chapter of the book, presenting a model of leadership that flows from the new relationship models explored in the previous chapter. It begins by describing how leadership through self-differentiation comes in at a tangent to the charisma/consensus dichotomy that is basic to almost all conventional leadership models—a notion that forces us into either/or choices regarding leader and follower. In chapter 6 I question the validity of concepts such as role-modeling, emulation, and identification, and describe other variables that affect those leadership styles. The key, in my view, is that by continually working on one's own self-differentiation, the leader optimizes his or her objectivity and decision-making capacity.

In chapter 7 I present a view of the emotional processes of organizations, framed in terms of a system of triangular relationships rather than through the linear formulations that emphasize dyadic relationships and people's inner workings. Emotional triangles are the molecules of any social system, and their laws are universal regardless of the makeup of the group. This chapter describes how these triangles function in various types of relationship systems. It also demonstrates their universality, shows how they transcend conventional social science categories such as gender and ethnicity, and explains that they are often the missing variable for a leader's stress and effectiveness. The concept offers both a perspective for differentiated functioning and a way of thinking that contributes to a leader's further differentiation.

Living with crisis is a major part of leaders' lives. The crises come in two major varieties: (1) those that are not of their own making but are imposed on them from outside or within the system; and (2) those that are actually triggered by the leaders through doing precisely what they should be doing. Chapter 8 addresses the handling of crises that are not of the leaders' making. Continuing with the notion of power through presence, I describe how all the factors that go into self-differentiated functioning help resolve crises in more fundamental ways than is accomplished by anxiety-driven quick fixes. Most crises cannot by their very nature be resolved (that is, fixed); they must simply be managed until they work their way through. This is generally a process that cannot be willed, any more than one can make a bean grow by pulling on it. This, of course, puts a premium on self-regulation and the management of anxiety instead of frantically seeking the right solution.

Using a health crisis of my own wherein I needed two different surgical procedures—one for my heart and one for my brain, each of which jeopardized the other organ—I highlight five separate principles that I applied to my own functioning as I made decisions and prepared for events. I have enabled leaders in a variety of organizational crises to apply the same principles. This final chapter emphasizes that sabotage is not simply something to be overcome; it comes with the territory. It describes the reasons for sabotage, the manifestations it usually takes with children, with marriage partners, or with managers and employees, and how leaders may best prepare for and deal with it.

All of this circles back to the kind of training leaders need in order to recognize and deal with emotional processes. The most striking parallel of all is this: Family problems can often be resolved by having the parents or partners focus on and work at unresolved issues in their families of origin. By the same token, leaders must not only develop vision, persistence, and stamina, but also understand that the problems they encounter may stem from their own unresolved family issues, their organization's past, sabotage in response to their effective leadership, or a combination of these factors.

In closing, let the reader beware how subtly radical some of the ideas that follow may be. Perhaps *subversive* is a better word, though not in an obviously confrontational way. Readers may find that the ideas here conflict with what they have always assumed to be the eternal truths of their profession, their politics, their understanding of life, or, sometimes (and perhaps most disturbing), their therapy. Some of the concepts that I will present—particularly with regard to how empathy has become a power tool, the totalitarian effects of consensus, the exaggerated importance of being informed, and the colossal failure of insight to bring change—will also be as jarring to "common sense" as Copernicus's notions were to even the most learned medieval mind.

We thus come to the following "catch 22." It has been my experience in presenting many of these ideas over the past decade that often the very emotional processes in society that this book will try to elucidate can work to prevent people from hearing precisely what I am trying to say about those processes. For example, given the volatile emotional climate of our time, some readers will look for a political slant. The very words *hierarchy* and *leadership* have become anathema in some circles. In addition, for many *self* is a four-letter word; for others, any disagreeable idea is dismissed by attributing it to the personality, gender, or ethnic background of its author. Let me state clearly, therefore, that I have no specific political agenda other than to line up with that spirit of radical thinking that inspired those who founded our land. And as near as I can tell, that was never a spirit that revered cloistered virtues. This book is not for those who seek political allies, but for those who are excited by the adventure of challenging ideas and who are concerned that our theories not get in the way of our survival.

While it is not my claim to be bringing some new truth, it is also not my intention merely to offer a new program. I seek, rather, to reformat the entire disc. Iconoclasm always sides with the doubters of perfect faith; so for my part, I will be quite content if all I have succeeded in accomplishing is to supply this century's best candidate for a book-burning.

The safest place for ships is in the harbor,
but that's not why ships were built.
—Anonymous

Chapter One

◆ IMAGINATIVE GRIDLOCK AND THE SPIRIT OF ADVENTURE

The *Nuremberg Chronicle* of 1493 describes Europe as depressed. Published in one of medieval Germany's most important centers of learning and innovation, the *Chronicle* epitomizes its era. On the one hand, pioneering with the new, innovative hardware of movable type, it faithfully reproduced engraved portraits of the major cities of Europe and the Holy Land. On the other hand, it described a civilization with little vision or hope. Referring to what they called "the calamity of our time," the publishers actually left several pages blank so that readers could record "the rest of the events until the end of the world."

Contributing to the general malaise was a combination of political, social, economic, and theological "downers." Late fifteenth-century Europe, despite its glorious cathedrals, emerging artists, and developing network of universities, was a society living in the wake of the plagues, the breakdown of the feudal order, and the increasing inability of an often hypocritical and corrupt church's capacity to ring true. In addition, the Moorish encirclement had proved invulnerable to centuries of crusades and now severely limited Europe's access to the riches and delights of the Far East. There had not been a major scientific discovery for a thousand years.

Then, as if suddenly, Europe is all agog. The depression lifts like a morning mist, novelty begins to shine everywhere, and the seeds of the Renaissance that had been germinating here and there for two hundred years sprout vigorously. The imaginative gridlock that had largely beclouded Europe's inventiveness for more than a millennium dissolves forever. Over the next half-century, more radical change occurred in every field of human endeavor than had ever happened before, or, with the possible exception of the first half of the twentieth century, since.

While there have been other half-centuries of extraordinary progress, few have involved such fundamental change of direction all across the board. A person born in 1492 could have witnessed in their lifetime:

- an extraordinary flowering of artistic imagination concerning form and perspective in painting, sculpture, literature, architecture;
- the Reformation led by Luther and Calvin, ramifying out into almost every subculture and presaging the way religious differences would be formulated for centuries thereafter;
- the invention of the watch, enabling an unheralded fine-tuning in the measurement and coordination of daily time periods;
- observations of space and experimentation with lenses that would lead to the creation of the telescope; and
- the dissemination of the first newspaper, initiating the effects of widespread information-sharing within a community.

Underlying all of this artistic, philosophical, and scientific upheaval was an even more basic, all-embracing change: the two worldviews by which European civilization had oriented itself for almost fifteen hundred years (based largely on the scholarship of the second-century Greek thinker and mapmaker, Ptolemy) were turned on their heads. One misperception was the view that the land mass on our planet was situated entirely *above* the equator, extending contiguously from western Europe to eastern Asia, with the Indian Ocean a land-locked lake. The other was the notion that our planet's relationship to the rest of the planets and other heavenly bodies was "geocentric"—that is, the other planets and stars revolved around the Earth, which according to this orientation was situated at the center of the universe.

It is appropriate that this "rebirth" of the human spirit has been referred to as the "Renaissance." But the tendency to attribute the Renaissance to a renewed interest in learning may, despite its origins, be the same kind of academic bias that focuses leadership training programs on data and technique rather than on emotional process. It certainly has not been my experience in working with imaginatively stuck marriages, families, corporations, or other institutions that an increase in information will necessarily enable a system to get unstuck. And the risk-averse are rarely emboldened by data.

Anyone who has ever been part of an imaginatively gridlocked relationship system knows that more learning will not, on its own, automatically change the way people see things or think. There must first be a shift in the emotional processes of that institution. Imagination and indeed even curiosity are at root emotional, not cognitive, phenomena. In order to imagine the unimaginable, people must be able to separate themselves from surrounding emotional processes before they can even begin to see (or hear) things differently. Without this understanding, it becomes impossible to realize how our learning can prevent us from learning more. After all, when Galileo, a century later, tried to reorient the cosmic perspective of his world, he offered in rebuttal to those who were unwilling to learn what he had learned a look for themselves through his telescope. And there were people who not only disagreed with his views but, when offered the opportunity, even refused to peek.

While it can be said that Columbus's voyage would not have been possible without some of the accumulated learning that preceded him, European history after 1493 (the period usually designated as the High Renaissance) does not logically follow from all the knowledge or creative imagination that had been gathering in the previous three centuries. The slow pace of advancement from Dante, Aquinas, Bacon, and Petrarch, from artists like Fra Lippi, Botticelli, van Eyck, and Della Robbia, and from architects such as Brunelleschi and

Giotto could have continued at that same slow rate of progress for another three or even five hundred years. Indeed, the luster of Florence had already dulled. The quantum leap, or, if you prefer, the "punctuated equilibrium" that occurred around 1500 was a direct result of a complete reorientation to reality initiated by Columbus's discoveries and the subsequent exploration of geography.

Similarly, though some have said that the Age of Discovery was merely symptomatic of the cultural and economic advances occurring at that time, I believe that the catalyst for those other imaginative breakthroughs was the "nerve" of the great navigators who led the way. Europe's imaginative capacity was unleashed not by the discovery of learning, as those with a vested interest in learning would have it, but by the discovery of the New World, while the enormous awakening of European civilization's inventiveness was a direct result of the effect those new horizons had on an Old World. Even as Columbus is returning from his fourth voyage (1504), Michelangelo is sculpting his *David* and Leonardo has completed the *Mona Lisa*; half a century later, by the time Drake has reached San Francisco (1570), Shakespeare, Cervantes, Rabelais, and El Greco are rising to the top. Opera has its beginnings. Tycho Brahe, Kepler, Galileo, and Harvey are beginning to set the stage for the next hundred years, which Alfred North Whitehead called the century of genius. All after a thousand years of almost complete darkness, illuminated almost solely by the great cathedrals.

Columbus's voyage was a hinge of time. It swung open a door barely ajar, and for the next hundred years after 1493, no significant cathedral, unless previously planned, was begun. The effect of America's discovery on the European imagination was as though God had been hiding a piece of land bigger than the known world since the dawn of creation. The great lesson of this turnaround is that when any relationship system is imaginatively gridlocked, it cannot get free simply through more thinking about the problem. Conceptually stuck systems cannot become unstuck simply by trying harder. For a fundamental reorientation to occur, that spirit of adventure which optimizes serendipity and which enables new perceptions beyond the control of our thinking processes must happen first. This is equally true regarding families, institutions, whole nations, and entire civilizations.

But for that type of change to occur, the system in turn must produce leaders who can both take the first step and maintain the stamina to follow through in the face of predictable resistance and sabotage. Any renaissance, anywhere, whether in a marriage or a business, depends primarily not only on new data and techniques, but on the capacity of leaders to separate themselves from the surrounding emotional climate so that they can break through the barriers that are keeping everyone from "going the other way."

This chapter will be an extended metaphor. Using the European discovery of the New World as an allegory of the human experience of getting unstuck, it will do the following:

◆ It will show the characteristics of imaginatively gridlocked relationship systems and how it is quite possible not only for families and other institutions but even for an entire civilization, including its most learned members, to be stuck in an orientation that confuses its own models with reality.
◆ It will illustrate the process and the difficulties involved in trying to re-map reality under those conditions.
◆ It will describe the kind of leadership that must arise before any relationship system (marriage, corporation, or entire nation) can undergo a fundamental reorientation.

In succeeding chapters I will draw more specific parallels to today. I will describe how the chronic anxiety that characterizes the emotional processes of contemporary American civilization influences our thoughts and our leaders toward safety and certainty rather than toward boldness and adventure. I will show how the factors that kept European civilization imaginatively stuck during its dark period are similar to the factors that keep contemporary American civilization gridlocked. For we too have our "equators." These imagination-inhibitors or emotional barriers that prevent new thinking about institutions in our time have the very same effect on limiting leaders' (and researchers') horizons today that the equator and a geocentric view of the universe had for the millennium before the Renaissance. The qualities of adventurous leadership that enabled Europe to escape its doldrums are exactly the leadership qualities necessary for breaking the imaginative gridlock of our civilization today. In fact, they are the same qualities of leadership necessary for dissolving imaginative gridlock in any relationship system anywhere, of any size or purpose, in any culture or at any time.

It is important to keep in mind, therefore, when comparing the sophisticated-appearing understandings of our day with the naïve-appearing conceptions of the medieval world, that just because an idea is sophisticated does not prevent it from functioning as a superstition when encompassing emotional processes put it to their regressive service. For example, information can function as superstition when encompassing emotional processes assert a regressive pull. Some of our most "common-sense" assumptions concerning the nature of human relationships upon which leadership training for both managers and parents is based today may be as off-course as the rarely questioned Ptolemaic views of heaven and Earth were, even for many of the most educated medieval minds.

◆ CHARACTERISTICS OF GRIDLOCKED SYSTEMS

There are three major, interlocking characteristics common to any relationship system that has become imaginatively gridlocked:

- ◆ an unending treadmill of trying harder;
- ◆ looking for answers rather than reframing questions; and
- ◆ either/or thinking that creates false dichotomies.

These attributes are both symptom and cause of a locked-in perspective. All three characterized fifteenth-century European civilization. All three describe any similarly stuck relationship system at any time, be it a marriage, a family, an organization, or an entire nation. And all three attributes, while appearing to be cognitive, are symptomatic of surrounding emotional processes rather than matters of the mind.

Trying Harder
The treadmill effect can be likened to a fly perpetually bouncing off a window it can see right through, with the result that despite its thousand eyes its perseverance gets it nowhere. The condition is well known to marriage partners who keep trying harder to change their partners, parents who keep trying harder to change their children,

therapists who keep trying harder to change their clients, teachers who keep trying harder to change their students, clergy who keep trying harder to change their congregations, managers who keep trying harder to change those they manage, CEOs who keep trying harder to change their managers, consultants who keep trying harder to change CEOs, and social scientists who keep trying harder to explain what is happening.

As I will show later, society itself can be on a treadmill when it becomes caught up in accumulating unending masses of data, because its models are inadequate to explain its processes. The treadmill of trying harder is driven by the assumption that failure is due to the fact that one did not try hard enough, use the right technique, or get enough information. This assumption overlooks the possibility that thinking processes themselves are stuck and imagination gridlocked, not because of cognitive strictures in the minds of those trying to solve a problem, but because of emotional processes within the wider relationship system. The failure to recognize those emotional processes, if not the outright denial of their existence, is what often initiates and ultimately perpetuates the treadmill effect.

But if fixation can influence behavior, perseverance can also perpetuate a fix. Whether it be a family, an institution, or an entire civilization, the treadmill process itself can evolve into the axis around which an entire world revolves, eventually going far beyond the original goal. Europe's orientation toward the Far East was just such a "fix." Frantic efforts to find a route to the Orient through the Northwest Passage perpetuated it, while centuries of combat with encircling Islam in the Near East and the increasing desire for the silks and spices of the Far East only reinforced it long after the western hemisphere had been revealed. In fact, it took European civilization almost three centuries to grasp fully that what it had found—North America—might be more important than what it was looking for.

So deeply fixed was Europe's attitude toward the East that despite the succeeding exploration and colonization, the land mass of the western hemisphere was considered largely "in the way." The well-known quest for a safe sea route to the East through the Northwest Passage—which began in the fifteenth century with Cabot in the north and continued through the sixteenth century with Verrazano along the Atlantic coast, Vespucci and Magellan to the south, and Drake, Juan de Fuca, and Bering approaching it from the west—extended for three hundred years. At the beginning of the nineteenth century, Thomas Jefferson dispatched Lewis and Clark to see if the wide Missouri, flowing eastwards, and the powerful Columbia, flowing to the west, linked up at their source.

The depth of this "fix" is illustrated by maps of the period, which provided the most reliable data explorers had. Maps were drawn to suit the prevailing concepts, with the Hudson River emptying into the Pacific Ocean. Some early maps showed the Northwest Passage at the top of the world, while in others, it went right through Toronto. The same mapmakers saw California as an island, its northern part (perhaps mistaken for Vancouver Island) being just below where the Northwest Passage was supposed to enter the Pacific. With great confidence the mapmaker wrote across the top, "A New and Accurate Map of the World Drawn according to the truest Descriptions, latest Discoveries and best Observations that have been made by English or Strangers."

The error about California came about rather innocently, but somehow it became so embedded in the imagination of cartographers that, with some exceptions, it remained "reality" for one hundred fifty years. The illusion began with a rumor on the part of a cartographer, Henry Briggs. He even wrote on his map, published in 1625, a report that one ship had met another coming down the west coast, and the latter informed the former that they had just found the western end of the Northwest Passage. On its own, Briggs's map might not have influenced others, but it was included as one of several foldouts in Samuel Purchase's *His Pilgrims*, a popular travelogue book of the day. And what had begun as a rumor was disseminated to the point at which it became a "virus" and entered everyone else's program.

Just why an entire civilization allowed itself to be so misled by one person's imagination is not clear, particularly since maps fifty years earlier had it right. What may be hard to understand today is that in those days, earlier researchers actually could have been more accurate in their information than those who came later, and that competition sometimes led those who recorded data to give in to sensationalism rather than being sure of their facts. The debate over whether or not California was an island became so heated that even after the error was conclusively disproved and eliminated from most maps, the belief in California's insularity had to be killed off by fiat. In 1747, King Ferdinand VII of Spain issued a royal decree stating flat out, "California is not an island." However, maps published as late as the eve of the American Revolution still promoted the myth, and it is an exquisite example of how the emotional processes of the treadmill effect influence cognitive capacity.

Answers Rather Than Questions

The second attribute of imaginatively gridlocked relationship systems is a continual search for new answers to old questions rather than an effort to reframe the questions themselves. In the search for the solution to any problem, questions are always more important than answers because the way one frames the question, or the problem, already predetermines the range of answers one can conceive in response.

The critical difference between what is now popularly called a *paradigm shift* and what might otherwise be simply an innovation involves precisely this change in focus from answer to question. For example, at some point in history someone realized that solid wheels could be made much lighter by cutting away pie-shaped slices and leaving only spokes. That was certainly a useful, facilitating innovation that produced a new answer to the question of how to overcome the cumbersomeness of wheels. But the paradigm shift of transportation that opened imaginative new ways of thinking was the wheel itself! Innovations are new answers to old questions; paradigm shifts reframe the question, change the information that is important, and generally eliminate previous dichotomies.

A more familiar example would be the mother who is perpetually trying to seek answers to the question of how to make her child more responsible. She will be on a frustrating treadmill until she is able to focus on her own development rather than her child's. For example, one mother spent years trying to find new ways of getting her kids to do their homework despite the fact that she knew she had been completely ineffectual. Finally one day she said to them, "This is crazy. You're going to save me a lot of money if you don't go to college. From now on, every time you catch me commenting on your schoolwork, you can fine me a dollar." As a result of reframing the question from "how do I motivate my kids" to "how do I regulate myself," she not only found them doing far better, but a chronic backache that had bothered her for years mysteriously disappeared.

Similarly, the understanding that one can get more change in a family or organization by working with the motivated members (the strengths) in the system than by focusing on the symptomatic or recalcitrant members totally obliterates the search for answers to the question of how to motivate the unmotivated. Thus employers who keep seeking answers to the question of what rewards or punishments will make their employees more productive will be on a trial-and-error treadmill until they can shift their thinking about owner/worker dichotomies and create profit-sharing plans. Similarly, the idea of a flat tax, whether or not you agree with its philosophy, would eliminate the search for answers to a huge number of deduction questions (although it might set up a whole array of new and more difficult ones).

As with the treadmill effect, the concern with finding the right answer is both contributory to a fixed orientation and symptomatic of it. And yet the problem is emotional, not cerebral. Perpetually seeking new answers to established questions rather than reframing the basic question itself not only betrays lack of distance on the part of the searcher; it also prevents obtaining the distance necessary for being able even to think, much less go, in new directions. Seeking answers can be its own treadmill. Changing the question enables one to step off.

Caught up in an intense struggle against the Moors, who were also "in the way" of a safe sea route to the trading partners of the East, Europe's obsession with the question of how to get past them prevented them from reframing the problem in a way that enabled them to think—not to mention go—in another direction. European civilization, oriented by a map of the world that had no backside, had framed the problem in such a way that it could only think in terms of finding the most direct route *through* the Moorish encirclement. In other words, while its picture of reality led to a misorientation, it was Europe's emotional climate, its locked-horns attitude toward the Moors, that kept it stuck. New alternatives cannot even be imagined, much less accepted or "heard," until the emotional processes that fix the orientation have changed. It was a long time before Europe realized that by going in the opposite direction, it had found more than it was looking for.

Either/Or Thinking

The third characteristic of gridlocked relationship systems is either/or, black-or-white, all-or-nothing ways of thinking that eventually restrict the options of the mind. Paradigms that might begin simply as theoretical differences become hardened into intense, oppositional, emotional commitments over even the most unemotional subject matter. Such polarized thinking and labeling is equally likely to occur in the fields of geology, biology, physics, economics, medicine, therapy, or jazz.

Such intense polarizations also are always symptomatic of underlying emotional processes rather than of the subject matter of the polarizing issue. And rigid dichotomies almost always hint that there is something wrong in the original orientation. Another way of putting this is that the differences in any system, whether it is a marriage or a legislature, rarely determine the nature or the intensity of the differing. Whether one is baking a cake or examining an institutional mix, the interaction of ingredients is almost always a function of the temperature and pressure of the environment. When troubled couples, for example, make a breakthrough, often the issues that they differed over have not gone away but the two sides have become less reactive to the differences. Whenever differences do polarize, it is always related to the same emotional processes that contribute to the treadmill effect and the failure to reframe the question.

The great either/or question in Columbus's time was: Is it three thousand or ten thousand miles from Europe to Japan? The Greeks had already measured the circumference of the earth accurately to within a few hundred miles. The cartographers before Columbus, starting with the Ptolemy map and adding Japan as a result of Marco Polo's voyages one hundred fifty years earlier, were fairly accurate in their depiction of what was known. But Columbus used a map that elongated Siberia to show that the Atlantic Ocean (the only ocean out there, to his world's way of thinking) was only five thousand miles across, which, if you subtract the distance from China to Japan (his destination), was, incidentally, just about how far his ships could go. Evidently in those days people seeking research grants fudged data in order to support their hypotheses. The funding committee in Isabella of Spain's court, however, said that Columbus's map was inaccurate, based on the experiences of world travelers such as Marco Polo and prominent Jewish and Arab travelers, as well as what was handed down from Greek civilization. The Atlantic Ocean is ten thousand miles across, said the funding committee.

With hindsight, it is hard for us today to conceive that neither side could imagine, in their day, a third possibility: another piece of land in between. That otherwise intelligent and learned men could have missed so obvious a third possibility cannot be explained in terms of ignorance, but only in terms of the emotional processes that create and sustain polarizations. And yet, despite these egregious errors—as well as more horrendous ones I shall describe shortly—the system worked. It worked because the spirit of adventure triumphed over the concern for safety and certainty.

The process of discovery that freed Europe from its imaginative gridlock of a thousand years is in large part about the relationship between risk and reality—which means it is also basically about leadership. It teaches the vital importance of leadership if a relationship system is to undergo a fundamental reorientation. And it gives a totally unambiguous answer to the perennial question, "Do times make the man (or woman), or does the person make the time?" Obviously, conditions must be propitious for imagination, boldness, or energy to bear fruit; but for ripe times to benefit from what they have to offer, someone simply must be able to separate himself or herself enough from surrounding emotional processes to go first— whether we are considering a marriage or a corporation.

◆ EXPANDING HORIZONS

The process of European civilization's reorientation to reality began almost half a century before Columbus with a Portuguese king who came to be known as Prince Henry the Navigator. Though not nearly as honored by history, he was Columbus's forebear in several ways: as a visionary, as an initiator of movements in new directions, as the promoter of adventures that created the seamanship experience Columbus eventually learned in his apprenticeship years with

Portuguese navigators, and as the one who induced mortals to break through the emotional barrier known as the equator. His government was, perhaps, the first to fund research.

Taking advantage of recent developments in technology, such as new rigging of sails, revised construction of ship hulls, and more refined instruments of navigation, Prince Henry began to send expeditions down the west coast of Africa. But emotional factors beyond technology were involved. After all, other seafaring nations also had both the new technology and the same economic interests. Portugal, situated on the edge of Europe, may have been less caught up in the dominant mind-set, as also would have been true of the Vikings.

But take nothing away from Prince Henry's own personal imaginativeness, boldness, and willingness to risk, for two of his successors, despite the fact that they also were situated outside of Europe's emotional processes, failed to seize the moment. Fifty years later, one of them rejected Columbus's "half-baked" idea with a guffaw similar to the Parker Pen Company's response to the first mention of a ballpoint.

As a result of Prince Henry's efforts, every few years Portuguese mariners made a new landfall further south down the west coast of Africa, including the crossing of the equator and the rounding of the Cape. To appreciate the boldness of this venture and the fears that had to be overcome, it is important to realize that the distance from Iberia to the southern tip of Africa is double the distance that has to be traversed to cross the great blue sea to America. The east-west bulge of Africa is almost one thousand miles long; as one approaches the equator the North Star appears to sink into the sea (perhaps the origin of the myth that here lies the end of the world); and there is strangeness everywhere. Around Cape Bojadar at the edge of the Sahara, the red sand turns the water blood red for miles. Much further down the coast, the enormous rush of the Congo River's descent creates a condition where the surface of the Atlantic is sweet for almost fifteen miles out. There was no way to measure longitude from a moving ship: captains were constantly having to go out to sea to avoid possible shoals, drive south to a given latitude, and then go back eastward until they sighted land again.

Two key points in this first part of the reorientation story deserve special note. The first is that around 1475, the legacy of Prince

Henry inspired an expedition to cross the equator, and instead of falling off the end of the Earth, everyone came back to tell their tale. The breaking of this emotional barrier was similar in what it unleashed to breaking the sound barrier, the four-minute-mile, the biblical prophets' rejection of polytheism, the shift to government by compact rather than divine right, and the movement from an individual model of psychology to a family systems conceptualization of relationships.

The second turning point occurred in 1488, when Bartolomeu Dias, after driving south along the coast for many leagues, turned east, failed to sight land, knew that Africa could be rounded, and proved that the Indian Ocean is not land-locked, as Ptolemy's map had indicated. Dias's discovery made Columbus's efforts possible. The Spanish, upon hearing that they have been beaten to Cathay (the orientation was still to the Orient), now realize they have nothing to lose. When money becomes available after the defeat of the Moors at Granada (they still think the Moors are the problem), they agree to fund Columbus, who for his part has all but given up on them and is thinking of trying his luck in France. Columbus makes four voyages between 1492 and 1504, exploring quite thoroughly the layout of islands in the Caribbean, though it is not until he finds the broad waters at the mouth of Venezuela's Orinoco in 1498 that he knows he has found a continent. And less than four years after Columbus's first voyage, the Portuguese launch Vasco da Gama in Dias's wake. He rounds the South African Cape with the aid of local navigators, heads northward up the coast past the long island of Madagascar, and then, launching out toward India, is out of sight of land twice as long as Columbus ever had been—all the while fighting the monsoons and crossing the course of Chinese Admiral Cheng Ho, who had come in the opposite direction several decades earlier.

Not to be left out, the British send Cabot to a New-found-land and eventually the French send Cartier and the English send Frobisher in a similar direction, where, to their surprise, they find industrious fishermen from La Rochelle already mining the Saint Lawrence. In between, Verrazano, the nobleman in the bunch, explores the entire Atlantic seaboard, the coast between Columbus and Cabot, while Amerigo Vespucci, the banker, going further to the south and discovers the Amazon. He writes up his travels and because he includes lurid details of exotic sexual practices to spice his adventures, his travelogues sell like wildfire. They make his name well known, and as a result Amerigo has half the world named after him.

For the last act in this initial reorientation process, Magellan, working his way south, finds in 1520 the fabled Northwest Passage in the southeast and, miraculously navigating one of our planet's most treacherous bodies of water without a chart, makes it all the way to the Philippines almost without seeing another island. It is not for another half-century, however, that the world comes to realize that Magellan did not have to go through the straits that bear his name, for South America does not touch Antarctica (or what was then called Australasia), as Sir Francis Drake found out. After navigating the same straits a half-century later, Drake is blown south of Tierra del Fuego against his will and finds the true southern end of South America, where what is now called the Drake Straits join the Atlantic and the Pacific and separate South America from Antarctica.

◆ RISK AND REALITY

Many have pointed to the relationship between risk and imagination and observed that it is safer to confine one's thoughts to the conventional. In the process of reorientation, however, the connection is far more fundamental. There is a relationship between risk and reality that involves not risk and one's *sense of reality,* which is a psychological concept, but nerve and *reality itself.* For if imagination involves risk, the willingness to risk is critical to validating one's perceptions.

Three facets of the discovery process I have described convey this relationship between risk and reality and add more evidence for the proposition that both being stuck and becoming reoriented are essentially emotional processes:

- ◆ the ultimate unimportance of mistakes when the quest is driven by adventure rather than certainty;
- ◆ the importance of serendipity in freeing oneself from one's own thinking processes; and
- ◆ the will to overcome imaginative barriers, like the equator.

The Freedom to Make Mistakes

To say, first of all, that mistakes are unimportant may overstate the case. Yet Europe's reorientation process clearly demonstrates that even though huge errors were made along the way, some lasting for more than a century, they turned out to be a small price to pay for getting the ships out of the harbor. For example, there were maps with islands in the Atlantic, tigers in the Appalachians, and a whole host of other demons, beasties, and cannibals decorating the cartography of the day. Some antique maps show Greenland joined to North America, and some have North America joined to Asia, or locate Japan in the middle of the Bering Straits between Russia and Alaska. Some show an unknown sea at the top of the world; others show the fabled Northwest Passage going through the Great Lakes. Indeed, it took two full centuries for Europe to get the Great Lakes straight. The development of that reality is its own metaphor for the problem of getting the right distance.

It is, however, Verrazano's map of 1509 that is the most startling. He was the first to explore what was eventually to become the most important part of the Atlantic coast—from Florida to Labrador. But being a nobleman and not an expert seaman, he was afraid to get too close to shore and so missed almost every major bay on the Atlantic coast, from the Chesapeake to the Bay of Fundy, including Delaware Bay and Narragansett Bay, even though he docked at its mouth. And when Verrazano entered the outskirts of New York Harbor, one hundred years before Henry Hudson, he apparently only went as far as "the Bridge" and missed having a whole river named after him. Actually, Verrazano's failure to thoroughly do his research resulted not only in his not seeing what is there; he also saw what is not. This resulted in later maps that contain the fabled "Sea of Verrazano." For when this overly cautious researcher came upon the Outer Banks of North Carolina and saw the Bay of Albemarle on the other side, but could not see the mainland through the fog, he assumed that this narrow strip was the entire width of this part of the New World and that he had discovered some new sea on the other side.

In this context, the role of cartographers in modeling reality deserves some mention. They, after all, are the publishers, the evaluators, and in some ways the censors of what is to be filtered into the public consciousness. Sometimes they seem to have had more power to determine reality than the explorers themselves. America, as was mentioned, was not named by some international tribunal or even a group of politicos but by the German mapmaker Waldseemüller, who said, "All the continents are named after women; it's about time we had a continent named after a man." Cartographers differed widely in their concern for accuracy, their ability to draw, their taste, and their honesty. They mixed fact, theory, and hypothesis according to their illusions, their fears, their wishes, their biases, and their political prejudices.

But the ability of mapmakers to determine reality is not only an ancient phenomenon. Compare, for example, the 1626 map showing California as an island, with all its claim to accuracy, with the evolving brain maps of today. When CAT-scans first appeared, their superiority over ordinary X-rays in depicting reality was lauded everywhere. But these images eventually gave way to the MRI as "the real representation of reality." In any field, then, is reality primarily what the "cartographers" of the day say it is? Answer: Only when the leaders of that age have deferred to the "mapmakers" because of their fear of making mistakes.

Yet despite the way the competition of mapmakers polarized them on specific issues, and despite the refusal of some cartographers to take on the expense of changing plates when new information became available, the system as a whole worked in the Age of Exploration. It worked because the all-encompassing, surrounding emotional atmosphere was conducive to excitement and adventure rather than the failure of nerve that always accompanies anxiety and a quest for certainty. Sixteenth- and seventeenth-century adventure was an open-ended search for novelty rather than a driven pursuit of truth. As I will show in subsequent chapters, our current age of discovery is very different.

The Value of Chance

My second point is that if making mistakes is relatively unimportant in an atmosphere of adventure, willingness to encounter serendipity is vital to its continuing spirit. The thinking processes of adventurers whose nerve fails them is depicted well in Virgil's *Aeneid*, the Latin epic that parallels Homer's *Odyssey* (both of which were read by

Columbus). Virgil describes the adventurer's decision-making dilemma with the following tale: According to the mythology of the time, every person's lifeline was spun out by three women called the three Fates. There was one sailor, however, who, lacking the confidence that he could influence the Fates, tried to fake them out. He would flip a coin before making any decision, but then do the opposite of what he said he was going to do depending on whether the coin came up heads or tails. Virgil tells us, however, that the Fates knew this was part of his destiny, so they always made the coin come up the opposite from the choice they wanted him to make.

Throughout this period of exploration, trips are beset by the unforeseen. Frobisher's ship is frozen in Hudson Bay. Columbus is told by natives in what is now Panama that there is another large body of water on the other side of the Isthmus, but he must meet another ship and has to leave it to Balboa to discover the Pacific. Verrazano ventures out of the range of the long bows on his ship and is captured and killed by cannibals in the West Indies. America is named for one of the least important of the explorers, who goes on to what becomes the less important of the two continents and has half the world named after him by a German cartographer. Drake, after navigating the Magellan Straits, is driven south, off course, and discovers the tip of South America, but his fate does not always come up "heads." When he passes the Golden Gate, the fog keeps him from discovering San Francisco Bay. The most serendipitous event of all, of course, is the discovery of America itself. After all, Columbus was really trying to reach Japan, and he died thinking he had.

The great lesson here for all imaginatively gridlocked systems is that the acceptance and even cherishing of uncertainty is critical to keeping the human mind from voyaging into the delusion of omniscience. The willingness to encounter serendipity is the best antidote we have for the arrogance of thinking we know. Exposing oneself to chance is often the only way to provide the kind of mind-jarring experience of novelty that can make us realize that what we thought was reality was only a mirror of our minds. Related here is the necessity of preserving ambiguity in artistic expression since, if the viewer's imagination is to flower, it is important not to solve the problem in advance.

The willingness to encounter the unexpected that Columbus and these other explorers manifested not only can free minds from their sets; it also enables us to imagine the unimaginable. And no society can continue to evolve as long as it makes cloistered virtues supreme. After all, the mistakes in reality that the discoverers of this period made, as outrageous as they might seem today, rarely lasted more than a hundred years. The totally erroneous grasp of reality that characterized European civilization's severely regressed, unadventurous, unimaginative thinking before 1493 lasted a thousand.

Emotional Barriers

The third lesson to be learned from the process of adventure that reoriented Europe actually came first, chronologically. As every school child knows, the belief that the equator defined the end of the world limited the spirit necessary to produce reality. The equator served as an emotional barrier, by which I mean a belief born of mythology and kept in place by anxiety. Such beliefs exist in every society and take hold to the extent that society is driven by anxiety rather than adventure.

I have called them *imaginative* or *emotional barriers* rather than simply myths, illusions, or erroneous beliefs because their effect is more than cerebral. For they are usually dissuasive in their influence, and their influence always spreads throughout society well beyond the content of their subject, much as family secrets affect relationships well beyond the subject of the secret itself. The proof of that fact is that, in both cases, when these barriers are broken (or the secret is revealed), more change occurs than could have been attributed to the specific content of the basic myth. These barriers can take hold in families, institutions, or entire civilizations. Emotional barriers as secrets in any "family" act as plaque in the arteries of communication and perception; that is, they stop up the entire artery, not just the location at which they are found.

The attempt to run a mile in less than four minutes serves as an excellent illustration of the power such emotional barriers can have. Back when the great Swedish runners Gunder Haag and Arnie Anderson kept failing to run a "four-minute mile," despite prodigious efforts, sports pages would actually ask the question whether it was physically possible for a man (not to mention a woman) to run a mile faster than four minutes. The goal seemed so beyond their endeavors that the four-minute mile took on the character of a constant, like the speed of light, a natural barrier. But when Roger Bannister finally broke that barrier in 1957, the following year three men broke it in the same race.

We tend to attribute Bannister's feat to new training techniques rather than a capacity to get outside the emotional processes of running. But in 1994 an African runner understood. When asked how he thought his colleague was able to lower the mile record by one of the largest amounts ever accomplished in one race, he replied, "He is not caught up in the mythology of Western runners." Similar stories can be told about how Chuck Yeager broke the sound barrier when he sped up at precisely the point where others slowed down because the plane began to rattle as it approached that "barrier."

Another example of a well-known emotional barrier was the belief in biblical times that a god was chained to a geographic area as well as to the fate of the god's people. The god would never, therefore, punish them. It was the breaking of that barrier that led to universal and ethical, rather than parochial and self-justifying, religion.

A contemporary emotional barrier beginning to be broken is the assumption that patients in hospitals should be forced to face pain stoically, for fear they will become addicted, rather than being given narcotics as needed or even having them under their own control. Perhaps we have witnessed the breaking of another contemporary emotional barrier that was just beginning to harden in the repeal of the arbitrary fifty-five-miles-per-hour speed limit. After all, if safety is the most important issue in life, let's get it down to forty-five (and keep the ships in the harbor).

The ramifying power of emotional barriers to restrict both the imaginative capacity and the adventure necessary for freeing the imagination is evidenced by what followed so quickly in the wake of the historic crossing of the equator. Once the inheritors of Prince Henry's spirit of adventure went beyond the "natural limit," what followed almost immediately was more than the discoveries of the western hemisphere. Within half a century, Magellan's circumnavigation had radically altered the fifteen-hundred-year-old Ptolemaic view of the entire planet. And less than twenty years after that,

Copernicus irrevocably changed Ptolemy's generally accepted view of the cosmos.

Copernicus, by the way—who was not from a seafaring nation but from Poznan, Poland—was studying in Italy around the time Magellan's men returned. He may have been emboldened to go forth with his imaginative ideas about the heavens upon seeing that Ptolemy was not so omniscient about the Earth. But none of this could have occurred had not Prince Henry set in motion the forces that ultimately broke through the emotional barrier of the equator, even though Columbus and many of the others did not actually have to cross the equator in order to go to the New World.

Future chapters will return to this theme of breaking the barriers, and discuss three imagination-limiting "equators" of contemporary American society's mind-sets (or, better, emotional sets) that I believe limit the horizons of leaders today. These emotional sets are generally accepted fallacies about

◆ *Data:* that data are more vital to leadership than the capacity to be decisive;
◆ *Empathy:* that feeling for others helps them mature or become more responsible; and
◆ *Self:* that selfishness is a greater danger to a community than the loss of integrity that comes from having no self.

Each of these myths will be discussed in terms of the ways in which it limits the thinking processes of family and institutional leaders and is nourished by the learned institutions of our day.

◈

To sum up, this is not a book that will play it safe. My thinking is based on the notion that contemporary American civilization is as misoriented about the environment of relationships as the medieval world was misoriented about the Earth and the sky. As indicated in the table below, every chapter in this book will be an adventure in thinking that offers new horizons for reorienting our conceptions of leadership.

REORIENTING OUR
CONCEPTIONS OF LEADERSHIP

Chapter Focus	"Old World" Orientation	"New World" Orientation
1. Adventure	Imagination is cerebral.	Imagination is emotional.
2. Anxiety	It's in the mind.	It's in between people.
3. Data	Be as informed as possible.	The capacity to be decisive is more critical.
4. Empathy	Foster feelings, sensitivity, rights.	Foster responsibility for one's own being and destiny.
5. Self	A leader's "selfishness" destroys community.	A leader's self is essential to the integrity of a community.
6. Models of Leadership	Linear; reality has to do with the nature of things; work to motivate others.	Systemic; reality is about relationships; work to differentiate self.
7. Stress	Results from hard work.	Results from position in relational triangles.
8. Crisis and Sabotage	Are basically dangers to be avoided; polarize the opposition.	Can be a sign of success; preserve self and stay connected.
Epilogue: The Past	It is prelude to the present.	It resides within the present.

For those who seek quick-fix answers to their leadership problems, such reframing may seem an impractical waste of precious time; but my experience has been that nothing is more relevant to the pragmatic than the way we tend to think. I do not presume to be a new Columbus, only a cartographer who has put some old data into new relationships and who hopes his "maps" might open unimagined vistas for leaders who are bold enough to set out in new directions.

A society cannot evolve,
no matter how much freedom is guaranteed,
when the citizenry is more focused on one another
than on their own beliefs and values.

Chapter Two

◈ A SOCIETY IN REGRESSION

At first glance, medieval Europe and contemporary America seem worlds apart. Our awareness in every field of knowledge is broader, our technology in every aspect of life from healing to war is far superior, our methods of communication and manufacturing are more proficient, our political and religious institutions are more sophisticated, the richness of our artistic expression is increasingly more varied, the complexity of our problems as well as of our solutions is infinitely more intricate. In fact, from the perspective of our more highly evolved technological state, the very term "medieval" has become a metaphor for ignorance and superstition.

However, describing families, institutions, and societies in categories of data, method, structure, and production while omitting the crucial variables of a society's emotional processes can obscure as much as it can inform. The technological differences between late-fifteenth-century medieval Europe and late-twentieth-century America are obviously great, but there are also some curious similarities between the anxious emotional processes of these two vastly different civilizations, five hundred years apart, that help highlight the factors that are toxic to leadership in our time.

Particularly striking are the similarity of forces that have been disruptive to the emotional balance of these two civilizations, and the symptomatic effects of such disruption. For example, there are forces to be found in both periods that are destructive of relationships and that are, by nature, anxiety-inducing. Each age comes at the end of a benchmark century. Each age has been destabilized by the breakdown of institutions around which society organized itself for centuries, and which may have been binding its anxiety, with feudalism and the papacy on the one hand, segregation and political chauvinism on the other. Both periods of time are characterized by radical power shifts in traditional alliances. In each age, a "global economy" makes many of the old, reliable rules irrelevant or inoperative. And whether your hero is Johann Gutenberg or Steve Jobs, a radical new technology for the transmission of information intensifies the connections of society's members.

But if there are similarities between the disruptive forces that might unleash anxiety throughout a society, there are also some curious similarities in the regressive symptoms that can result when such anxiety becomes chronic. Each age is marked by population drifts toward more concentration. Each epoch is characterized by a rising tide of purification: the Inquisition or "political correctness." Each period is scarred by a rampant plague: Black Death or AIDS. Each society is characterized by increasing polarization, rigidity of belief, clouded vision, and an inability to change direction. There is cynical pessimism about the future, despite the tremendous potential offered by new technology and social change. What both periods have in common is what I shall call a tendency toward societal regression.

Whereas medieval Europe's lack of cohesion eventually enabled individuals to separate themselves from its regressive emotional climate, precisely because our technologically advanced society constantly keeps us in often-simultaneous touch with one another it may be more difficult today not to become caught up in the surrounding systemic anxiety. Ironically, the very advances in technology that mark our era tend to intensify the "herding instinct" characteristic of an anxious society. This kind of enmeshment inhibits further the kind of individuation that is the essential precondition for bold leadership and imaginative thinking. As I shall demonstrate below, these regressive processes are pervasive throughout American civilization today in families, in institutions, and in society at large. In fact, it is the automatic and reciprocal feedback among these three emotional fields that makes society's anxiety systemic.

My thesis here is that the climate of contemporary America has become so chronically anxious that our society has gone into an emotional regression that is toxic to well-defined leadership. This regression, despite the plethora of self-help literature and the many well-intentioned human rights movements, is characterized principally by a devaluing and denigration of the well-differentiated self. It has lowered people's pain thresholds, with the result that comfort is valued over the rewards of facing challenge, symptoms come in fads, and cures go in and out of style like clothing fashions.

Perhaps most important, however, is this: in contrast to the Renaissance spirit of adventure that was excited by encounter with novelty, American civilization's emotional regression has perverted the *élan* of risk-taking discovery and pioneering that originally led to the foundations of our nation, shaping much of its fundamental character into an illusive and often compulsive search for safety and certainty. This is occurring equally in parenting, medicine, and management. The anxiety is so deep within the emotional processes of our nation that it is almost as though a neurosis has become nationalized.

I will begin by describing the nature of an emotional regression and showing how in any society, no matter how advanced its state of technology, chronic anxiety can induce an approach to life that is counter-evolutionary. One does not need dictators in order to create a totalitarian (that, is totalistic) society. Then, employing five characteristics of chronically anxious personal families, I will illustrate how those same characteristics are manifest throughout the greater American family today, demonstrating their regressive effects on the thinking and functioning, the formation and the expression, of leadership among parents and presidents. Those five characteristics are:

◆ I. *Reactivity:* the vicious cycle of intense reactions of each member to events and to one another.

◆ 2. *Herding:* a process through which the forces for togetherness triumph over the forces for individuality and move
everyone to adapt to the least mature members.

◆ 3. *Blame displacement:* an emotional state in which family
members focus on forces that have victimized them rather
than taking responsibility for their own being and destiny.

◆ 4. *A quick-fix mentality:* a low threshold for pain that
constantly seeks symptom relief rather than fundamental
change.

◆ 5. *Lack of well-differentiated leadership:* a failure of nerve that both
stems from and contributes to the first four.

To reorient oneself away from a focus on technology toward a
focus on emotional process requires that, like Columbus, we think in
ways that not only are different from traditional routes but that also
sometimes go in the opposite direction. This chapter will thus also
serve as prelude to the three that follow, which describe the "equators" we have to cross in our time: the "learned" fallacies or
emotional barriers that keep an Old World orientation in place and
cause both family and institutional leaders to regress rather than
venture in new directions.

By the term *regression* I mean to convey something far more
profound than a mere loss of progress. Societal regression is about
the perversion of progress into a counter-evolutionary mode. In a
societal regression, evolutionary principles of life that have been
basic to the development of our species become distorted, perverted,
or actually reversed. Chief among those evolutionary principles are:

◆ self-regulation of instinctual drive;
◆ adaptation to strength rather than weakness;
◆ a growth-producing response to challenge;
◆ allowing time for maturing processes to evolve; and
◆ the preservation of individuality and integrity.

Emotional regression, therefore, is more of a "going down" than a
"going back"; it is devolution rather than evolution. It has to do with
a lowering of maturity, rather than a reduction in the gross national
product. One needs to view societal regression in three dimensions,
not two. At the same time that a society is "pro-gressing" technologically it can be "re-gressing" emotionally.

What follows will not be a description of society as a "dysfunctional family." Families can be quite functional and still be operating in a mode that is emotionally regressed, if not outright psychotic. The focus on symptoms such as drinking, abuse, conflict, and divorce distracts from the possibility that a family can be totally absent of those symptoms and still live in a distorted reality that is ultimately more destructive. People can function quite well in the midst of a full-blown psychosis while a garden-variety neurosis can put them to bed for weeks. When a society (or any institution) is in a state of emotional regression, it will put its technological advances to the service of its regression, so that the more it advances on one level the more it regresses on another. Furthermore, a civilization's major technological advances can become perverted into a force for irresponsibility, if not immorality, as in modern warfare. The very same distortion can occur far more subtly in a state of peace with regard to advances in science, management, parenting, healing, education, research, or even the most well-meaning efforts to form community.

The ultimate irony of societal regression, however, is that eventually it co-opts the very institutions that train and support the leaders who could pull a society out of its devolution. It does this by concentrating their focus on *data* and *technique* rather than on emotional process and the leader's own self. These always go hand-in-hand. One result is erosion of the individuation necessary for well-defined leadership to arise or express itself. Another result is that parents and presidents then fail to recognize that in the shaping of any institution, emotional processes are more powerful than the nature of its structure or makeup. This widespread misperception is more than a failure to observe, however. The focus on data and technique is itself a characteristic of emotional regression: namely, avoidance or denial of the fact that it is happening.

◆ BOWEN FAMILY THEORY

The concept of an emotionally regressed society was first developed in the mid-twentieth century by Dr. Murray Bowen of Georgetown Medical School. One of the seminal thinkers in what was then the relatively new field of family therapy, he had begun to apply his observations of deeply disturbed families to society itself. What enabled him to make this transition was that for Bowen, family therapy was not simply some new technique for "fixing" families. It was, rather, a radically different way of understanding the universal emotional processes found everywhere in families, institutions, nations, civilizations. In making this conceptual leap, like Columbus, he went in a direction that was opposite to most thinking in his time. Rather than trying to understand families in terms of their cultural, class, or ethnic distinctions or how they differed from other kinds of human institutions, Bowen focused instead on the underlying natural systems principles that all families share, even though they might express those universal principles in different cultural garb.

From this "reversed" perspective, the most critical issues in understanding human institutions are not their customs, rituals, and ceremonies but rather how well families or other institutions are able to handle the natural tension between individuality and togetherness, their ability to maintain their integrity during crisis, and their capacity to produce well-differentiated leadership. While families and other institutions obviously differ in these regards, from this vantage point the key variables in that difference have less to do with their respective cultural traditions or sociological niche than with the way their members are connected emotionally, as well as how they have handled crises in the past. One cannot say, after all, that the families of any given ethnic or even class distinction are more mature than those of another background. It is rather the multigenerational emotional process, transmitted from generation to generation uniquely by each family, that puts aspects of its cultural or ethnic background to its own emotional service.

By going in the opposite direction, Bowen was able to observe new horizons, in particular the ways in which the principles found universally in family life also manifest themselves in the emotional processes of other institutions as well as in society itself. Drawing on observations from his pioneering research at the National Institutes of Mental Health, as well as a professional lifetime of working with severely impaired families, Bowen was struck by similarities between what he had been observing with increasing frequency in American society everywhere and what he had been used to seeing in chronically anxious families of various backgrounds—especially those with acting-out children.

Extrapolating from his broad experience, he went on to develop the idea that as with individual families, the anxiety curve of an entire civilization also goes through periods when it rises or falls. And, as with individual families, Bowen suggested, an entire society could lose its ability to cope with change when certain factors occur simultaneously:

◆ Anxiety escalates as society is overwhelmed by the quantity and speed of change.
◆ The institutions or individuals (whether scapegoat or symptomatic) traditionally used to absorb or bind off society's anxiety are no longer are available to absorb it.

In family life the major destabilizing changes are birth and death, marriage and divorce, geographical relocation, retirement, and a significant relational, health, economic, or legal crisis. Physical or "mental" symptoms surface in any given nuclear family (irrespective of cultural background) within six months of these two factors, reaching critical thresholds somewhere within that family's extended relational field.

An example from society is the treatment of Jews in medieval Europe, where they were alternatively driven out and allowed to reenter. This vacillation has been attributed to their economic importance as moneylenders in an incipient capitalist economy where it was un-Christian to lend money at interest. By keeping Jews in a pariah position (the so-called identified patient position in family therapy thinking), medieval Europe was able to bind off its anxiety by focusing on the alienated group. It was the rise in anxiety that occurred after Jews were no longer available to absorb this anxiety that induced nations to allow them back. This notion of anxiety-binding also suggests that when nations go from discrimination to extermination or ethnic cleansing, they can be unwittingly upsetting their own emotional balance to such an extent that one result of success at "ethnic cleansing" would be more internal polarizations and internecine struggles.

When both of these factors occur at the same time, suggested Bowen, the societal leaders (including parents) lose their capacity to lead, and the relationship system of that society, irrespective of culture or era, begins to exhibit the same patterns of thinking and relating that one tends to find in families with severely impaired members or in those in which the fabric of coherence has begun to disintegrate. Principally, that regression would show up in a lessened capacity of a society's "family" members to operate on the basis of principle; their response to challenge would become narrow and lose its resiliency, and their overall imaginative capacity would become stuck. To use the metaphors of the previous chapter, the "family's" orbit would become circumscribed as it feared mistakes; it would fail to expose itself to serendipity; and, in its unwillingness to risk, it would live in a distorted reality. "Family" members, therefore, would soon find themselves on a treadmill of efforts to get free, unable to obtain the distance that could shift their orientation and polarized on anxiety-driven issues.

◆ THE SPECTER OF CHRONIC ANXIETY

The kind of anxiety Bowen was referring to is not what is usually meant by therapists or psychologists who are diagnosing individuals nor the existential "angst" of philosophers—the anxiety that is a byproduct of being mortal, the fact that we are neither omniscient nor omnipotent. Nor is it the anxiety that is meant by political commentators who refer to our era as "an age of anxiety," pointing to economic worries or fears of violence or nuclear holocaust— although it might include such fears. Chronic anxiety is systemic; it is deeper and more embracing than community nervousness. Rather than something that resides within the psyche of each one, it is something that can envelope, if not actually connect, people. It is a regressive emotional process that is quite different from the more familiar, acute anxiety we experience over specific concerns. Its expression is not dependent on time or events, even though specific happenings could seem to trigger it, and it has a way of reinforcing its own momentum. Chronic anxiety might be compared to the volatile atmosphere of a room filled with gas fumes, where any sparking incident could set off a conflagration, and where people would then blame the person who struck the match rather trying to disperse the fumes.

The issues over which chronically anxious systems become concerned, therefore, are more likely to be the *focus* of their anxiety rather than its cause. This is why, for example, counselors, educators, and consultants who offer technical solutions for how to manage whatever brought the family in—conflict, money, parents, children, aging, sex—will rarely succeed in changing that family in any fundamental way. The anxiety that drives the problem simply switches to another focus. Assuming that what a family is worried about is what is "causing" its anxiety is tantamount to blaming a blown-away tree or house for attracting the tornado that uprooted it.

As with the families they are trying to help, "change artists" often confuse cause with effect. In fact, there is reason to believe that the very effort to offer quick-fix technical solutions, rather than encouraging the client family to become engaged in the much slower and more painful process of modifying its anxious emotional processes, is itself evidence that the consultant has become caught up in his or her client's anxiety. And that, in turn, says something about the importance of the *being* of the consultant, no matter how superior his or her eloquence, knowledge, or method.

As long as the focus is on technique, the being of the consultant is irrelevant. It is only when the focus is on emotional process that the consultant's presence can be considered an important variable—which is perhaps why focus on technique is so seductive. Clients can rarely rise above the maturity level of their helpers, however.

All the same would be true, of course, regarding the failure of consultants to change governmental, business, non-profit, religious, or medical institutions. Administrative, technical, and managerial solutions (such as centralizing, decentralizing, recentralizing, deconstructing, downsizing, right-sizing, or otherwise re-engineering) may often alleviate the symptoms of an organization. But they rarely modify the malignant chronic anxiety that could have been part of that institution's "corporation culture" for generations, and that, if left unmodified, will resurface periodically in different shapes and forms. Malignant conditions are rarely cured by "new blood" or radical surgery. It becomes all the more difficult to keep this principle in mind while focusing on the microcosm of a given institution within society when the macrocosm of society is itself in a state of emotional regression.

Extending this way of thinking to society at large, the issues upon which a chronically anxious civilization concentrates are also less the cause of its anxiety than its focus. When families get fixed on their symptoms—abuse, alcoholism, delinquency, marital conflict, or chronic physical illness—rather than on the emotional processes that keep those symptoms chronic, they will recycle their problems perpetually no matter what technical changes they make, how much advice they receive from experts, or how hard they try to understand their symptoms.

The same is the case when an entire society stays focused on the acute symptoms of its chronic anxiety—violence, drugs, teenagers smoking, crime, ethnic and gender polarization, economic factors such as inflation and unemployment, bureaucratic obstruction, an entangling tax code, and so on—rather than on the emotional processes that promote those symptoms and keep them chronic. In that case, the society will continue to recycle its problems, no matter how much legislation it passes, how it redistributes its resources, how many agencies it creates or dismantles, how many forms it finds for reinventing itself, or how many wars it engages in as a way of binding that anxiety off.

The process feeds back upon itself. For the more systemic chronic anxiety becomes in any "family," the more likely that relationship system is to stay oriented toward its symptoms, or the more likely it is to engage in "foreign" entanglements—wars and international crises for nations; intense struggles at neighborhood swimming pools, religious institutions, or school boards for families—as a way to avoid facing the emotional processes that are driving that "family" to become symptomatic.

This distinction between acute and chronic anxiety has major ramifications for the functioning and being of leaders. For there is no way out of a chronic condition unless one is willing to go through an acute, temporarily more painful, phase. This is another universal principle of emotional process that transcends the social science construction of reality. Whether we are considering a toothache, a tumor, a relational bind, a technical problem, crime, or the economy, most individuals and most social systems, irrespective of their culture, gender, or ethnic background, will "naturally" choose or revert to chronic conditions of bearable pain rather than face the temporarily more intense anguish of acute conditions that are the gateway to becoming free. But what is also universally true is that over time, chronic conditions, precisely because they are more bearable, also tend to be more withering.

◆ CHARACTERISTICS OF CHRONICALLY ANXIOUS FAMILIES

The following pages contain a description of five interlocking characteristics of chronically anxious individual families and their regressive parallels in the greater American family of today. Each is regressive because it subverts a major principle of the way life on this planet has survived and evolved, as shown below.

CHARACTERISTIC	EVOLUTIONARY PROCESS SUBVERTED
1. Reactivity	Self-regulation of instinctual drive
2. Herding	Adaptation toward strength
3. Blame Displacement	A growth-producing response to challenge
4. A Quick-Fix Mentality	Allowing time for processes to mature
5. Failure of Nerve in Leadership	All of the above

All five characteristics contribute to one another, although the fifth, lack of leadership, may be the link among them all. For the first four all share two factors in common that always tend to compromise effective leadership: denial of emotional process and a devaluing of the individuality that is necessary for summoning "nerve." Conversely, as I will demonstrate later, well-differentiated leadership tends to diminish the intensity of all four. All families will at times exhibit these characteristics when their anxiety reaches certain thresholds, and probably no family or institution is more than seventy percent free of them over an extended period of time. But there are some families that are only free of those characteristics thirty percent of the time, and even that number may be too high. I suggest that America's leadership difficulties are due to the fact that at this point in the history of the greater American family we are closer to the thirty percent than the seventy percent. Similarly, many of the events that are used to illustrate the chronic anxiety in contemporary American society have occurred in other eras. It is not the specific illustrations but their volume, their intensity, and their interconnections that single out our time.

According to E. O. Wilson, author of *Sociobiology*, the three essential characteristics for an enduring society, whether it consists of ants or humans, are *cooperation, cohesiveness,* and *altruism.* In civilized human societies these characteristics have been made possible by the development of our ability to regulate our instincts rather than let them drive us automatically. Under conditions of chronic anxiety, however, that capacity is eroded, and with it go cooperation, cohesiveness, and altruism.

1. Reactivity

The most blatant characteristic of chronically anxious families is the vicious cycle of intense *reactivity* of each member to events and to one another. It is as though the family were contained in a "feeling plasma," with everyone's nervous system constantly bombarded by the emissions of everyone else's. This state is not to be confused with "emotionality": dogged passivity can also be a reactive response.

Responses in a chronically anxious family can be framed and phrased quite rationally and with impeccable logic and charm, but it is as though they were driven by forces that had totally bypassed the cortex, and they tend to be triggered by outside stimuli rather than from within. For example, members of chronically anxious families will be quick to interrupt one another, if not to jump in and complete one another's sentences, and they are constantly taking and making things "personal." Communication is marked more by diagnostic or labeling "you" positions rather than by self-defining "I" statements. Rather than saying, "This is what I believe," "Here is how I perceive it," "This is what I will do," family members stay focused on the other: "You're just like your mother." "You're a control freak." "You're insensitive, unfeeling, irrational, missing the point, or just don't get it." The family is thus easily "heated up" as feelings are confused with opinions. Those inclined to become hysterical and those inclined to be passive-aggressive will both find their tendencies promoted.

Family members, therefore, are easily brought to loggerheads over the most inconsequential issues. The more aggressive members are in a perpetually argumentative stance, and the more passive are in a constant state of flinch. Attempts by any one member to express a well-defined stand calmly will be disrupted before he or she has reached a semi-colon. In such families anxiety circuits become super-conductive; there is little resistance within the system to its surges. Highly reactive families are a panic in search of a trigger. And the quickest trigger is any issue that involves a child. In fact, many chronically anxious families can be described as "child-focused."

The fact that it is difficult for any one member of a chronically anxious family to remain calm enough to think out a well-defined position perpetuates the momentum. The very calmness of one member often creates more reactivity in the other members, as they perceive calmness to be lack of concern and confuse reactivity with passion. Members of highly reactive families, therefore, wind up constantly focused on the latest, most immediate crisis, and they remain almost totally incapable of gaining the distance that would enable them to see the emotional processes in which they are engulfed. The emotionally regressed family will stay fixed on its symptoms, and family thinking processes will become stuck on the content of specific issues rather than on the emotional processes that are driving those matters to become "issues." The systemic anxiety thus locks everyone into a pessimistic focus on the pathology within the family, and it becomes almost impossible for such systems to reorient themselves to a focus on their inherent strengths.

What also contributes to this loss of perspective is the disappearance of *playfulness*, an attribute that originally evolved with mammals and which is an ingredient in both intimacy and the ability to maintain distance. You can, after all, play with your pet cat, horse, or dog, but it is absolutely impossible to develop a playful relationship with a reptile, whether it is your pet salamander, no matter how cute, or your pet turtle, snake, or alligator. They are deadly serious (that is, purposive) creatures.

Chronically anxious families (including institutions and whole societies) tend to mimic the reptilian response: Lacking the capacity to be playful, their perspective is narrow. Lacking perspective, their repertoire of responses is thin. Neither apology nor forgiveness is within their ken. When they try to work things out, their meetings wind up as brain-stem storming sessions. Indeed, in any family or organization, seriousness is so commonly an attribute of the most anxious (read "difficult") members that they can quite appropriately be considered to be functioning out of a reptilian regression. Broadening the perspective, the relationship between anxiety and seriousness is so predictable that the absence of playfulness in any institution is almost always a clue to the degree of its emotional regression.

In an atmosphere where everything is dire, a vicious cycle develops as a loss of playfulness destroys perspective. When that circular process reaches unbearable thresholds, the chronically anxious family will not be able to contain its reactivity within its own boundaries, and some members will begin transmitting the family's intensity beyond the family (acting out violently, combatively, or sexually) into a broad range of society's other institutions, such as church choirs, synagogue religious schools, traffic, PTA meetings, a condominium association, or any office or place of business.

But the most damaging effect of intense reactivity in any family is on its capacity to produce or support a leader. As the capacity of any member to achieve self-regulation or distance disintegrates, so does the ability, or desire, to lead. Reactivity, therefore, eventually makes chronically anxious families leaderless, either because it prevents potential leaders from emerging in the first place or because it wears leaders down by sabotaging their initiatives and resolve with constant automatic responses.

In the greater American family we call society, all of the same attributes of reactivity are rife today: the automatic response, the pessimistic focus on pathology rather than strength, the intrusiveness into the boundaries of others, the loss of playfulness, the wearing down of leaders. As with any chronically anxious family, there is in American society today an intense quickness to interfere in another's self-expression, to overreact to any perceived hurt, to take all disagreement too seriously, and to brand the opposition with *ad hominem* personal epithets (chauvinist, ethnocentric, homophobic, and so on). As in personal families, this hardens hearts and leaves little room for forgiveness or balanced accommodation.

The following example shows how our communities adapt themselves to the least mature and most dependent person. While turning a corner, a woman driver clips the edge of a stopped car and continues to drive away in front of several bystanders. The driver of the hit car, a young teenager, runs after the hit-and-run car, catches up to it at the next stop sign, reaches in and takes the driver's keys, saying, "We are calling the police." But when she says to him, "*You* hit *my* car," he realizes how crazy she is, gives her back the keys, and starts to drive off, while she stands in front of his car waving madly in an effort to prevent him from moving. He swerves around her, however, and leaves, but notices in his rear-view mirror that she is sitting in the middle of the street beating her breast. Two months later, he is arraigned by police for hitting her in the jaw when he reached in and took the keys. At the trial, the judge says he never saw so many witnesses come forth voluntarily, and he scolds the woman for making such mischief.

Why did it get that far? Relentlessly, she had gone to the police, week after week, talking to the person who decides if a charge should be honored and sent on to trial. This officer of the court finally gave in against his better judgment and let it go to trial just to be rid of her, even though that decision wound up costing the young driver thousands of dollars in attorney fees and lost work time.

With chronic social anxiety, the major regressive effect on leaders is the same as in families. They remain in a reactive stance themselves, led by each emerging crisis rather than being able to take a proactive stance that develops out of an objective perspective or principle. Being constantly engaged in the chronically anxious reactive climate, the leaders of the greater American family are almost completely incapable of gaining the distance necessary for objectivity. The constant engagement also prevents leaders from being able to take the necessary time out to become clear about their own vision and prepare new initiatives. Ultimately, even the desire to lead is eroded.

Almost everywhere I have traveled, whether the leaders are at the state level or the local level, whether their bailiwick is finances or education, the complaint is always the same: "I am constantly barraged by competing activist groups whether I do, or do not, take a stand, and no matter what stand I take. Efforts to establish reasonable discussion of the issues are a waste, and efforts to mold a working consensus are impossible. Something is going on that is more than the right to dissent. There are always some disaffected people out there that just won't let go. I thought I could make a difference, but there's no way to get a handle on the damn thing." This kind of statement was made to me by both a school official in a small community and the governor of a very large state, on different sides of the Mississippi. Both, after years of dedicated public service, decided not to fight for reelection when their term was up.

Finally, as the following story illustrates, the reactivity that is characteristic of emotionally regressed America today can induce a more "dis-courag-ing" failure of nerve among society's most individualistic leaders than did the Communist hysteria forty years ago that involved issues far more critical to the survival of the Republic. A prominent attorney, known for his passionate defense of justice and his courage in defending unpopular sides, disagreed strongly with a newspaper story that argued for nullifying the constitutional guarantee of freedom of speech when it came to politically incorrect stands on pornography. The article, written in a provocative style, also slurred, backhandedly with pointed *ad hominem* arguments, those who disagreed with the author's views, questioning their loyalty to democracy.

Driving to his office the next morning, the attorney, who had a long history of civil rights defenses going all the way back to the days of McCarthy, mentally composed a letter to the editor showing how his own longstanding commitment to the right of free speech had increased rather than decreased after he had defended a client on similar issues. But then, after further consideration, he never went through with the letter, saying to himself, "Who needs all those phone calls?" Yet he had never flinched when it came to the red-baiters who accused him of treason.

2. The Herd Instinct
Since the emergence of the earliest self-reproducing life forms, a critical principle of evolution has been that as new forms develop, life

evolves in the direction of its strengths by preserving a balance between togetherness and individuality. The herding instinct in a chronically anxious family upsets that balance, however, by encouraging the force for togetherness to smother the force for individuality. It does so by reversing the direction of adaptation toward strength, and it winds up organizing its existence around the least mature, the most dependent, or the most dysfunctional members of the "colony."

A major byproduct of the reactivity in chronically anxious families is the dominance of the forces for "togetherness." For the more automatic the responses in any relationship system become, and the less time-lapse there is between reactions, the more likely it is that everyone will be emotionally fused with everyone else. This emotional herding reinforces many of the factors mentioned above regarding the loss of space and distance. When chronic anxiety reaches systemic proportions, the desire for good feelings rather than progress will on its own promote togetherness over individuality.

The "togetherness" that forms under such circumstances is an undifferentiated togetherness. It is more a stuck-togetherness, similar to the kind of oneness that is characteristic of cults. The chronically anxious, herding family almost seems to develop a "self" of its own to which everyone is expected to adapt. As its regression deepens, it will turn the togetherness principle into the supreme goal that rules every member and transcends all other values. In the herding family, dissent is discouraged, feelings are more important than ideas, peace will be valued over progress, comfort over novelty, and cloistered virtues over adventure. Problems are formulated in rigid either/or, black-and-white, all-or-nothing categories. In this cult-like atmosphere, members of the family will tend to pressure both outsiders and "their own" to adapt to the centrality of its togetherness principle. This behavior is always short-sighted since it promotes contrariness, conflicts of will, and perversity. In fact, the constant pressure of various members to coerce one another to adapt, whether through threats or charm, is often characteristic of the families with the most severe physical and emotional problems.

The alternative, however, is not to promote compromise and consensus but to develop the kind of self-differentiation in each member that will increase their toleration of every other member's differentiation. Actually, the polarizing potential of the chronically anxious family's all-or-nothing attitudes makes the family more likely to split and increases the possibility that alienated members will cut off from one another. While the latter may seem to go against the desire for togetherness, it has a selective effect that preserves the homogeneity of the herd, for only those who are willing to surrender their self to the family's self will be comfortable in the homogenized togetherness. And where the family does not break up, the intense, locked-in polarization between members can also be understood as another kind of emotional fusion. Perhaps the major goal of family counselors ought to be to help people separate so that they do not have to "separate."

The overall effect of herding is circular: if reactivity causes people to herd, then herding increases the conditions for reactivity. To the extent that members of an emotionally fused family become caught up in one another, the process inhibits the individuation of its members. This loss of self in turn lessens the capacity of any one member to gain the distance and perspective that are needed to maintain self-regulation, thus diminishing further the imaginative capacity of anyone to even see things differently from the rest of the "herd." All the more so when the herd is in a reactive stampede.

The herding effect, therefore, militates even further against the kind of genuine self-definition that is a *sine qua non* for well-defined leadership. In addition, the overall atmosphere of conflict seduces leaders into thinking that the way to bring change is by exerting their will upon the family rather than by modifying its resistance through the nature of their own being and presence.

But the most important ramification of the herding phenomenon for leadership is its counter-evolutionary effect. In order to be "inclusive," the herding family will wind up adopting an appeasement strategy toward its most troublesome members while sabotaging those with the most strength to stand up to the troublemakers. The chronically anxious, herding family will be far more willing to risk losing its leadership than to lose those who disturb their togetherness with their immature responses. Always striving for consensus, it will react against any threat to its togetherness by those who stand on principle rather than good feelings. The herding instinct will move an emotionally regressed family to a position where it endeavors to accommodate the disruptions of the immature and of those who think in terms of their rights rather than their responsibilities. So rather than take stands with the most disturbed members and support those who stand tall, the herding family will adapt to the symptom-bearer (alcoholic, delinquent, substance abuser, gambler, hot-tempered one) and at the same time undercut anyone who attempts to define himself or herself against the forces of togetherness. They often characterize that person as "cruel," "heartless," "insensitive," "unfeeling," "uncooperative," "selfish," and "cold."

Actually, this tendency to adapt to immaturity and to sabotage strength is so often characteristic of chronically anxious systems that a good rule of thumb for leaders who are trying to pull any institution out of its regression is that when people start calling you "cruel," "autocratic," "heartless," "hardheaded," "unfeeling," "uncooperative," "selfish," and "cold," there is a good chance you are going in the right direction. Carried to its ultimate extreme, the herding instinct of the chronically anxious family will eventually lead it to organize itself around the symptomatic member rather than around its (potential) leader. The former will then become the axis around which the family's entire life revolves, the "squeaky wheel" perpetually getting the "grease." It is always easier to be the least mature member of a highly mature family than the most mature member of a highly regressed system.

The major effect of this system on leadership is that it hinders, if not cripples, the capacity to be decisive. The word *decisive* comes from the Latin root *cedere*, "to cut," as in incision, recision, or precision. The word *decision* means literally "to cut away." When one makes a decision, one is making choices, which includes the choice of being willing to give something up. When families are in a herding mode, however, the fusion in the togetherness force inhibits the capacity and the willingness to conceptualize solutions in such terms. The resulting indecisiveness of leaders is also reinforced by the herding force's erosion of self. Most of the decisions we make in life turn out to be right or wrong not because we were prescient about the future—which, after all, does not exist yet—but because of what we do after we make the decision. And the less confidence leaders have in their ability to stand alone after they make a decision, the less likely they are to make one.

The herding instinct in chronically anxious America has the same effect of furthering adaptation to the least mature, to those who are most unwilling to take responsibility for their own emotional being and destiny. Its influence on leaders is several-fold. It discourages them from expressing "politically incorrect" opinions and encourages them to play it safe generally; it undermines excellence by encouraging society to organize around its most dysfunctional elements; it forces leaders to engage in countless arguments that are dilatory; and it makes it more difficult for leaders to be clear, much less decisive. Leaders in chronically anxious America today— whether they are black or white, Jewish or Christian, liberal or conservative, young or old, male or female—tend to support or adapt to the most incessantly demanding members of their following.

The effects show up in language usage, in the administration of justice, in education and welfare policy, in divorce settlements, in the emphasis those who specialize in conflict resolution put on compromise, in the conduct of public meetings, and even in the world of sports. And in some institutions the togetherness forces put such a premium on inclusivity that those who do not agree with making it the overriding principle of the organization are isolated or rejected, thus creating Orwellian "Animal Farms" in which diversity is eliminated in the name of diversity.

One of the most extraordinary examples of adaptation to immaturity in contemporary American society today is how the word *abusive* has replaced the words *nasty* and *objectionable*. The latter two words suggest that a person has done something distasteful, always a matter of judgment. But the use of the word *abusive* suggests, instead, that the person who heard or read the objectionable, nasty, or even offensive remark was somehow victimized by dint of the word entering their mind. This confusion of being "hurt" with being damaged makes it seem as though the feelings of the listener or reader were not their own responsibility, or as though they had been helplessly violated by another person's opinion. If our bodies responded that way to "insults," we would not make it very far past birth.

The use of *abusive* rather than *objectionable* has enabled those who do not want to take responsibility for their own efforts to tyrannize others, especially leaders, with their "sensitivity." The desire to be "inoffensive" has resulted in more than one news medium producing long lists of words, few of which are really nasty, that reporters should avoid using for fear of "hurting" someone. Obviously there are some words that are downright impolite if not always hostile and disparaging, but making everyone sensitive to the sensitivities of others plays into the hands of those who feel powerless. And the notion that one can change attitudes by changing the way people express themselves is highly questionable. As I shall elaborate in chapter 4, often the shoe is actually on the other foot. It has been my impression that at any gathering, whether it be public or private, those who are quickest to inject words like *sensitivity, empathy, consensus, trust, confidentiality,* and *togetherness* into their arguments have perverted these humanitarian words into power tools to get others to adapt to them.

Here is a series of vignettes, each of which metaphorizes the adaptation to immaturity rather than to strength that has become so widespread throughout the "greater American family."

◆

One day, after I had spent a full day in court, I asked a small group of judges about a repeated pattern that appalled me. I noticed a variety of people brought before the bar on various charges from disturbing the peace to traffic violations. In each case, after the judge made his decision the citizens, whether they were professional persons, someone engaged in business, or a garden-variety mother and housewife, generally accepted the verdict without argument.

But almost every time irresponsible, flaky, often drug-addicted drifters (most of whom were there for the second or third time because they did not follow the judge's decree the first time) received a new decree, they tried to bargain with the judge, complaining help-lessly that it was unfair and that they didn't think they would be able to follow such a stringent order.

Every one of these irresponsible people seemed to dip into the same storehouse of explanations for why they had not followed the

judge's order the first time. Each one came across compliant and
repentant, but they all also focused on their rights rather than their
responsibilities. What astounded me most, however, was that the
judge on the bench constantly was willing to engage in the
bargaining! When I mentioned this incident to the judges they
sighed, rolled their eyes, and talked about how helpless they felt to
bring about a change in a community that would not back up
"harsh" treatment.

A very large community organization situated near the ghetto of a
metropolitan area was known for giving free food to the "poverty
stricken" and homeless in the community. The director, who had
been there for several years and had not seen much evidence that this
charity furthered responsibility, suggested a change: that a list of
work projects be drawn up that the community needed, and that all
those who came for meals should be told that they would have to
sign up for one of the projects before they could receive a free meal.
The negative reaction of some members of his board to the proposal
was so severe that he almost had to leave in order to prevent the
opposition from leaving and forming a new (rival) organization.

A group of clergy came to me from one of the major religious
denominations in our society and said, "We are about to start a
project that will raise fifty million dollars for our five hundred most
troubled ministers. How would you spend it?" I responded, "Why
would you put the fifty million into your five hundred most troubled? You will advance your denomination and our society far more
if you put it into your five hundred best." They answered, "But we
could never raise the money for that."

A woman, age thirty-two, who had twice left her husband because of
his controlling ways but who returned each time because of his

promises to change, finally took her three children and left. The man, age thirty-four, who had been used to getting his way, a charmer who was pleasing when he wanted something but a "killer" when he could not get his way, could not deal with her differentiation. At first, seemingly in a panic, he called everyone who knew her, literally anywhere in the world, and urged them to talk her into coming back. When she was adamant about not returning, he cut off her funds completely. Next, he began to sabotage her at work by calling and leaving false messages. He hired the most notoriously vicious lawyer he could find. He stopped payments on their house after borrowing heavily against it, and saddled her with half the debt. He locked her out of the house, kept the kids' toys, and stored their furniture where she could not find it. He sold her wedding gifts. He kept telling lies to their children about their mother's reputation. He tried to have her declared an unfit mother and ran up thousands of dollars in psychological consultation bills for their children, which he also never paid.

Despite the fact that everyone involved was clearly on her side, the husband continued to flout the courts, the banks, and whoever else in society was in a position to "bring the laws down" on him. Instead of doing just that, they all kept pressuring her to go half-way every time he made a new demand. The response of their children's therapist captured it all. When asked why she had not made a stronger report to the court about the father's unfitness to be a father and his obstructiveness of the mother-child relationship, she expressed what everyone else had evidently also felt: "Frankly, I don't want to have to deal with him."

◈

One wintry afternoon in a large Midwestern metropolis, I gave a presentation before an audience of several hundred people entitled "Lessons from the Holocaust for Survival Today." Throughout my talk I focused on the strengths of those who had survived, and I tried to show how weak leadership could create a totalitarian society as quickly as autocratic leadership. The subversion of democracy, I suggested, could come about not only from the abrogation of civil liberties but also from a failure of nerve among its leaders to stand up to uncompromising factions that wanted everyone else to adapt to them.

After the intermission, a panel representing various institutions in the community assembled to respond to questions, and people began to form lines at several microphones scattered throughout the audience. At one point, someone asked the panel a question concerning the difficulty he was experiencing in applying his artistic talents to the subject matter of the Holocaust. When it came my turn to respond, I said that the problem might be that he was trying to use his art in a utilitarian way, to send a message, and that this attitude tends to make artists more prosaic. Perhaps things would go better, I added, if he did not focus on a pointed message, but just let his soul express itself, and let the medium of his artistry be the message. Returning to my major theme of the day, I added that this was a problem with some feminist and other politically purposed art today, in that it was more concerned to make a statement than to let the artist's imagination flower individually.

As soon as I had expressed my point of view, a woman in the front row literally ran up to one of the audience microphones and, squeezing in front of the line of people that was waiting patiently to ask their questions, grabbed the microphone herself and exclaimed that she just could not sit still and listen to this abuse of women. She justified her subversion of the democratic process with her zeal and then made an impassioned attack on chauvinism. This then engaged all the members of the panel for the next fifteen minutes on a subject that was irrelevant to the day. Moreover, what happened was an example of precisely what I had been talking about, as they reactively tried to soothe her and in the process let her reactivity steal the agenda.

The reason for this sidetracking was not due to my comment nor the woman's retort, however. The regression came about because the moderator (that is, the leader) of the panel was a "nice guy" (a former minister and president of a local educational institution) who did not have the temerity to set limits on this person's invasiveness. He was more concerned to assuage her hurt feelings, to right her perceived slight, and to keep good feelings going in the community. By letting her speak and guiding the panel in a discussion of her remarks, he thereby adapted the entire community to her demands rather than "keep her in line." He might have said, "Madam, I can see that this is a very important subject to you, but we have set up a protocol for how this afternoon is to proceed, and if you will kindly wait your turn, I can promise you that you will have the opportunity to state your views." Or, he might have even said, "Madam, not only are you impolite, but it is you who are being *abusive:* of the audience, of the speaker, and of those members of your community who are waiting behind you."

It is interesting to contrast the view on adaptation to strength of another leader from a different part of society, a sports coach. Appalled at the coddling of complaining athletes, this football coach exclaimed, "When I coach, if receivers complain that the quarterback throws the ball too hard, I don't go to the quarterback and tell him to let up. I tell him to throw it as hard as he can, and I then tell the receivers they had better hang on to his passes if they want to hang on to the team. If those who cover punts complain that the punter kicks it too far, I don't go to the punter and tell him not to kick it so far. I tell the punter to kick it as far as he can, and I'll try to find players who can get down the field and cover his kicks. And if blockers say that they have trouble keeping up with a running back because he's too fast or too slippery, I don't get on the running back and tell him to go slower; I tell him to do his thing as best as he is able, and I get on his blockers to keep up with his agility."

What would it take to get CEOs, parents, judges, therapists, and those who specialize in conflict resolution to establish a similar pattern of adaptation?

3. Blame Displacement

One of the major advances in modern medicine has been the effort to stamp out disease not by trying to eliminate all the disease agents in the environment, but by enabling the body to limit a toxic agent's invasiveness. This immunological approach to disease is in line with what has worked for life from the beginning, for the toxicity of an environment is only one variable in survival. Another often more determining factor is the response of the endangered organism or species. The chronically anxious family, however, seems to be devoid of an immune response. It will not draw on its own resources, but will remain focused on what it perceives to be the outside agent.

Chronically anxious families encourage blaming rather than "owning it." This is a natural byproduct of the erosion of well-differentiated self that results from their herding attitude. The capacity to take responsibility for one's own being and destiny requires integrity, which in this context means not only honesty but being "put together well."

The projection process of casting blame outward rather than taking responsibility for one's own condition shows up with regard to both other family members and other institutions and forces. Within the family, members will take turns accusing one another of controlling them, hurting them, causing them to fail, being an obstacle to their own life goals, or even dropping something in the kitchen. The blaming attitude also feeds into the previously mentioned reactivity that spawns accusatory, binding, "you" statements ("Why did you have to embarrass me again last night with your drinking?") rather than responsible "I" positions of self-definition ("I have decided that you have the right to make a fool of yourself. But from now on, I am going in my own car"). *Ad hominem* retorts that displace the problem onto another's personality are almost always an indication not only of the anxiety of the person expressing them but also of their helplessness, if not emptiness.

Another favorite way that chronically anxious families avoid responsibility is to bind off their anxiety by coalescing around "displacement issues." If it is an internal displacement, the issue might be money, sex, an in-law, an ex-spouse, an illness, or a troublesome child. If it is an external displacement, it might be an institution to which the family belongs or a professional person from whom they have desperately been seeking assurance or magical solutions. The effect of the displacement issue is to distract family members from more painful matters that would focus them on themselves or their own relationships. And the effect on the object of displacement is that it then becomes extremely difficult to be objective about the nature and extent of its real problems, since so much added anxiety has been "grafted" onto it.

The chronically anxious family is caught in the following bind: The same avoidance of looking inward that leads members to cast blame outside the family also prevents family members from looking inward for the support of their own natural resources. The focus is constantly on pathology rather than strength. In addition, its constant search for certainty often results in too much emotional dependency on an outside resource, and its unrealistic expectations of professionals perpetually lead family members to feeling "let down." Accusations of malpractice are often a breach-of-promise suit, and the chronically anxious family will constantly "snooker" the helpful helper into making an unrealistic promise.

In this sense, litigiousness and violence are twin symptoms of regressed families. In fact, litigiousness may have become a middle-class form of violence, having in common with it the effect of displacing the anxiety, the reactivity, the problems, and the irresponsibility of the family onto other systems often all too willing to absorb it.

In a middle-sized New England town the parents of a five-year-old girl were having trouble keeping their daughter in her own bed at night. She screamed "uncontrollably" when left alone and constantly disturbed her parents' sleep by insinuating herself between them. After sending their child to a therapist, they concluded that the "cause" of their daughter's fears was a "horror" movie (*Poltergeist*) shown at a Halloween party by a day-care center to which they had been sending her.

After the child had visited the therapist for three months, they proceeded to sue the day-care center, even though the parents of all the children had been notified and asked for permission slips in advance. The day-care center, the only one in town, was led by a woman known for her principles, and she did not take this "lying down." She mobilized her colleagues, her friends, and her associates, splitting the community in half. Eventually, she ran out of money defending herself and finally left the town bereft of her talents or a day-care center. The parents eventually spent thousands more on their daughter's therapy, never going themselves. But then it came out that the wife had been having an affair all along. Both now began accusing one another of being the cause of their daughter's problems, and they soon became involved in a very messy divorce—focused on child custody, of course.

What chronically anxious families are largely incapable of seeing is that trauma is often, and perhaps usually, less the result of the impacting agent than of the family's own evolving emotional processes. A fairly new way of thinking in contemporary physics, which has been termed "self-organized criticality," has significant application for conceptualizing responsibility in family life. Basically, the idea is that when an outside force triggers dysfunction or disintegration within a system, the degree of disruption, the consequent symptomatology, or the resulting regression is not simply proportional to the strength of the impacting agent. The extent of the damage is rather the consequence of the way the system had been organizing itself to that point. For example, if one allows a sand pile to build up, grain by grain, at some point one more grain will cause an avalanche. But the origin of the avalanche, its speed, and its disruptive effect on the pile are not "caused" by the additional grain. It is not a case of one more straw on the camel's back. The influence that might be projected onto the outside agent belongs to the system's processes of self-organization.

When the thinking associated with self-organizing criticality is applied to families, it leads to the notion that much of what has been labeled "post-traumatic stress" is not simply the result of an event but has much to do with the way the family, or the person, had been developing before the event as well as with the way it responds to the shocking experience afterwards. If, for example, one takes a sampling of ten children, age ten, who are abused, or any ten adults who suddenly lose their jobs, the resulting long-range effects of the incident on the family and on the "victim" will only partially be due to the conditions of the event itself. A major, often determining, variable in the ultimate outcome of that victim's health (physical or emotional) will be the family's response which, in turn, is directly connected to the way it had been organizing itself; and that, in turn, always includes the way it was being led. This way of thinking may even be extended to battlefield hospitals, hospital emergency rooms, and maybe even complications after surgery and side-effects of medication.

While every crisis has its own context, there is one universal: to focus on the outside agent rather than on their own response. This in turn furthers a family's regression by reinforcing all of the factors mentioned earlier, particularly the focus on pathology rather than strength, the adaptation to immaturity, the tendency to take things in a way that precludes apology and forgiveness, and the narrowing of a family's repertoire of responses. Every crisis has a different context, of course, but what can be said of all families of any culture is that to the extent that families deal with crisis by focusing on the impacting agent or condition, they usually remain stuck as a result. More mature families that focus primarily on their own response to a trauma generally heal faster. They sometimes even grow—that is, evolve—to a higher capacity for dealing with trauma as a result of their encounter with challenge. As I will elaborate in the following chapters, this is precisely how the immune system (and the self of any human being) "grows"—by broadening the repertoire of its responses.

Well-defined leaders, of course, are not to be found in displacing, blaming families, and not only because they might have to take a lot of flack. It is built into those families' emotional processes. By the nature of the case, families that can produce well-defined leaders are not given to engaging in such childishness. Indeed, the concept of leadership, as I have been defining it, is totally incompatible with displacing blame. What is needed is pre-traumatic stress leadership.

All the characteristics of blame displacement we find in families are also prevalent throughout the greater American family today: focus on the other, disregard of personal resources, personal attacks on the opposition, a desperate quest for certainty, and a variety of pet (that is, favorite) displacement issues. Perhaps the outstanding example of blame displacement in chronically anxious America is what has come to be called *anti-incumbency*, the tendency of voters to reject whoever is in office almost irrespective of their party affiliation. This flailing at the political winds amounts to a collective irresponsibility on the part of voters seeking magical, quick-fix answers to a complex range of the problems of existence. Instead of focusing on their own response to the challenges of change, these voters find fault in their political stars. And it is not just a political phenomenon; it is occurring with regard to coaches, educators, CEOs, and clergy, not to mention marriage partners and parents.

To be sure, the critical importance of leadership for the health of an organization justifies the action of members of any institution to replace poorly defined leaders. But anti-incumbency is not that sort of rational search. It is more a reactive response to the voter's own inner emptiness, personal frustration, general unhappiness, loss of hope, and feelings of helplessness. Anti-incumbency is akin to a malpractice suit. Its roots have a lot in common with the failed promise that is the natural manure of litigiousness.

Supporting this atmosphere is the proliferation of revisionist history that focuses on the clay feet of yesterday's heroes, from Columbus to Pasteur to Freud to Churchill. This "Monday morning quarterbacking" when the "game" is already over is both a symptom of the anti-leadership phenomenon and contributes to it, by focusing on pathology rather than on strength, and on unverifiable motivation rather than on the solid reality of deeds.

The displacement of blame on leaders may be even more salient in churches and synagogues than in the political arena. Over the last ten to fifteen years I have witnessed a tremendous increase in the collective reactivity of religious congregations to their ministers, irrespective of gender or belief. As America's emotional regression has deepened, the clergy of every denomination have been increasingly thrust into a panicky national game of musical chairs, as each minister leaves one disappointed congregation only to be eagerly snatched up by another in the false hope that this new one will be better than the last. The former minister, in the meantime, has now found a new opportunity to be a displacement focus for a congregation that had become disaffected with its previous minister, who is presently about to take the place of the first, the anxiety still unabated and the focused issues still unresolved. This game is not confined to the world of religion, of course, and is played equally well with coaches, CEOs, school superintendents, police chiefs, and place-kickers in the National Football League. And in some locations, the round robin is played with the marriage partners of neighbors.

Indeed, the skyrocketing divorce rate also can be seen as an effect of the national tendency to displace blame. While it has plateaued in recent years, at one point it almost seemed to indicate a nation of quitters, and this includes both marriage partners and their counselors. What has led me to this conclusion is the number of people I have counseled years after a divorce who, in retrospect, might have saved their marriages had they understood how "to hang in there" in a less reactive manner. Many quit because the other partner did not seem motivated; others left because they did not have the stamina to see it through. Many others ended the marriage because their counselors' nerve failed them. These are counselors whose own chronic anxiety prevented them from enduring an unresolved or highly conflictual situation, thus impelling them to fix things or force a solution rather than bringing a non-anxious, and perhaps challenging, presence to the counseling session.

Contrary to popular thinking, it does not require two people working on a marriage to change it. Rarely are both partners equally motivated. But changing a marriage fundamentally does require that someone function as a leader in the sense in which I have been using that term. Where one partner can be taught to regulate his or her own reactivity, the other will often begin to imitate that behavior, and adaptation can ultimately be reversed. But for this shift to occur a critical point of departure must be reached: the more motivated partner must also be able to stop shifting blame to the other and to look more at his or her own input. This does not mean that they should look more at their own faults, but rather at how they have been compounding the situation.

This "coaching" approach to marriage counseling is a far more fundamental change in direction than might at first appear, and it is in keeping with the other reorientations illustrated in this book. It also shows how even marriage counseling has been caught up in societal regression, for it requires changing the criterion from "Who has the problem?" to "Who has the motivation to focus on strength, not weakness, and on leadership, not pathology?"

The focus on pathology rather than strength throughout our society is itself a form of displacement, since it protects us from the far more difficult task of personal accountability. The media, after all, are far more likely to report the details of a person who has been victimized by events than one who has overcome obstacles. For example, one evening a news channel showed an electrical engineering Ph.D. in California pumping gasoline. A recession that had overwhelmed Silicon Valley had cost him his job, and this white-male-over-thirty had to sell his house, keep his kids from going to camp that summer, and send his oldest child to a state school rather than to the private institution upon which she had set her heart. The message was that his plight metaphorized the hardships of many who had been "victimized" by the sudden downturn in the local economy. But the reason he was reduced to pumping gas was not that he had lost his job; it was that, unlike more resourceful others whose stories did not seem "newsworthy," he did not have the "nerve" to leave California.

Almost simultaneously, another channel's news program was interviewing a mother of about age thirty who, with her three young children huddled next to her, described helplessly how she had no place to go because she was being victimized by her landlord. The background for that story was that landlords who had received low-interest loans many years previously if they agreed to rent controls now found it was worth paying higher interest rates in order to get higher rents. But the landlord in this particular case had not suddenly kicked everyone out. He had both mailed and posted clearly his intention, and had given all his tenants several months' warning. What had this mother been doing all those months? This kind of blame displacement has reached truly creative proportions. A list of culprits could include parlor games like "Dungeons and Dragons," candy bars with too high a sugar content (the "Twinkie defense"), passive smoking, anything that gives off rays, and of course violence on television.

Television, in fact, is a good example of how displacement works to avoid dealing with personal resources. The most pernicious violence on television is actually in the story line—how the simplistic concept of human struggles "does violence" to the nature of life. The most insidious message that children—and adults—get from the average television program is the notion that motivation is singular, that all questions have answers, that justice always triumphs, that love conquers all, that life is unambiguous, and that there will always be a *deus ex machine* "in the wings" waiting to rush in. This view of existence is a far more dangerous addiction for a regressed society than escape into vicarious violence. Thus the worry of parents that violent television shows will affect their children adversely is the epitome of a chronically anxious society focusing on outside forces rather than inner strength. Parents cannot possibly hope to insulate their children against all the pathogenic forces and ideas in the environment. That way of thinking has to lead to unending cycles of anxiety. Where does it end? But they can "inoculate," so to speak, their children against those noxious forces by the maturity they instill in them through their own well-differentiated leadership. The immune response is always about self, strength, and integrity.

As with the nuclear family, the greater American family has also has its favorite displacement issues. These are not false issues; they are real and important in their own right. But for one reason or another, usually the result of how they are positioned in the emotional processes of a relationship system, they also attract to them—and are energized by—the surrounding, free-floating, general anxiety in the "family." This makes it harder to be objective about the extent of the real danger. It injects into these issues an increased intensity and allows them to serve as a distraction from personal responsibility elsewhere. The phenomenon of displacement thus works in two directions. On the one hand, the issue binds off, or absorbs, anxiety that is not directly related to the issue. On the other hand, in the course of serving that function, it frees other parts of the family or society from having to confront issues they do not want to face but which may be even more critical to the health of that "family."

Today the issues most vulnerable to becoming displacements are, first of all, anything related to safety: product safety, traffic safety, bicycle safety, motorboat safety, jet-ski safety, workplace safety, nutritional safety, nuclear power station safety, toxic waste safety, and so on and so on. This focus on safety has become so omnipresent in our chronically anxious civilization that there is real danger we will come to believe that safety is the most important value in life. It is certainly important as a modifier of other initiatives, but if a society is to evolve, or if leaders are to arise, then safety can never be allowed to become more important than adventure. We are on our way to becoming a nation of "skimmers," living off the risks of previous generations and constantly taking from the top without adding significantly to its essence. Everything we enjoy as part of our advanced civilization, including the discovery, exploration, and development of our country, came about because previous generations made adventure more important than safety.

4. The Quick-Fix Mentality
Life processes evolve by taking their time. It took half a billion years for the first self-replicating life-forms, almost three billion more for

the first multicellular organisms, still another half a billion for the rise of hominids, and another half a million until the appearance of our species, *Homo sapiens.* Growth, whether of a flower or of a baby, follows similar laws to this day; and growth, meaning *maturation,* evolves in the same way. There is no gene for maturity. But the chronically anxious family thinks it can modify life with technique.

The chronically anxious family is impatient. The same escapist thinking that leads it to the displacement of blame also leads it to assume that problems can be fixed in a linear way. The quick-fix mentality is the other side of the coin of displacement. Both are a flight from challenge, simplistic in their conception of life, and outwardly focused. Both avoid dealing with emotional process and devalue the self. And ultimately, both depreciate the integrity of the leader. All the characteristics of the chronically anxious family that have been mentioned previously come together to create the quick-fix mentality. What points them in the same direction is that regressed families have a very low threshold for pain. In fact, the amount of chronic anxiety in a family is inversely proportional to its capacity for enduring pain. What makes the chronically anxious family's anxiety chronic is not its pain, but the way it deals with its pain, In fact, the root of the word *anxiety* means pain, as in *angina, anger, anguish,* or *angst.*

As mentioned previously, there is no way out of a chronic condition without being willing to go through a temporarily more acute phase. And since anxiety is not something one wills away except by numbing drugs or stuck-together relationships, chronically anxious families will seek out those professionals who promise the most comfort, not those who offer the most opportunities for maturation. They will seek those professionals who help them avoid or reduce their pain as quickly as possible, not those who would encourage them to endure their pain in order to move steadfastly toward higher goals. The quick-fix attitude, therefore, will affect their choice of physicians, therapists, ministers, and politicians, as they are drawn to the snake oil of quick-fix elixirs that masquerade as technical solutions.

Focused always on symptom relief rather than on fundamental change in the emotional processes that underlie their symptoms, the chronically anxious family will constantly seek saviors, then pressure the expert—whether medical, educational, therapeutic, legal, or political—for magical administrative solutions. When engaged in therapy, such families only ask "how to" questions, constantly searching for techniques to manage conflict, manage money, manage sex, manage illness, manage children, manage teenagers, manage parents, manage in-laws. The quick-fix mentality therefore provides the ideal atmosphere for the proliferation of demagoguery and quacks, since it wants more than speed; it wants certainty. This search for easy answers drives the family to catch professionals up in an endless game of reassurance for problems that cannot be changed except by interventions that focus on their own emotional being, a game that circles back to their tendency to sue for malpractice, itself often a quick-fix solution for unresolved emotional processes.

This orientation to life is materialistic to the core. Even when a chronically anxious family is a pillar of its church or synagogue, its orientation to life is never really spiritual. It is the low threshold for pain, however, that is in many ways the key to the family members' regression, inhibiting both the ability to grow from experience and the responses that help other family members mature. The degree of pain we are experiencing at any time almost always includes two variables: the stimulus "causing" the discomfort, and the threshold for tolerance—that is, the capacity to overcome or perhaps reduce the sensation itself. It can sometimes be difficult to discern, when our pain has decreased or increased, whether what has changed is the stimulus or our threshold. But what is clear about pain universally is this: To the extent that we are motivated to get on with life, we seem to be able to tolerate more pain; in other words, our threshold seems to increase. Conversely, to the extent that we are unmotivated to get out of our chair, our threshold seems to go down.

This connection between pain and motivation also has a relational slant and plays a role in the aforementioned herding adaptation to immaturity. Raising our own threshold for the pain another is experiencing can often motivate the other to take more responsibility for his or her life. There is even the possibility that the challenge of having to deal with their pain will, in the most natural way, make their own threshold rise as well. By the same token, to the extent that our threshold for another's pain is too low, perhaps because we are unable to distinguish theirs from our own, their threshold for their own pain is likely to go down as well, and with it

their own motivation for maturing. This is precisely what I was referring to above when I said that many marriages break up because their
counselors cannot tolerate the couple's pain.

An illustration of the connection between pain and motivation
comes from one highly aggressive CEO who told the following story
about himself:

> I used to be an avid stamp collector, and once every ten years there
> is a huge international exhibition. Unfortunately, as the decennial
> event approached this time, I injured my knee and was limping
> around painfully on crutches with my leg in a cast up to my hip and
> my armpits burning from the upward push of my supports. But I
> wasn't going to let this once-in-a-decade opportunity go by. I there-
> fore managed to travel one hundred fifty miles by train, hobble my
> way in and out of cabs at both ends, wait in the vestibule of this
> huge armory for half an hour closely pressed to thousands of others
> in a herd "mooing" to be let in, let the stampede carry me through
> as the doors finally opened, crutched around for two hours. I was
> having the time of my life, hardly noticing that my arms or my legs
> were sore. I then returned that evening in a state of utterly satisfied
> exhaustion.
>
> The next evening, however, my wife asked me to take out the
> garbage, and I cried foul. "Can't you see how difficult it is for me to
> get around? I had a miserable day at the office. My armpits are
> killing me; I can't stand the awkward position of my leg. I really
> need some rest. How can you be so insensitive? Sometimes I think
> you don't appreciate how really painful this whole situation is."

An illustration of the relational side of pain, of the incapacity to
tolerate pain in others, comes from the principal of a school in
which one teacher's classroom was constantly out of control. No
matter what practical advice or moral support she gave the teacher,
the story was always the same. The teacher never seemed to be able
to sustain the kinds of stands that regulated her children's behavior.
Then one Christmas the teacher had a party at her home. When the
principal arrived, she could not help noticing all the tables in the
house had protective padding on their corners. Their youngest had
started to walk and his head was just getting up to the level of the
tables. Fearing that he would injure himself on one of the corners,

she had protected him from that danger—which was fine as long as they did not take him to anyone else's home.

What chronically anxious families require, of course, is a leader who does not give in to their demands. Should such a leader somehow arise, these families will be relentless in undercutting his or her resolve, and outside the family circle they will continually try to adapt other systems and professionals to their needs. And this is the link to the quick-fix mentality in the "greater American family." Once again, the principle stated above applies: People rarely can rise above the level of the maturity of their leaders or mentors. In every major area of American civilization today, leaders and mentors are adapting to this demand for quick fixes, technical solutions for problems that actually have to do with emotional processes. This mentality spares no part of American civilization. It manifests itself equally in healing, in politics, in people's belief systems, in management, in personal relationships, and of course in dealing with anxiety. It can be observed in the increasing popularity of brief, solution-oriented therapy and in the effort to discover a gene for everything that is not "normal." As with personal families, the desire for a quick fix throughout the greater American family evidences a search for certainty, a penchant for easy answers, an avoidance of the struggles that go into growth, and an unwillingness to accept the short-term acute pain that one must experience in order to reduce chronic anxiety.

Our obsession with method and technique affects education, healing, therapy, parenting, and management equally. Ironically, it leads leaders by the nose. Whether the issue is evaluating, analyzing, hiring, firing, team-building, or motivating, leaders everywhere seek the "instrument" that will do their work for them. This is epitomized by the V-chip for television sets that will enable parents not to have to worry about how the emotional processes in their family determine the effects of the programs to which their children are exposed. To really make them safe, why not try to put a chip in their brain? It is already being suggested that such a chip might improve memory storage. A mother reported entering the family room as her nine-year-old daughter inserted a tape she had rented. To everyone's shock, a spout of four-letter words came streaming from an actor's mouth. "Turn that off immediately!" shouted the horrified mother.

"I didn't know that was on the tape, Mother, honestly," apologized the embarrassed daughter. But that child recognized the words, and it was the parent's response that fixed the traumatic effects. Maybe parents can get "off the hook" altogether if only someone will invent an implantable chip that can cleanse children's brains as we used to wash out their mouths with soap.

The effect on leaders of this widespread demand for a quick fix is that it turns them from professionals into hacks. For as long as leaders cater to the demand that they fix things quickly rather than encourage, promote, or even force their clients to deal with their own emotional being, then these leaders—be they parents or presidents—also miss out on challenging opportunities to grow. The difference between a professional and a hack is not in their degree or training. Both may do what they do with polish; but the hack is not transformed by his experience.

To paraphrase one of my own characters from *Friedman's Fables*, Cassandra the Greek prophetess, discussing denial in an anxious society:

> The quest for certainty has produced a fascination with reducing everything to its basic components; everything must have an answer. Only the poets are unafraid of ambiguity; everyone else goes to experts. It is true that in my day we sought oracles, but today people still want the oracular, whether from their therapist, physician, minister, or politician. The helping professions have been turned into certain-tizers. At least at Delphi they had the good sense not to be too specific.

5. *Poorly Defined Leadership*

The four major characteristics of chronically anxious families all conspire to produce the fifth, the lack of well-differentiated leadership—although to the extent that the fifth applies, it also promotes the first four. This effect is uniform across the board for all "parents and presidents" irrespective of their personality profile, their cultural background, or their place in society. The major regressive effects on leadership of chronic anxiety in both personal families and in the greater American family are these:

◆ Leaders lack the distance to think out their vision clearly.
◆ Leaders are led hither and yon by crisis after crisis.
◆ Leaders are reluctant to take well-defined stands, if they have any convictions at all.
◆ Leaders are selected who lack the maturity and sense of self to deal with sabotage.

These are in stark contrast to the major principles of leadership mentioned earlier that were characteristic of the great Renaissance explorers:

◆ the capacity to separate oneself from surrounding emotional processes;
◆ the capacity to obtain clarity about one's principles and vision;
◆ the willingness to be exposed and to be vulnerable;
◆ persistence in the face of inertial resistance; and
◆ self-regulation in the face of reactive sabotage.

The fact that chronically anxious families will always lack well-differentiated leadership is absolutely universal. I have never seen an exception to this rule. After many years of working with troubled families from a vast variety of cultures and backgrounds, I have found that the single most important factor distinguishing those families that became hopelessly stuck or disintegrated into crisis from those that recovered was the presence of a well-defined leader. And again, by leader I do not mean someone who tells others what to do, but someone who can maintain the kind of non-anxious, well-principled presence I have been describing.

What is always absent from chronically anxious, regressed families is a member who can get himself or herself outside of its reactive, herding, blaming, quick-fix processes sufficiently to take stands. It has to be someone who is not so much in need of approval that being called "cruel," "cold," "unfeeling," "uncooperative," "insensitive," "selfish," "strong-willed," or "hard-headed" immediately subverts their individuality. I believe that the universality of this principle lies in the fact that it is not some abstraction or guideline from a manual, but it is the way life works. It is a principle of all natural systems. All forms of social organization require leadership, whether one is considering herds, flocks, swarms, pods, packs, or schools. It is this natural systems basis that makes it an evolutionary principle; for this reason, when chronic anxiety in any family works to regress this principle, the effect is counter-evolutionary.

On the following pages are three tables that show the reciprocal relationship between regressed societies and poorly differentiated leadership. Table 1 sums up the characteristics of chronically anxious families and American civilization that I have been describing and lists their effects on leadership.

Table 2 lists the regressive characteristics of thinking and relating that all leaders have to contend with in any chronically anxious relationship system.

Table 3 displays the overall connection between chronic anxiety, the perversion of evolutionary principles, and its regressive effects on both society and leadership.

TABLE I
CHARACTERISTICS OF CHRONIC ANXIETY
IN FAMILIES AND AMERICAN CIVILIZATION,
AND THEIR MAJOR EFFECTS ON LEADERSHIP

CHARACTERISTICS OF CHRONICALLY ANXIOUS FAMILIES	MANIFESTATIONS IN CHRONICALLY ANXIOUS AMERICA
1. Reactivity	
◆ automatic responses	◆ uproars over perceived slights
◆ boundary erosion	◆ bureaucratic entanglements
◆ exaggeration of extremes	◆ *ad hominem* retorts
◆ loss of resiliency (playfulness)	◆ disruption, interference, and censorship of opposition

Effect on Leadership: Leaders become less imaginative, are eventually worn down, and resign or "go through the motions."

2. Herding	
◆ togetherness as supreme value	◆ uncompromising special interests
◆ totalism in thinking and relating	◆ courts lose base in principles
◆ wills conflict, polarization, and cut-offs	◆ funding for weakness, not strength
◆ organizes around dysfunction	◆ politically correct language
◆ adapts to immaturity	◆ dignifying of immaturity (sexual acting-out)

Effect on Leadership: Leaders become indecisive because, tyrannized by sensibilities, they function to soothe rather than challenge and to seek peace rather than progress.

3. Blame Displacement

- loss of integrity and accountability
- fault projected outside
- quickness to blame (sue)
- cynical pessimism
- focus on safety rather than adventure

- anti-incumbency
- litigiousness and violence
- rising divorce rate
- national displacement issues
- carcinogens, abuse, environment

Effect on Leadership: The least mature are selected while those with the greatest integrity, precisely those who have the best capacity to pull a society out of a regression, do not even seek office.

4. Quick-Fix Mentality

- low pain threshold
- simple answers

- vulnerability to snake-oil fads
- quest for certainty

- drug culture
- fundamentalism and reductionism
- proliferation of data
- emphasis on technique

Effect on Leadership: Leaders are not challenged to grow.

TABLE 2
REGRESSIVE CHARACTERISTICS
OF THINKING AND RELATING TO BE FOUND IN ALL
CHRONICALLY ANXIOUS RELATIONSHIP SYSTEMS

THINKING CHARACTERISTICS	RELATIONSHIP CHARACTERISTICS
◆ polarized and totalistic (black-and-white, either/or, all-or-nothing)	◆ with us or against us polarizations
◆ reactive rather than stemming from principle	◆ members homogenized or cut off
◆ reductionist	◆ adapts to the most immature member
◆ given to *ad hominem* reasoning	◆ organizes around the dysfunctional
◆ oriented toward pathology, not strength	◆ sabotages differentiation
◆ focused externally rather than internally	◆ loss of integrity and individuality (self)
◆ oriented toward crisis, not opportunity	◆ oriented toward comfort, not challenge
◆ magical	◆ functions for peace over progress
◆ serious	◆ scapegoats to bind the anxiety
◆ no curiosity	◆ judges caring by getting a reaction (hurting)
◆ given to "group think"	◆ focuses on rights rather than responsibilities

TABLE 3

OVERVIEW OF THE CONNECTION BETWEEN CHRONIC ANXIETY,
ITS PERVERSION OF EVOLUTIONARY PRINCIPLES,
AND THE REGRESSIVE EFFECTS OF COUNTER-EVOLUTIONARY FORCES
ON BOTH SOCIETY AND LEADERSHIP

CHRONIC ANXIETY	PRINCIPLE PERVERTED	EFFECT ON SOCIETY	EFFECT ON LEADERS
Reactivity	regulation of instinct	inhibition of self-differentiation	perspective on leadership clouded
Herding	adaptation to strength	organization around immaturity	indecisiveness
Blaming	response to challenge	disintegration	sabotage
Quick-Fix Mentality	maturation takes time	recycled stuckness	least mature selected

Imagination is more important than information.
—Albert Einstein

Chapter Three

◆ DATA JUNKYARDS
AND DATA JUNKIES:

THE FALLACY OF EXPERTISE

If you went back in history by a factor of ten to the year 206 or
207, the amount of information that existed in the world then
would fit in perhaps a single library or two. You would find the
two Testaments, early rabbinic and church commentaries, Hindu and
Norse Vedas, Sumerian and Egyptian poems and codes, Roman and
Greek writings, various political and scientific treatises, the sayings
of Buddha and Confucius. You might also imagine a large oral
collection of tribal tales from Africa, America, and other far-flung
regions. But not much more.

Ten times that number of years later, the quantity of data that is
available to leaders is not ten times greater but a number so huge as
to be unimaginable. Indeed, with present computer technology, every
time a new bit of information is conceived, it has the potential
immediately to cross-pollinate with all existing data and to double—
and that is happening in a myriad of situations every nanosecond.
Moreover, we are just beginning to realize the computational potential in exploiting naturally occurring biological systems such as DNA
that can organize and rearrange sequences of information a trillion

times faster and at a billionth of the cost in energy. Data today expand at a proportion so much greater than time passes that the expansion is becoming a quantum phenomenon. Terms like *exponential* and *logarithmic* have become understatements.

Now, instead of going back almost two thousand years, suppose you were to project forward two thousand years. How much data (I use the word interchangeably with "information") will there be? Even with the latest advances in information retrieval or the envisioned concept of storage within cells or between atoms, data may eventually outweigh the planet. And, in that distant future, someone will give a report at a conference on healing or education or economics or parenting or leadership and say, "We did a complete literature search on our subject to make sure that we have discovered something completely new. In fact, we went all the way back to the beginning of recorded history, although we all know that nothing of lasting importance could possibly have been thought of before now."

What I am driving at is this: As long as leaders—parents, healers, managers—base their confidence on how much data they have acquired, they are doomed to feeling inadequate, forever. They will never catch up. The situation can only get worse. Yet everywhere in our society, the social science construction of reality has confused information with expertise, know-how with wisdom, change with almost anything new, and complexity with profundity. Neither parents nor presidents will ever be able to escape the flood of data that engulfs them, either by trying to limit its expansion or by trying to keep up with its flow. Nor is specialization the way out, since it only sends the avalanche of information in the opposite direction.

The data deluge can only be harnessed to the extent that leaders can recognize that not all information is worth gathering, and also to the extent they can develop criteria for discerning what information is important to leadership. It has been calculated that human beings exchange one hundred thousand bits of information every minute; but how much of that information is significant? Without the development of such criteria, leaders will constantly be caught in a wearying bind wherein the quick-fix orientation of a chronically anxious society spawns unlimited quantities of data and technique, while leaders, in their effort to "stay on top of things," will continually be made more anxious by their efforts to keep up, if not feeling more guilty over the fact that they are not all current.

It is not advancing technology that is creating the information bind, however; it is societal regression, first by perverting the natural instincts of curiosity and adventure into a dogged quest for certainty, and second by focusing on pathology rather than on strength. The thinking processes in an age of discovery that is marked by a spirit of wonder are quite different from those that characterize an anxiety-driven dash for "the truth." The latter is more likely to lead to reductionist thinking, the reification of models, and an overbearing seriousness, all of which rigidify rather than free the imaginative capacity.

As for the focus on pathology, data-gathering in a society oriented toward pathology rather than strength eventually winds up, like the very nature of pathology, as a process that is unable to set limits on itself. In contrast, as I shall demonstrate throughout this work, the categories of strength are well defined, and the pursuit of information in this area promotes the self-differentiation necessary for harnessing the data deluge.

Developing new criteria for judging the importance of information, therefore, is not a matter of changing one's "database." What is required is a fundamental reorientation of our thinking processes, one that allows leaders to evaluate information in the context of emotional variables, along with the leaders' self-differentiation. Ultimately, the capacity of leaders to distinguish what information is important depends less on the development of new techniques for sorting data than on a leader's ability to avoid being driven by the regressive anxiety that is often the source of the unregulated data proliferation to begin with.

This chapter begins a series of three discussions on what I have called the "equators" of modern society. These are *myths, emotional barriers,* and *learned superstitions* which, because of their hold on our imagination, keep our thinking processes stuck and preserve "old world" views, thus limiting our horizons and range. The illusion that is the subject of this chapter is the fallacy that orients leaders toward "know-how" rather than the nature of their own being. The great myth of our data-gathering era that affects leaders, parents, and healers alike has two sides: "If only we knew enough, we could do (or fix) anything," and its obverse, "If we failed, it is because we did not use the right method."

A further consequence of our orientation toward data and technique rather than toward emotional process devalues the self in several related ways that affect leadership:

◆ It overwhelms leaders.
◆ It confuses them with contradictory results.
◆ It emphasizes weakness rather than strength.
◆ It de-selfs them by ignoring the variable of individuation.

In this chapter I will describe the effects of the data deluge on all members of society generally and how it erodes the confidence, judgment, and decisiveness of leaders in particular. Then I will show the paradoxical side of the data deluge. Despite its anxiety-provoking effects, the proliferation of data also has an addictive quality. Leaders, healers, and parents "imbibe" data as a way of dealing with their own chronic anxiety. The pursuit of data, in almost any field, has come to resemble a form of substance abuse, accompanied by all the usual problems of addiction: self-doubt, denial, temptation, relapse, and withdrawal. Leadership training programs thus wind up in the codependent position of enablers, with publishers often in the role of "suppliers." What does it take to get parents, healers, and managers, when they hear of the latest quick-fix fad that has just been published, to "just say no"?

The next part of the chapter will begin the process of reorientation. The latest understandings of the nature of the human brain have out-distanced the "old world" knowledge on which most contemporary leadership theory is based. And it is precisely the "old world" focus on data and technique rather than emotional process that contributes to that fundamental misunderstanding. I will describe how new orientations toward the brain integrate data and emotional process at the most fundamental levels of brain functioning. This has revolutionary consequences for leadership, both with regard to leadership's major categories—motivation, insight, communication, values, resistance, perversity, and madness—and with regard to the very nature of the leadership process itself. For in any age, models of leadership ultimately must square with the latest understanding of the connection between the brain and the body.

Whether one is a parent or a president, the "new world" understanding of that connection offers a model for the relationship between a "head" and a "body politic" that is radically different from the leadership theory that is based on the social science construction of reality. The "new world" view of the brain suggests that in any data-gathering process, attempts to separate out the intellect from emotional processes not only omit a crucial variable, but in effect become anti-intellectual and actually may be downright "stupid."

Furthermore, there is a strange perversity here. The development of the human brain has been a major vehicle for our species' evolution. But conventional models of the brain that separate out the brain's cognitive functioning from our broader emotional heritage—that which connects us with the universal natural processes that govern all life on this planet—is, ironically, in danger of subverting the brain into a counter-evolutionary force. For paradoxically, to the extent that the variables of emotional process are omitted in any family or organizational data-gathering activity, and the more successful the human brain becomes in its endeavors to produce more "knowledge," the more stuck the human animal will become in the knowledge it produces. And this brings us back to the three characteristics of an imaginatively gridlocked society: a treadmill of always trying harder, a focus on finding answers rather than reframing questions, and a polarization into false dichotomies. At times it seems as though the chronic anxiety in modern America has turned the brain into a sorcerer's apprentice that is outputting more than our species can meaningfully handle. The resulting overflow eventually creates a backwash that begins to drown out the entire process to the very extent it becomes more productive.

In 1993, the person in charge of computerizing all the information being spun off by the human genome project in its aim to map totally the location and function of the one hundred thousand genes in a human organism commented on the work being done. She said that because it was not clear just what would eventually be done with all this information, they were often not sure how to record it in the first place. There was the danger, she continued, that without such criteria of meaning, we would wind up with what she labeled *data junkyards*.

Below are a number of illustrations of her point from medicine and the mental health professions, followed by parallels in parenting, business, and management. I begin with healing because the amount of responsibility one takes for his or her own life is the quintessential issue of leadership and self. The thinking involved in how anyone "manages" his or her own health encapsulates all critical issues of management. It is both reflective of and ramifies out to the way society encourages us to "manage" our selves and others in all areas of our life.

◆ MEDICINE

In 1990, the number of indexed articles that a physician could refer to had reached six hundred thousand. At that point, Octo Barnett (the gentleman in charge of computerizing all information from all medical journals so that the average physician can learn all there is to know about your problem by turning on his kitchen PC in the midst of microwaving a quick dinner) said that for a physician to read two articles a day from these journals would be a prodigious task. Moreover, if a doctor were able to keep that up for twelve months, at the end of the year the physician would be eight hundred years further behind than when he started. Coming from the opposite direction but conveying the same point was the head of a major accounting firm who said, "You don't want to learn too much, because there is so much you are going to have to forget."

This huge volume of "knowledge" has affected the very core of medical training as each specialty, during the relatively short period of time students are exposed to a department, tries to stuff as much information as possible about that field into their budding physicians' brains. Once again the problem can only get worse, and recent efforts to revamp medical school curricula rather than changing the paradigm of healing will only slow, not stem, the tide. Yet deans of medical schools have been overheard to tell incoming students that the way to tackle the problem is to make sure they memorize fifteen facts a day.

This focus on data continues throughout the physician's life, and has a significant effect not only on how the healer practices his or her own art but also on the response of patients to their condition.

The proliferation of data (and the denial of emotional process) begins with the well-known intake forms with over one hundred questions, and goes further on standardized insurance forms which—in the case of neurology, dermatology, and orthopedics—list more disease syndromes than one could ever have thought possible. It cannot be that whoever or whatever organized this universe set it up in such a way that this much information would be necessary in order to function effectively.

While it might at first appear that such refinement of data simply represents the increasing sophistication of scientific knowledge, this way of organizing one's mind—that is, solely in terms of data categories that omit the emotional variables that might influence a patient's response—can have a significant de-selfing effect on both doctor and patient. Concerning physicians, the data deluge can distract them from focusing on the healing power contained within their own presence. This includes not only their overall objectivity and diagnostic astuteness but also their capacity to regulate their own anxiety with regard to both their patients' anxiety and their attorney's. How physicians manage their own anxiety can be a vital component in a patient's will and recovery, and it often influences, and is influenced by, how much they rely on or pursue the unending amount of data that modern medical technology is prepared to offer.

Just as important, the data orientation also affects the "nerve" of patients directly. The mere reading of intake forms is an invitation to anxiety: first, because they tend to be totally focused on pathology. Second, because they focus patients passively on their body to the exclusion of their minds (that is, will). Third, when the emotional set established by the pathology content of intake forms is combined with the statistical data patients learn about their illness, they are inexorably led to the assumption that their condition is part of some roulette game played by life which has made them "victims" of a disease. This obscures the possibility that the course of most illness, as with any other crisis, is a much more complex process that also includes the patient's own response to his or her condition.

Nowhere on the ubiquitous medical intake forms are questions that would inform physicians of a given patient's capacity for recuperation, questions which might by their very asking challenge patients to be more responsible for their own condition. No one seems to know how these forms originated, nor how they became so conventionally standardized. But their proliferation certainly has expanded with societal regression.

A practice of medicine that was less overwhelmed by the deadly seriousness of data accumulation might also ask questions like:

◆ "How long do you think it will take for you to get over this?"

◆ "How have you tended to deal with crises in the past?"

◆ "What relational binds do you now find complicating your life, either in your family or your business, that might have a compromising effect on your integrity and therefore on the natural ability of your body to mobilize an optimal response?"

◆ "Who will suffer most because of your condition?"

◆ "Who would be likely to benefit most from your demise?"

While such questions might in some cases "cause" additional anxiety initially, we are back to low pain thresholds. The temporary increase in acute pain that challenging questions induce is usually a small price to pay if those questions can elicit a self-differentiating response. Specific (acute) anxieties generally only upset people. Chronic anxiety, on the other hand—the unrealized kind that is deep within the emotional processes of a family, an institution, or a healing practice—not only is more likely to induce a failure of nerve, but it has far more power to "dis-integrate."

This omission of the variable of the patient's own response on forms and in statistics gives all data a morbidly deterministic quality and puts the patient into an emotional bind that is similar to the dilemma of the indecisiveness of leaders. No matter what the statistical reality of a patient's affliction, his or her own personal future is not there yet, and in many cases it will be influenced by how the patient functions after he or she finds out what disease he or she has.

For example, a patient is being prepared for an angioplasty procedure to unclog one or more arteries and is told about the possibility of inserting stents to help keep the arteries open. The patient is also told that there is a thirty-percent chance of re-stenosis (reclogging)

within a month if stents are used, for stents may, by their intrusiveness, alert a kind of immune response that fosters re-stenosis faster
than might have occurred over the next five years if they had not
been inserted.

Which way should the patient bet? The statistical odds (seventy
percent) may be with the patient, but they will be presented as data
apart from the emotional processes currently affecting the patient.
Worse, the statistics upon which the patient is expected to make an
"informed" choice were gathered, in the first place, by gatherers who
left out those same differentiating variables when counting the
results of that procedure on other patients.

Once one begins to include emotional variables in the overall
data, such as current emotional binds, past tendencies in crisis, the
ability to differentiate self from the emotional reactivity of relatives,
and the capacity to maintain resolve, then it becomes possible to
realize that the same procedure is never the same procedure, even if
it is technically identical. The focus on data to the exclusion of
emotional variables leaves the patient to hope that he or she "falls"
into the right category. This atmosphere not only turns patients into
statistics; ultimately it turns them into data.

Of course, not every physician has lost his or her self to the data
deluge. After the lungs of a patient with advanced emphysema
collapsed, he was told that his only chance of staying off a respirator
was to undergo a procedure that would adhere his lung to his chest
wall. The family wondered whether the procedure was worth the risk,
since they were told privately by their pulmonologist that based on
the data of medicine's experience with this procedure, the operation
would only give him a year or two at best. Six years later, when the
patient, who had since found out about his two-year prognosis,
mentioned it to a more street-savvy pulmonologist, the latter
responded, "We doctors are real good at predicting death within six
months; after that, forget it."

The de-differentiating effects of data are not, however, confined to
the physician's office. They are part and parcel of the chronic anxiety
in society. Daily, the media publish the latest results of some "scientific" discovery showing a relationship between your most feared
disease and something you ingest or do, or they bring false promise of
a quick fix to one of the more serious illnesses that "plague" humanity.

The overall nerve-wracking effect on patients is many-fold. First, as already mentioned, the sheer amount of the data is overwhelming. Second, the studies are confusing because they are often contradictory. Third, the data themselves are formatted in anxiety-provoking formulas that, precisely because they leave out emotional variables, give a deterministic impression. In part, this is a result of the way they are phrased, but, in large part, these results are due to the fact that the statistics generally omit the differentiating variable of the organism's own response. In short, the extrapolations ignore the exceptions, but it is precisely in the exceptions that we often find the key to the role of an organism's response in its own survival.

The overwhelming and confusing effects of data on the general public can also be illustrated with examples from coronary conditions and cancer. In recent years the public has been told that heart problems can be significantly reduced by the ingestion of polyunsaturated oils, red wine, margarine, Vitamin A, Vitamin E, Vitamin D, fish oils, oat bran, wheat bran, all whole grains, vigorous exercise, HDL increasers, legumes, vegetables, soybean products, niacin…and most things that don't taste good. But "studies" have also shown that

- Constant dieting is bad.
- Vitamin E, while an antioxidant that eliminates the free radicals that promote atherosclerosis, also raises the risk of cancer.
- Margarine may be worse than farm-fresh butter because of its high trans-fatty-acid content.
- Low-fat diets may not have that much effect on cholesterol over the long run.
- "French pressed" coffee raises cholesterol more than percolated coffee.
- Cholesterol below 160 might lead to depression and suicide.
- For exercise to make a difference it does not have to be vigorous.
- Fatty (stearic) acids in chocolate do not raise serum cholesterol.
- Cholesterol in egg yolks is balanced out by its other nutrient benefits.
- Not all HDL is healthy.
- The benefits of seafood may be a fish tale.

This sense that we are playing Russian roulette also applies to cancer, which has been correlated with almost anything, sometimes positively and negatively simultaneously, from cell phones to antihistamines and smoking. Ultraviolet waves, on the one hand, have been implicated in melanoma (a skin cancer) and, on the other hand, have been "shown" to have preventative effects on prostate cancer. Broccoli is now said to have a prophylactic effect on carcinogenesis because it reduces estrogen. Vitamin A was "shown" in one study to ward off cancer but to be associated with higher levels of lung cancer in another. As for coronary conditions, studies of women correlating estrogen levels positively to cancer and negatively to heart conditions suggest that what is beneficial to one condition can be harmful to the other.

But scientists now know that oncogenesis, the original mutation that can lead to a malignant process, is not the same as the clinical entity we call cancer. Autopsies have uncovered cancers that had remained contained and never became symptomatic. The response of the organism to malignant cells is a factor in the course of the disease. As with genetic research, the desire for simple cause-and-effect certainty gives these studies a deterministic aura. And in this context, also to be mentioned is the oft-quoted remission waiting period of "five" years that discounts the patient's own individuality in the outcome of cancer. It is in danger of becoming yet another equator-like, anxiety-driven emotional barrier that seems to have taken on a reality of its own. It is almost as though the more knowledgeable one tries to be, the more anxious one must necessarily become. As CPAs and anyone else who has tried to stay knowledgeable about the tax code have come to realize, the great danger of acquiring too much data, as already stated, is that there is then going to be that much more data that one is soon going to have to forget. As with the 1626 map of California as an island, everyone is claiming to have an "accurate map of the world drawn according to the latest discoveries and best observations." Will it take a century and a half, as it did then, to finally get things straight?

What should give us all pause about living life by correlation is that studies have also been published that "show" that we have a greater chance of having a heart attack working on Mondays and that our cars, particularly if they are red, have the most chance of

being stolen on Thursday or Saturday night. It has even been calculated that the amount of radioactivity coming out of a hospital daily
in its waste material due to patients' excreta would not be allowed if
the source were a power station.

The propensity of such studies to induce a "failure of nerve" lies
not only in their sheer volume, but also by the way a regressed civilization's focus on pathology and drive for certainty causes them to
be formatted in the first place. They are always phrased in a way that
stresses the damage (which is so much more easily measured) rather
than the chances for survival. For example, the focus on pathology
rather than survival might emphasize that asbestos workers develop
certain kinds of lung cancer at up to five times the rate of the general
population; what will be left out is that far less than five percent of
asbestos workers develop the disease at all. Statistics phrased in terms
of the rate of death rather than the pure number always seem
ominously determinative. Studies will constantly conclude that your
chances of obtaining a particular disease are three or even five times
greater if you eat this or do that. Even though the numbers of people
involved in almost all of these studies are very small, a chronically
anxious public mind concerned with certainty extrapolates that proportion out in real numbers to a very large portion of the population.

For example, a study is reported in the media that eating fish that
are rich in omega-3 fatty acids reduces your chance of sudden heart
failure by fifty percent. The study is reported with the usual scientific statistical data that include control groups. But what is not
stated is that the number of people who die suddenly of such conditions is two in ten thousand, so that what this study means in real
numbers is that instead of 9,998 people not dying of such conditions it would now be 9,999 people who would not have died of
such conditions. In other words, by focusing on the pathology side,
not only is the result more anxiety-provoking, but the larger the
extrapolation, the greater the failure to account for the response of
an individual organism. As with the maps used by Columbus and
Magellan, everyone shows the evidence they want to believe or that
increases the possibility that they will get funding for their "voyage."

While epidemiologists will state that epidemiology is not an
exact science, and researchers will often try to hedge their bets by
using the term "risk factors" (which both protects their hypotheses

and leaves an escape hatch for contrary evidence that would put them on the spot), it is precisely the factors that go into the *exceptions* that are the basis for a self-differentiating approach to the determinism of data. The term "statistically significant," when isolated from emotional process factors, belongs to the same breadbasket as the idea that identical surgical procedures are really identical. Instead we need to ask, What are the variables that make for the individual differences? What about the possibility that, while necessary, physical factors are rarely sufficient conditions? Where is the study of emotional risk factors that might tip the balance of the capacity of any "body" to mount an immune response? Factors such as a child's position in the family or the state of the parents' relationship are never included. One of the reasons for this is that much effort is made to correlate disease with personality types—such as Type A men and coronary disease, or cancer and repressed anger—but these studies leave so many exceptions that in the focus on personality, variables such as the position of people in the emotional triangles of their families and work systems are ignored.

But the statisticians and physicians are no less at fault than the way societal regression has put that field to its own neurotic service. What I have described here about medicine is not about medicine; it is about a chronically anxious society. The factors that make it difficult for a person to be clear, decisive, and non-anxiously reactive with regard to his or her own health are the same factors in society that affect any leader's ability to be clear, decisive, and non-anxious regarding what he or she is managing. While health and managing might appear to be different areas of life, the issues of self-regulation and self-definition are equally affected by societal anxiety whether what one is trying to manage is a corporation or one's own health. Whether it is medicine or management, it is precisely the omission of the emotional variables that turns most collections of data into junkyards, and that account for why the problems of the data deluge cannot be solved by limiting the data. Only by adding emotional variables can people be led to a more responsible position for their responses.

The best evidence for the fact that this pathology-focused view of illness is deeply connected to other thinking in our emotionally regressed society is illustrated by the way we have tended to deal with the great tragedies of World War II—the Holocaust and Hiroshima. In both cases, the research and historical emphasis of the social science construction of reality has been overwhelmingly focused on the pathological nature or effects of these events, not on the type of response that went into survival, during either the trauma or the aftermath. We are far more likely to hear about the man who has been a hollow shell the rest of his life because he lost his family and his fortune than of the man who, having lost his family and his fortune, built another family and another fortune in the decades that followed. Similarly, the regeneration of Hiroshima within fifty years into a thriving, modern metropolis of a million people (four times the population of 1945) is almost totally neglected. While studies of pathology are useful in the treatment and prevention of disease (or evil), there are equally great lessons to be learned from those tragedies about the tenacity of life and the capacity of members of the human race to endure and overcome.

Researchers who emphasize the tragic consequences of these events, however, see the effort to focus on the recovery as *denial* of the tragedy or its pain. The focus on pathology has become such a natural part of the thinking of social science researchers that the idea that such a focus is itself pathological is totally out of their ken. After the Kobe earthquake, twelve Japanese women tried to offer counseling help to the homeless housed in schools and other institutions, only to be rejected by most, who said in effect, "Get me some sake and sushi and I'll feel fine." A psychotherapist from the more sophisticated metropolis of Tokyo said, "You have to understand that talking about your feelings is not culturally accepted here." But if that is true, then we have to accept the opposite as also being true, namely, that talking about our feelings is also a cultural phenomenon rather than the only path to recovery. The people of Kobe were unbelievably imaginative in the way they responded to the tragedy, such as finding a ship in Hong Kong that had cranes on the ship, since all dock cranes had been destroyed; working out three-sides-of-a-square railroad pathways to get around the destruction; and creating commuter routes that combined taking trains and walking. The notion that talking out one's grief rather than working it out through creative behaviors is denial with long-lasting consequences is exactly the kind of learned superstition that infects the thinking processes of the social science construction of reality.

◆ MENTAL HEALTH

Even more overwhelming and de-selfing than the data deluge in physical medicine is the proliferation of information concerning "syndromes" and "disorders" that afflicts those in the interrelated fields of mental health: therapists, educators, clergy, employee assistance counselors, and attorneys, and by extension parents and managers at any level. And once again it is not just a matter of the quantity of data, but of how the models used for formatting the data affect the thinking processes of leaders everywhere. Even here, where the basic thrust is supposed to be the relational or psychological side of life, the tendency is to categorize life according to data while omitting the emotional variables that leave room for differentiated responses. In fact, *The Diagnostic and Statistical Manual of Mental Disorders*, originally intended as a guide for members of the treating professions, now needs its own "guide" for the perplexed. It has become so voluminous that enterprising publishers are publishing guides to understand the guide, and enterprising professionals are conducting workshops to guide one through it. After all, the National Institutes of Health has released (self-serving) "data" to show that half of our population has suffered some mental disorder in their lives, and that one-third have experienced depression. But it has not published data on how many of these people overcame their "neurosis" without outside help, or how many have been able to function responsibly in society despite their "condition."

A major reason for the growth of this guide is that, as one of the institutions caught up in societal regression, therapy has shifted its focus from the presence of the therapist to the problem of the day, with a moving fashion show of symptoms and cures. It is as though the entire mental health profession suffered from its own form of attention deficit disorder. For example, when the family therapy movement began in the 1960s, Masters and Johnson had just published their books on sexual dysfunction. For a while every family therapy conference anywhere began to have as its keynote speaker an expert on sexual dysfunction. Families were going to be made healthy through lack of frustration. And then, suddenly, the issue receded into the background. Did everyone suddenly become sexually satisfied? The focus on sex was replaced for a while by anorexia, then attention deficit disorder, then repressed memory syndrome, and today it is either post-traumatic stress disorder or child abuse. These issues do not get cured; rather, everyone gets bored because the issue itself is a symptom. The intensity surrounding it is not due to its own nature but to the fact that it has taken center stage for a while as a focus of societal anxiety.

What turns these categories of information into data junkyards is once again the omission of the emotional variables that lead to the differentiation of individual responses, both the patient's and the therapist's. If one is interested in the more fundamental goal of maturation rather than a quick fix for a patient's pain, then the critical factor in mental health healing (as with all leadership) is not the proper categorization of the problem, nor the right technique for alleviating symptoms, but the nature of the counselor's own being, in particular his or her capacity to maintain an objective distance and a non-anxious, challenging presence. But psychotherapy is no different from any other American institution in its ability to get caught up in the characteristics of our society's emotional regression.

The notion that one has to be able to understand the background of people in order to help them is *ad hominem* thinking in reverse. While such information can be useful on a macro scale to help various groups preserve their traditions or benefit from government entitlements, the bottom line in efforts to help people grow still is (as has been mentioned) that patients cannot rise above the maturity (or anxiety) level of their counselor, no matter what the form of therapy. What the focus on the data of cultural differences does is to permit the patient not to take responsibility for his or her own behavior and responses, and to enable the therapist not to have to focus on his or her own personal struggles of growth.

I first noticed this kind of cultural camouflage within my own ethnic community when I heard Jewish people inadvertently attribute a broad array of factors in their life to their Jewish background. Examples of such comments were: "Boating is a Gentile sport," or "Jews think distance is fundamentally a non-Jewish concept." "Jews don't live near forests...like contemporary homes...let their kids sit in the living room." Or, "Jewish women don't tell their ages...are dirty fighters...can't keep secrets...don't tell secrets...are built small on top and big on the bottom." Then I began to see how universal the process was:

◆ My husband has a typical Syrian temper.
◆ That's a typical Prussian way of distancing.
◆ German men are pushy.
◆ If you're Catholic, you carry your cross till you die.
◆ Pakistani women have no sense of romance.
◆ It is my English reserve; one doesn't wear dirty linen in public.
◆ My parents were Methodists; they always paid cash.
◆ The Irish don't bring up divorce at a wake.
◆ It was a garden variety, close Huguenot family.
◆ In those days Australian families didn't get divorced.

People tend to generalize from their experience in their own personal family and attribute its emotional characteristics to its cultural and sociological background, rather than to the way in which members of that particular family are connected. Rare is the culture in which all or even half of its members follow all of its customs. Family members tend to select from their culture's repertoire of customs and ceremonies those behaviors that support their own idiosyncratic patterns, whether they are healthy patterns or neurotic, and pay most attention to those values in their tradition that *prevent* change. Cultural or environmental factors can no more be the sufficient conditions for the creation of pathology than paint and canvas can produce a masterpiece. Culture does not "cause" family process so much as *stain* it and make it visible. Even if we knew all the ethnic and other sociological factors in a given family's background, we still could not predict the emotional health of that family or of any given member. But if we knew nothing about a family's cultural background, we could posit the future of that family with a great deal of accuracy if we knew all the dynamics of that family's emotional processes for several generations. It is their position within the triangles of their family's emotional processes that, although it may wear different garb in different cultures, is the true "culturing medium," not the culture itself.

◆ PARENTING

Parents today can learn about techniques of parenting from programs and lectures in churches and synagogues, universities, hospitals, libraries, PTAs, and community programs at mental health institutions. In addition, bookstores have large sections devoted to their "needs," while newspapers often have weekly columns to catch them up on the latest theories and research. Even the United States Government Printing Office has pamphlets about "A Teenager in Your House" which, like "Termites in Your Basement," is designed to teach parents what to be wary of. Yet there is absolutely no evidence that the most successful parents are those who are most "knowledgeable" of either the "proper" techniques or the latest data on the children who are either most troubled or most happy. One would be hard-pressed to show that members of the mental health professions, who presumably have far more data and knowledge of child-rearing techniques at their fingertips than the average "lay" parent, are doing a better job of raising their children.

Everything I have said above holds true for parenting as well. Over the years I found parents so engulfed in data and techniques that I stopped trying to educate them and started trying to free them from this "syndrome." I developed a presentation entitled "How to Get Your Kid to Drop Out and Save $100,000 in Tuition" (it was $30,000 when I began). I always mention at the very beginning that all the specific "techniques" I am going to offer such as how to escalate conflict, screw up communication, and increase the generation gap will work better if parents will commit themselves to reading all they can about raising children. This, I point out, will help make them more anxious, more inconsistent, less self-confident, and far less the kind of non-anxious, challenging presence that could ultimately cost them a bundle of tuition. The advantages of trying to keep up, I point out, are that they can consistently worry if they are reading the right book, if the real truth has just come out and they do not even know about it, and if there are experts out there who "know" how to do it.

Parenting is no different from any other kind of "managing." The critical issues in raising children have far less to do with proper technique than with the nature of the parents' presence and the type of emotional processes they engender. I have, for example, almost never seen a mother who had a mature relationship with her own mother have trouble with her daughter. Similarly, I never saw a highly reactive or hypercritical father who was not distant from his own family of origin (and who, thereby, made the members of his new nuclear family too important to him).

Where parents are willing to take responsibility for their own unworked-out relationships either with their own parents or with one another, children rarely develop serious symptoms. Symptoms in a child are most likely to develop in the areas of the parent's own traumatization where they, therefore, have the least emotional flexibility. (Parents never seem to get the problems they can handle.) And to the extent child-focus enables parents not to have to deal with their own relationships or their own unresolved issues, that projection process will retard if not nullify all techniques and well-meaning efforts to improve the child, including the aid they seek from tutors and counselors.

To expect parents to focus on the emotional processes in their own relationships rather than focus on their children requires having counselors (therapists, educators, clergy, and so on) who are willing to do likewise. And it is much easier for everyone to conspire to focus on data and technique instead. The social science construction of reality that would diagnose children instead of family emotional process, and that would allow parents to blame their ethnic background rather than take responsibility for their own responses, furthers the anxiety.

◆ MANAGEMENT

It is remarkable how the explosion of books in recent years about management resembles the similar explosion that occurred in the 1960s regarding premarital counseling. As society became anxious about the rising divorce rate and everyone talked about the demise of the family, the number of books being written for the clergy in this country on premarital counseling seemed to be exceeding the number of people getting married. Similarly, the number of books being written today on management far exceeds the number of managers, whether they are on the subject of total quality control, climbing mountains, the learning organization, the Japanese way of management, or team-building.

But there is another side to the data deluge. For the greatest mental health problem in America today may be the substance abuse of data. If the data deluge puts all leaders on an anxious treadmill of pursuing more information in order to "stay on top of things," the pursuit of information also offers family and institutional leaders and healers an easy escape from having to deal with society's chronic anxiety as well as with their own personal being.

Leaders are smack in the middle of an exquisite double bind, precisely the kind of relational position in a family that escalates stress exponentially. They are both overwhelmed and seduced by the data. In a chronically anxious family this type of bind could easily lead a family leader to seek a way out through an indiscriminate and panicky abuse of alcohol, nicotine, drugs, or sex; in chronically anxious America the constant imbibing of data and technique offers a similar quick fix. Data thus become a substance that is at first eagerly sought and then ultimately abused. Almost every family troubled with substance abuse is chronically anxious because it is unable to deal directly with, or even face, its problems. Recovery begins with "admitting there's a problem."

One reason that the abuse metaphor is appropriate is that all forms of addiction are related to the major themes of this book: anxiety, lack of nerve, and poorly differentiated self. Almost all addictions come about because of some combination of these factors. In fact it may be said that whatever "drives people to drink" also drives people to data. The far more critical parallel, however, is this: the vicious cycle that is always characteristic of addiction—the fact that the reliance on the substance erodes the very strengths that have to be mobilized in order to break free from the substance—is remarkably descriptive of what has happened to America's leaders and healers with regard to data and technique. The addiction metaphor, if it is only a metaphor, applies to the etiology, the nature of the "disease," and the problems of lasting "recovery."

Quite often substance abusers can appear otherwise normal, even hold down jobs and remain with their families. There is great debate about the proper classifying of substance abuse. Is it a behavior problem, a vice, a disease, a genetic proclivity, or a personality disorder? What is less open to question is that those who become addicted tend to create relationships that are "pseudo-mutual" (codependent), tend to see the world in a distorted reality, often have trouble distinguishing what is normal, live a life that is organized around their symptom, tend to be mired in guilt, and are "enabled" to remain helpless by the helpfulness of codependent others.

Again, all these attributes apply to the data addiction. The relationships established at conferences devoted to technique and data often resemble the pseudo-mutuality of people sharing a "binge"; after the party is over, things go right back to "normal." The assumption that data and technique are the keys to life is a major distortion of reality; many professionals organize their entire life around the symptom of imbibing more of the substance; and all are enabled to continue on this path by those who organize professional conferences. The guilt, however, comes from the other direction. It is not over having surrendered to the "substance" but over not having "imbibed" enough. After presentations on the themes of this chapter, one of the comments I have heard most frequently from members of the audience who have been trying desperately to keep up with their professional journals, annual conferences, the latest recommended book, or their children has been, "Thank you for relieving my guilt. I would love to feel it's okay when I don't read all the literature I receive or when I decide to go skiing rather than attend every workshop."

Some readers may wish to object at this point, "The analogy is cute, but data abuse does not have the same hold as chemical dependency, where the body has adapted physiologically to the substance, if not made that person vulnerable to the addiction in the first place." But this response is another denial of emotional process. Anyone who thinks the difficulties involved in de-toxing are primarily a physiological matter has just never observed the problems of withdrawal involved in trying to separate a golfer, a stamp collector, a gambler, or a fisherman from his habit. And it can be much harder to break a relational addiction than one that is chemical.

"Kicking" any habit is difficult—all the more so to the extent the surrounding atmosphere promotes escape and the substance is easily accessible, not to mention energetically "pushed." Moreover, since one of the keys to recovery is a system of support, where does one find a support system in a society where almost everyone else also seems to be addicted and is chorusing, "I'll start tomorrow"? "Detoxing" from data and technique is no exception. There is no quick fix for avoiding a quick fix. It always requires resolve, vision, commitment, stamina, persistence. But now we have come full circle, since those are the very qualities of leadership that are eroded by the substance. Will the information superhighway become the next skid-row? What would sobriety look like in a data-addicted leader or parent? What about a therapist or CEO in recovery?

Those who specialize in substance abuse have generally agreed that there is no basic sobering agent, that there must be admission of the fact that there is a problem, recognition of the role the addiction plays in the substance abuser's life, and a commitment to self-regulation. In addition, at the heart of most twelve-step programs is an emphasis on the need for a spiritual awakening that begins with surrender to a Higher Power, however one defines it.

Facing the pain of anxiety and growth, not denying the emotional processes that erode self-differentiation, being willing to risk and be vulnerable—these are the keys to overcoming the addiction to data, as well as the way to avoid being overwhelmed by the data deluge. Or, to use a spiritual metaphor, the worship of data and technique is very simply a form of idolatry. The sin of idolatry may lie less in the actual action of worshiping a foreign god than in the denial of universals that such worship implies. The higher power to be surrendered to here is the natural connection between all forms of life.

Finally, one other parallel to addiction is worth noting: the long-term effects of any addiction on both the brain of an addicted parent and the brains of their children. Long-term abuse of a chemical substance can eventually effect actual changes in the neuronal pathways of the brain. Could that be happening with regard to data? Could contemporary American society's "fix" on data and technique in the denial of emotional process and personal being actually affect the way the pathways of our brains will evolve? And is it too far-fetched to assume that a civilization that teaches its leaders to rely on data rather than maturity would also produce a similar evolutionary change that is transmitted to the next generation? Is there an analogue to Fetal Alcohol Syndrome? What will be the effect on the brains or nervous systems of succeeding generations who have been nurtured in a civilization where its leaders have become addicted to data as a way of avoiding the problems of maturing?

◆ A NEW WORLDVIEW OF THE BRAIN

As debilitating and anxiety-provoking as the information overload can be for anyone, and as misleading and addictive as the focus on data and technique can become for leaders especially, there is still a third aspect of our society's orientation toward data rather than emotional process that is misleading in a very fundamental way. That third aspect is our tendency to conceptualize the organ we call the brain as some kind of central processing unit.

Study of the brain has become one of the most adventurous new research frontiers of our age. The cartography that describes the latest findings produces, almost daily, new understandings of the relationship of its parts and their reciprocal communication with the body. While there is some difference of agreement among the "cartographers," most concur on one point: the brain takes emotional factors into account during the very process of cerebrating, and not just after one has produced thoughts. Emotions do not simply modify thinking, reasoning, or decision-making processes; they are part and parcel of the *process* of reasoning. Cerebration, in other words, involves more than logic, and thinking involves more than cerebration. "Mental" includes feelings. And the brain's method of processing data always includes emotional variables.

The tendency to equate the brain with only one of its subsystems, the cortex, leads us into the assumption that what we label "thinking" is primarily about the intellect. There is, in fact, a striking parallel between the way data and technique are separated out from emotional processes in our data-gathering endeavors and the way we have traditionally categorized cognitive processes and emotional processes separately in our understanding of how the brain functions.

The new orientations toward the brain, which do not compartmentalize data and emotional process, have important ramifications for the way parents and presidents are taught to conceptualize problems of leadership, such as role-modeling, emulation, and identification. Newer (systemic) understandings of the brain that show how emotional processes are part of thinking processes lead to a more systemic—that is, organic—model of leadership itself, and shift the entire paradigm of how information is gathered, correlated, and given meaning.

Leadership, therefore, is doubly affected by these new orientations toward the brain that do not separate out data from emotional process. Not only do they offer new ways of conceptualizing a whole range of traditional leadership problems, from communication to motivation to resistance; they also offer a different model for the way in which leaders and followers (and parents and children) are connected. And, in keeping with the major thrust of this chapter, they provide new criteria for what information is important, as well as for how to weigh its significance.

While there has always been some awareness that feelings or instincts can affect judgment, the assumption generally has been that these "non-intellectual" phenomena come from the body or are processed independently by a different part of the brain than that which produces thinking. Emotions and feelings, in this view, may act upon or filter the results of what has been considered a central cerebral processing unit; but they do not function as part of it. The newest systemic understandings of the brain, however, suggest that analogizing the brain, or some key part, to the central processing unit of a computer is quite off-base.

New maps of the brain constantly lead to unification, not bifurcation. This unity applies to the most conventional dichotomies and it almost turns the whole notion of psychology "on its head." It totally invalidates the false dichotomy *psychosomatic*. It plays havoc with the meaning of testing results and evaluations; it reworks our understanding of communication as a skill that has to do with rhetoric, syntax, and articulation, or the idea that change has to do with insight and awareness, or the notion that resistance and sabotage have to do with differing opinions. In addition, it questions the trickle-down notions of leadership, and it highlights the illusion of assuming that by simply gaining enough information one has become "informed." In short, the new maps of the brain not only suggest a new way of thinking about these leadership categories, they suggest a new way of thinking about thinking.

Four new maps of the brain suggest a more unified, that is, organic, orientation of this crucial organ, and show the unreality of separating out data from emotional process in any formulations of life. Two of the maps are focused inward and have to do with the brain's "infra-structure"; two have an outward focus and have to do with the brain's relationship to the body. They begin with a view of the brain as the repository of all evolution and therefore of the human connection to all other forms of life, itself a link to universal emotional processes. And they progress to a relational understanding that not only is the brain intimately connected to the body that houses it, but also, within any relationship system whatsoever, the brain of one individual is connected to the bodies—and the brains— of other individuals through its involvement in the emotional processes between them.

All the maps point to similar conclusions that have enormous consequence for the relationship of data and emotional process:

- ◆ The brain does not contain a central processing unit for information.
- ◆ The brain always processes emotional factors and data simultaneously.
- ◆ Thinking always involves the self of the entire organism.

Map 1: The Triune Brain—An Evolutionary Perspective

In 1990 Dr. Paul McLean, who had studied the human brain for more than thirty years at the National Institutes of Health, published a monumental volume entitled *The Triune Brain*. His thesis is that the human brain has three distinct parts, each of which developed at a different stage of evolution but evolved in an interconnected fashion, with information flowing reciprocally in both directions between all three parts. The brain, in other words, is itself a history, if not a manifestation, of the evolution of our species.

Other organs such as the kidneys, the lungs, the pancreas, or the bladder seem to have ceased evolving after reaching a form that fit their function. The brain, on the other hand, keeps changing its size and shape as animal life has evolved, so that the brain appears to be a hodgepodge. It is as though the Creator or Evolution had afterthoughts. The human brain has grown in weight from the few ounces found in reptiles to the "enormous" full pound found in early humans to its present "whopping" size of three pounds. But Dr.

McLean has shown that the earliest brains have not simply been replaced by newer models. Rather, they remain as the substructure onto which new forms have been built, and into which new forms have been plugged. In fact, the older brain forms that still reside beneath, or at the base of, the modern human brain are structurally and chemically identical to their forerunners in reptiles and mammals.

At the base of the human brain, says McLean, is a bundle of nerve connections that is totally absent of thought processes. Its bailiwick is instinct. He has dubbed this the "reptilian brain." Above that is the part of the brain that fills most of the cranium. It allows for thinking on rudimentary levels and evolved with early mammals. He has called this the "mammalian brain." It is in the mammalian part of the brain that we find the apparatus for creating lasting relationships and therefore families. For it is in the mammalian brain that we first find the seat for nurturing, for playfulness, and for vocal communication.

The third part of the brain is the cortex, the half-inch layer at the top that most people think of as the "real" brain, and its frontal lobe, known as the neo-cortex. It is the cortex that is the center of intellectual activity, and it is the neo-cortex that allows for philosophical speculation, deep problem-solving, intricate strategies, leaders, healers, and, eventually, leadership training programs. But, as mentioned, even the cortex is not really a "central processing unit." For the most part, the cortex functions interdependently with its reptilian and mammalian precursors. This is as true in gathering data as in making decisions. The information each part processes is to some extent modified by the information simultaneously being processed by the other two parts.

The major significance of McLean's work for leadership is its implication that while the modern, human animal is capable of deep thought and, like its mammalian forebears, can nurture and play, it also is capable of behaving in an absolutely "reptilian" manner. While that last feature may sound simply like more evidence for the fact that humans have an instinctual side or that their judgment is influenced by feelings, McLean's theory has a slightly different spin that creates a new perspective on reactivity, madness, and regression. Dr. Michael Kerr, of the Bowen Center for the Study of the Family, compares McLean's view of the connection between the cortex and the lower parts of the brain to a driver-training car with two sets of controls. Normally the cortex does all the steering, but *when anxiety reaches certain thresholds* the instinctual, reptilian systems can take over the other set of controls and override the steering of the cortex. The problem is that after the reptilian brain takes over, the cortex continues steering, assuming it is still in charge.

Madness, therefore, cannot be judged by strange ideas, outlandish theories, unpopular values, or even irrational beliefs—the favorite categories of the social scientists. While these matters of the intellect are products of the cortex, when conditions are right, the cortex can be working at the service of the lower brain. This shows up blatantly with highly intelligent families whose brilliance, instead of serving them well in their efforts to function in more healthy ways, actually seems to intensify their unhealthy ways of thinking and relating. Madness has more to do with how people function in a relationship system than with products of their intellect. After all, judging madness on the basis of beliefs and values puts one in a relativistic position. In addition, if everything is relative, in any family or institutional disagreement a leader cannot go around simply dismissing all disagreement as madness.

If, however, a leader focuses on the way people function in a relationship system rather than on their stated values and beliefs, he or she can develop a more objective perspective on the madness of others. The three criteria of reptilian functioning that leaders of any family or institution can always rely on to judge madness (of others or their own) are:

◆ interfering in the relationships of others;
◆ unceasingly trying to convert others to their own point of view; and
◆ being unable to relate to people who do not agree with them.

These criteria are universal rather than relative and totally transcend the social science categories of virtual reality. They are evidence of regression in all cultures, genders, ages, and races, at any period in the history of our species. For they are all products of anxiety and therefore are rooted in the automatic reactivity of the reptilian brain rather than the more considered deliberations of the cortex, no matter how rationally they are phrased or how deliberately they are delivered. Furthermore, it is not as though some people exhibit these characteristics and some do not; we all have areas of, or moments in, our lives where, when we become anxious enough, we tend to behave in a "reptilian" manner.

As a CEO from Texas put it after hearing about McLean's views on the brain:

> I was fond of using the circle-the-herd model when I wanted to "round up" my managers. If you bring in the herd, and find you have left one or two stragglers, it is very hard to get them to come in alone unless you take the entire herd out, circle them 'round again, and have the togetherness forces gather the stragglers in with their "colleagues." I never knew why it didn't work with some of my branch chiefs, but now I understand. Circling the herd works on the mammalian brain, and I've been trying to use it on reptiles—rattlers, no less.

Map 2: The Brain's Interconnections

Support for the interconnectedness of brain divisions, as well as for an organic understanding of thinking, comes from another perspective also: the work of neurologists such as Dr. Antonio Damasio and others who have been tracing the internal pathways of communication between various parts of the brain. Their new cartography shows that while various parts of the brain such as the amygdala, the thalamus, the hypothalamus, or the pituitary may have different functions, they do not simply act upon one another's results as much as interact all along the way, so that the data which any of these parts produces have been influenced by their interactions within the overall process. In drawing their new maps of the brain, Dr. Damasio and other cartographers have not been able to find one central processing unit that organizes or integrates the output of the other units, even though their output converges at various points. The brain, says Damasio, is "a supersystem of subsystems" and the cortex, the subsystem that is usually credited with thinking, is only one of those units. Therefore a given brain unit's contribution is not just in its structure but also in its position in the system.

As with McLean's concept of the triune brain, from this systemic perspective thought processes are not simply affected by emotional processes; rather, these processes are the constituent of the "intellectual" process by which information is acquired and judgments made. Or, as Damasio puts it, "Feelings are as cognitive as precepts," and by extension, biological regulation of the entire organism interlocks with reasoning and decision-making.

Not only are the brain's various parts interactive with one another, but the brain's connection with the body is also interactive. The brain, in fact, suggests Damasio, is "the body's captive audience." Rejecting Descartes's famous dictum, "I think, therefore I am," which is basically a philosophical understanding of existence, Damasio has shown that we could not be without our bodies—that is, our brains could not be grounded in reality without our bodies. The body is the "ground reference for reality" and "the mind had first to be about the body." In other words, neither brain nor body interacts with the environment alone, without the participation of the other. Thus, all the images that our brains collect are only obtainable through messages sent to the brain by our body's interaction with the environment. And, of course, how those data are then processed ultimately feeds back to affect our bodies.

If McLean's brain maps bring data and emotional process together from an evolutionary perspective, the maps of Damasio and others have been based on adventures into the world of people whose brains were damaged at birth, by accident, by lesions, or by disease. A major result of this research that strongly supports the overall hypothesis of the interrelatedness of brain parts (and therefore the intimate connection between data and emotional process) is the concept that sound judgment turns out to be related to parts of the brain that do not deal with data, or what we normally consider matters of the intellect. There are people whose brain damage did not affect their capacity for calculation, memory, logic, knowledge, attention span, and perception but who wind up making poor judgments. In other words, being informed was not enough. The significance of this finding for leadership is that, while all the situations which Damasio studied involved physical damage to the brain, my own experience in working with leaders is that chronic anxiety can have the same effects. I will go further: every single skewing of perception, reasoning, discernment, decisions, judgments, and thought processes observed in physically brain-damaged people who otherwise seem to have their intellects intact can also be the result of sustained chronic anxiety.

The findings of McLean and Damasio thus dovetail. Their research into the infrastructure of the brain raises many questions about what we have tended to call "psychological" and about the conventional understanding of intelligence that informs leadership training programs. They suggest that some kind of conceptual leap is needed beyond what has come to be termed *emotional intelligence.* In fact, the very term shows how difficult it is to get away from models of the brain that are not reduced to psychological concepts. Actually, the brain maps of McLean and Damasio suggest that the entire emphasis on right brain/left brain, or on gender distinctions in the brain, exemplify how the categories of the social science construction of reality can be misleading. No doubt these differences do exist. But they are not the differences that count when it comes to the emotional processes of well-differentiated leadership.

One can, after all, be as reactive with one's right brain as with one's left, and the differences between male and female brains do not correlate with the capacity of members of either gender to be imaginative, self-defined, or self-regulated. The data-gathering about right brain/left brain differences, because it tends to leave out the variables of emotional process and self-differentiation, is potentially another junkyard. It is not nearly as important for leadership as the information that can be obtained about people's functioning by focusing on the distinction between top brain and bottom brain.

Map 3: A Liquid Nervous System

The brain cartography of Damasio and McLean is drawn from an internal perspective, the relationship of brain parts to one another. There is also a new brain cartography drawn from an *external* perspective: the relationship of the entire brain itself to other body parts, if not to other bodies. This perspective also supports the inextricable relationship between data and emotional process, and it, too, leads to new ways of conceptualizing leadership problems and leadership functioning.

For many years the major model used in explaining our nervous systems has been electrical. In such brain maps, a charge travels down a neuron and jumps a synapse (gap), thereby communicating with the network next door. In recent years, however, more and more attention has been given to the fact that nerves also communicate with one another through liquid pathways. For when nerves fire, they release substances called neurotransmitters that travel via the body's fluids and eventually dock at receptor sites that have the right molecular lock and key connection. While there has been some awareness of this brain/body connection throughout most of the twentieth century, it was the discovery in the 1970s of endorphins—analgesic substances stored in the brain and released to kill pain in the body—that heightened everyone's awareness of the widespread "presence" of the brain in the body. More recently, receptor sites for serotonin, a neurotransmitter integral to the regulation of mood and violence, have been found in the gastrointestinal tract, while antidepressant medications that modify serotonin also regulate diarrhea and constipation.

But it is a two-way street. Dr. Candace Pert, former head of brain chemistry at the National Institutes of Health and a pioneer on these new voyages, points out that for every substance that the brain releases, there is the appropriate receptor site somewhere within the various parts of the immune system, and vice versa. In fact, Pert's findings of the interconnections between brain and body so influenced her that she no longer uses the terms separately in her writings, but employs the construction *brain/body* instead.

Communication between glands and other organs throughout the body is, therefore, more a systemic process than a mere matter of communication relays. Body parts can have an impact on one another from a distance. In fact, *hormone* is the Greek word for *impact*. Since the brain has the largest number of nerve connections, it also releases the most "impacting agents." The brain, in fact, turns out to be, or to function like, a gland, and in sheer quantity releases more substances than other well-known glands such as the thymus or the pancreas. The brain even manufactures and stores its own insulin. The more one begins to orient oneself to this view of the brain, the more it seems that its major function is to preserve the health of the organism in which it is situated—so that thinking may actually be a bonus!

This brain/body orientation toward the brain points to several new ways of thinking about both data-processing and leadership. First, it suggests that to be effective, a "head" must find a way to be present in the body it is leading, but that presence does not have to be communicated by a chain of command. Second, the nature of that presence is felt through its impact, not its messages. *Hormone* means "impact," not "messenger," as some who try to base their approach to leadership on "information theory" have erroneously stated. The importance of this distinction for leadership is that information does not consist of energy, and leadership is all about energy, that is, about making an impact. Basing leadership on information theory disempowers leaders and is part of the bias toward data that was discussed earlier in this chapter. Impact, to the contrary, is about emotional process.

Third, if the relationship between a "head" and a body is organic rather than hierarchical (a word that has almost become the *sine qua non* of leadership training programs), proximity or even contiguity is not nearly as important as we are wont to think. The head of an organization, as the head of an organism, can affect many parts of the body politic simultaneously. (How else did George S. Patton convey his presence to a quarter-million men—or Genghis Khan, for that matter?) This understanding of the connection between the brain and the body shows that, through his or her own self-definition, self-regulation, non-reactivity, and capacity to remain connected, a leader can make a critical difference. He or she can transmit a presence that has every bit as much capacity to regulate the emotional processes of a family or organization as the brain's capacity to regulate the various "members" of the organism it is leading through the substances it is transmitting and through the way it responds to the substances it is receiving.

Fourth, there are some ramifications here for consultants. One of the spin-offs of this new understanding of the relationship of the brain and the body is the field of biofeedback, where it has been shown that people can, by changing the nature of their thought processes through trial and error, affect various parts of their body that were once thought to be "involuntary" (for example, the "smooth" muscle cells that line the nervous system, arteries, and digestive tract). They can even modify through their thinking processes the circulation paths of the body's fluids and therefore the delivery of neurotransmitters.

Consultation for leaders (parents or presidents) can be viewed as biofeedback rather than a dispensing of cures. Successful medical biofeedback requires an information source. The person who is trying to regulate (become the leader of) his or her own body must have a way of knowing to what extent he or she is being successful. If, instead of anxiously providing data or offering advice and new techniques, a consultant can provide the kind of inquisitive, non-anxious climate that helps clients view the effects of their own thinking and input into the system they are leading, those clients, whether parents or presidents, can often begin to develop more objectivity and self-regulation with regard to that relationship system. Actually, those practitioners of medical biofeedback who also focus their clients on family relationship processes have found that the same capacity for self-regulation that develops with regard to their own body immediately carries over to their functioning in the relationships of all their "families."

Map 4: The Brain and Other Bodies
The notion that the brain of one body can be connected to other bodies requires a conceptual leap greater than the one required to integrate data and emotional process, though it is a parallel leap. That quantum jump forward was provided by the pioneers of the family therapy movement who began to focus on relationship processes rather than discrete personalities. People in any family or institution, therefore, are connected by the emotional processes between them, and the relationship system is understood to be a self-organizing unit.

This systemic understanding of human relationships leads logically to the conclusion that one cannot understand one body's brain without understanding the relationship of that body to other bodies. Whereas thinking from the perspective of an individual personality model tends to isolate the thinking processes of each individual and then sees how they come together, it is possible to view the thinking processes of each individual in a family or institution as constantly interactive. From this perspective, just as data are processed within the brain simultaneously along with emotional variables, so it is also

possible to view the thinking in each individual part of a relationship system as being processed simultaneously in a context of reciprocal feedback.

Here are two examples of how the brain of one human being is
influenced by the connection of its body to other bodies in a relationship system.

First, the notion that *communication* is essentially about ideas is
basic to all training programs about leadership. Whether the training
is for clergy or attorneys, educators or therapists, managers or
administrators, the assumption is that ideas come raw and unpack-
aged. Leaders in all professions, as well as parents, are therefore
coached on how to articulate their ideas more clearly, the focus being
on syntax, semantics, rhetoric, and diction. While there is general
awareness that emotions are involved in the way people "hear" an
idea, the emphasis is on how to deal with those feelings in the nature
of one's presentation.

A "new world" view of the brain suggests instead that communication is itself an emotional phenomenon, rather than a matter of
the intellect that is influenced by feelings or the emotions, and that
it depends on three interrelational rather than "mental" variables:
direction, distance, and anxiety. Whether you are a parent, a minister,
a healer, or a CEO, your communicant's capacity to hear you
depends primarily on the emotional variables of direction, distance,
and anxiety. Others can only hear you when they are moving toward
you, no matter how eloquently you phrase the message. In other
words, as long as you are in the pursuing, rescuing, or coercive position, your message, no matter how eloquently broadcast, will never
catch up. And as for anxiety, it is the static in any communication
system and can distort or scramble any message. It cannot be eliminated simply by turning up the volume, since that invariably also
turns up the static. Messages in families, in the consultation process,
or in organizational directives come through less because of the
quality of their content than because of the emotional envelope in
which they are delivered. (To say "the medium is the message" is not
the same thing.)

My second example has to do with *secrets*. If most of the members
of a family or an organization are privy to a secret, the person who
is not will find his or her thought processes begin to take on a para-

noid tinge that has nothing to do with his or her personality. At a dinner party, after a presentation to the staff of a large community psychiatric clinic, I found myself worrying that I had somehow failed even though I could not think of anything I had done differently from similar presentations that were generally well received. No one was going out of their way to talk to me. Everyone seemed to be huddling together in small groups that did not invite me in, and my thoughts became an avalanche of insecurity: "Did I not provide enough examples? Was I unclear? Had I mentioned something I shouldn't have?" Finally, someone came up to me and said, "I don't know if you realize what is going on, but we all just found out that our executive director, of whom we are very fond, has terminal cancer."

Perhaps the most powerful evidence for the fact that the thinking processes of the brain in one body are affected by the emotional processes of others is everything I have said about renaissance and regression in chapters 1 and 2:

◆ The Renaissance was not caused by the learning of new data, but rather that learning and the imaginative capacity flowered after a change in the emotional processes of Europe brought about by the discovery of a New World.
◆ The thinking processes that produce a failure of nerve and a quick-fix mentality in contemporary America are the result of a decline in maturity in an anxiously regressed society.

The new brain horizons described in this chapter lead to a more organic definition of thinking, one that involves the *functioning* and the *integrity* of an entire being, not simply one that understands thinking as mere mental activity. Another way of putting this is that we must distinguish between "thinking" and "cerebration," and the difference lies in the self-definition and self-regulation of the overall organism. For example, cerebration that occurs in a reactive mode should not truly be labeled "thinking." The key to thinking lies in an emotional category, the differentiation of the thinker's self. The ramification for leaders is this: the "old world" view separates data from emotional process and focuses leaders on the "talking heads" of others, while the "new world" view focuses leaders on the nature of their own presence.

Finally, it is important to note one other aspect of the emphasis on data and technique, rather than on emotional process and self-differentiation: its effect on the training of parents and presidents. The emotional processes of societal regression influence not only the formulas we formulate, but the way we are prone to formulate. One result is that the theories and models leaders are currently being taught to use in framing leadership issues are often formatted by society's chronic anxiety, and they can even wind up being put to its service. When dealing with chronically anxious families, for example, it is not unusual to find members expressing themselves intelligently and rationally while being totally invulnerable to the kind of awareness that could produce change. That is because, as I have demonstrated, what is coming out of the top part of their brains (the cortex) is being driven by much deeper processes that emanate from the instinctive, non-thinking, automatically reactive, reptilian, lower part of their brains that is so vulnerable to surrounding anxiety.

If we were to conceive of the academic institutions of our civilization as its "cortex," then a parallel process could be seen in society at large. Data that are being published may be magnificently formulated and accurate, but they will still be of little help in producing change because they are irrelevant to the larger emotional processes driving that "cortex" to produce all the data. Actually, as I described above, the emotional and the theoretical can be connected in such a way that even when thinking processes are articulated in the most logical manner, they could be driven by emotional processes that are really quite mad. As one very bright woman who had been in supervision with me for a year before she took her certification boards said (after having difficulty passing the examination), "I should never have come to you before I took my boards; to pass their examination you have to think 'anxious.'"

It is often said that new ways of seeing or cohering things must originate from outside of a system. My experience with families and institutions, however, is that truly novel concepts can begin from within, provided someone can get "outside" of its emotional processes even while remaining physically inside. The "catch 22" is this: in order to be able to identify those processes, one must be able to think differently in the first place. The capacity to "hear" new ideas in a family, in an institution, or in an entire civilization thus depends to a large extent on the capacity to avoid being automatically regulated by that system's emotional processes. And the more reactive the surrounding climate, the more that society in its anxious efforts to seek certainty will reify its models and eventually confuse them with reality itself.

The rejection of empathy is not the rejection of emotions.
—Bertolt Brecht

Chapter Four

◆ SURVIVAL IN A HOSTILE ENVIRONMENT:

THE FALLACY OF EMPATHY

One day I made a presentation to a large group of community leaders about my ideas on imaginative gridlock and the
great sixteenth-century explorers. It was illustrated with
slides of the early maps, and was received enthusiastically by the
audience. Then someone arose and said, "That was one of the most
boring presentations I have ever heard, and I am deeply hurt by your
ethnocentric bias."

I decided that I would respond in a way that went in the face of
his sensitivities. I told him directly that I couldn't care less about his
feelings and that I was trying to present universal, challenging ideas
about the orientations of stuck civilizations and the evolutionary
value of adventure. Then, returning to my interest in the creative
process, I said, "It seems to me that any artist has no choice but to
express himself in the medium of his own background; if he touches
the microcosm of experience, it will flower into something universal.
My views may not always be correct," I added, "but if anyone in the
audience is having trouble getting in touch with the universal themes
of human existence that I am trying to portray because of the

cultural context in which I have drawn my metaphor, then it seems to me that there is some serious question to be raised about whose ethnocentricity is getting in the way."

At this point another member of the audience went to the first person's aid, saying, "You are still avoiding his feelings." This time I responded, "He may have been 'hurt,' but he wasn't damaged. My purpose here is to expand your minds with previously unimagined concepts. I am trying to inspire by focusing on what we all share in common with life's natural processes. The previous questioner, in my view, is creating a diversion by introducing political rhetoric, and I don't intend to let him steal my agenda, nor will I take responsibility for his feelings or be tyrannized by his sensibilities. If, on the other hand," I continued, "he wants to express his opinions about my ideas, I will be completely open to such dialogue. But dialogue is only possible when we can learn to distinguish feelings from opinions and recognize that the background or personality of a person is totally irrelevant to the validity of what he or she is saying."

My decision to confront the empathists in the audience with "harshness" was aimed at more than those who spoke up. I wanted to pierce the general illusions of empathy which so disorient American society today and give license to undercutting well-defined leadership everywhere.

As lofty and noble as the concept of empathy may sound, and as well-intentioned as those may be who make it the linchpin idea of their theories of healing, education, or management, societal regression has too often perverted the use of empathy into a disguise for anxiety, a rationalization for the failure to define a position, and a power tool in the hands of the "sensitive." It has generally been my experience that in any community or family discussion, those who are the first to introduce concern for empathy feel powerless, and are trying to use the togetherness force of a regressed society to get those whom they perceive to have power to adapt to them. I have consistently found the introduction of the subject of "empathy" into family, institutional, and community meetings to be reflective of, as well as an effort to induce, a failure of nerve among its leadership.

This chapter will describe the second emotional barrier to reorienting leadership in our time: the focus on empathy rather than responsibility. The great myth here is that feeling deeply for others

increases their ability to mature and survive; its corollary is that the
effort to understand another should take precedence over the
endeavor to make one's own self clear. The constant effort to understand (or feel for) another, however, can be as invasive as any form of
emotional coercion. As I overheard one precocious eleven-year-old
say to his up-to-date mother, "Hit me with the book, Mommy, but
please stop using it on me."

While a focus on feelings would seem to be the exact opposite of
a focus on data, it has an equally regressive effect on leadership.
What the orientation toward data and the orientation toward feelings share in common is a focus on weakness or immaturity rather
than on strength, an orientation toward others rather than toward
self, and a way of avoiding issues of personal accountability. But the
most deleterious effect of empathy's subversion on leaders is more
fundamental. It has to do with the way we conceptualize the forces
of light and darkness. The focus on empathy rather than responsibility has contributed to a major misorientation in our society about
the nature of what is toxic to life itself and, therefore, the factors
that go into survival. Thus, on the most fundamental level, this
chapter is about the struggle between good and evil, between life and
death, between what is destructive and what is creative, between
dependency and responsibility, and, consequently, in the deepest
realms of personal existence, between what is evolutionary and what
is regressive.

The chapter is divided into two major sections. The first is
devoted to the nature of a hostile environment. I will show that in
any relationship system, from the cellular level to the international
level, and whether we are considering families or other institutions,
all disintegrative forces have one essential characteristic in common,
and it is totally unresponsive to empathy. That characteristic is the
un-self-regulating invasiveness of another's space. There is a remarkable similarity between the regressive effects on life processes of (1)
malignancy in a human organism; (2) the continual disruption of a
family's integrity by its most immature members; (3) the preempting
of time and energy by chronic troublemakers in institutions; and (4)
the wanton destructiveness of organized crime or totalitarian
nations. Forces that are un-self-regulating can never be made to
adapt toward the strength in a system by trying to understand or

appreciate their nature. This was Chamberlain's great mistake at Munich in trying to empathize with Hitler. Priding himself on his own reasonableness and his unwavering belief in the value of achieving consensus, Chamberlain was trying to "understand Hitler's needs." He tried to project himself into, that is, feel for, Hitler's position, so that they could work out a mutual accommodation. It never seems to have occurred to him that there are forces on this planet that, because of their inability or unwillingness to self-regulate, are by nature all take and no give.

The significance for leadership of the folly of trying to be reasonable with a "virus" is that when parents and presidents put their primary focus on their own self rather than on the needs of another, that endeavor, far from being "selfish," has much in common with the latest understanding of the immune response. Its basic purpose is the preservation of an organism's integrity, that is, the self. It is self-regulation, not feeling for others, that is critical in the face of entities which lack that quality. There is a third alternative that is both caring *and* self-preserving—one that frees healers, leaders, and parents from this either/or choice. It is promoting responsibility for self in another through challenge. But that requires raising one's threshold for their pain and not being sensitive to their sensitivities.

In the second section, devoted to resources for survival, I will develop this thesis from the other direction by demonstrating that in any hostile environment whatsoever, whether the toxic force is outside or inside the person, most often the critical variable in survival has less to do with the strength or number of toxic factors in that environment than with the response of the endangered organism. Once again, it is responsibility, not empathy, that is the crucial variable in this equation. Indeed, the focus on being empathic toward others, rather than on being responsible for one's own integrity, can actually lessen the odds for an organism's survival by lowering the other's pain thresholds, helping them to avoid challenge and compromising the mobilization of their "nerve." And when it is the leader who has fallen into the empathy trap, sometimes it is not only the survival of the follower (patient, child, client, or institution) that is compromised and put at risk, but also the survival of the leader.

The word *empathy* is used so often today by teachers, parents, healers, and managers that few realize it only entered the English language in the twentieth century (compared to *sympathy*, which is four hundred fifty years old, and *compassion*, which goes back to 1340). According to the *Oxford English Dictionary* the word *empathy* was first employed in 1922, when a need arose to translate a German word in the field of aesthetics (*einfurlang*, "to feel in"). The original intent of the word *empathy* was to convey how projecting oneself into a work of art (painting, sculpture, theater) would enable a viewer to appreciate better the creation being observed. In fact, the word *empathy* does not appear in the original edition of the *Oxford English Dictionary* published in 1931 after fifty years of painstaking research into the breadth and particulars of the tongue (without the aid of word processors). The first editors were either unaware of *empathy* or thought it too rarified, too new, or too technical to include it.

While the adjective *empathetic* appears in some psychological essays at the beginning of the twentieth century, it was not until after World War II that the word *empathy* itself became part of common parlance, as it jumped from the realm of art appreciation to that of human relationships. It promised that projecting one's own person into the skin of another would enable one to understand the other person fully, to be more sensitive to his or her condition, and to better appreciate his or her dilemma. Empathy, "to feel in," therefore, was intended to be an advance over old-fashioned concepts such as sympathy or compassion, which mean only "to feel or to suffer with." But, if *sympathy* has been in use for at least four hundred fifty years and *compassion* goes back almost seven centuries, are we to assume that English-speaking people suddenly became more sensitive to others in the middle of the twentieth century? Or does the popularity of the word signify something else?

I believe that the increasing popularity of empathy over the past few decades is symptomatic of the herding/togetherness force characteristic of an anxious society. And I say this knowing that empathy has achieved such inviolable, holy status in the thinking of some that to even question its value will be considered as irreverent, if not sacrilegious, as denying the Trinity or cursing the Land of Israel.

On the one hand, there can be no question that the notion of feeling for others, caring for others, identifying with others, being responsive to others, and perhaps even sharing their pain exquisitely or excruciatingly is heartfelt, humanitarian, highly spiritual, and an essential component in a leader's response repertoire. But it has rarely been my experience that being sensitive to others will enable those "others" to be more self-aware, that being more "understanding" of others causes them to mature, or that appreciating the plight of others will make them more responsible for their being, their condition, or their destiny.

It is possible, of course, to define empathy in a way that tries to nullify these effects, but I am concerned here not with the "true" meaning of the word *empathy* but with its use, and thus with what it has come to mean. As understood today, empathy may be a luxury afforded only to those who do not have to make tough decisions. For "tough decisions" are decisions the consequence of which will be painful to others (although not *harmful* to others—an important distinction). The focus on "need fulfillment" that so often accompanies an emphasis on empathy leaves out the possibility that what another may really "need" (in order to become more responsible) is *not* to have their needs fulfilled. Indeed, it is not even clear that feeling for others is a more caring stance (or even a more ethical stance) than challenging them to take responsibility for themselves. As mentioned earlier, increasing one's threshold for another's pain (which is necessary before one can challenge them) is often the only way the other will become motivated to increase their own threshold, thus becoming better equipped to face the challenges of life.

Ultimately, societies, families, and organizations are able to evolve out of a state of regression not because their leaders "feel" for or "understand" their followers, but because their leaders are able, by their well defined presence, to regulate the systemic anxiety in the relationship system they are leading and to inhibit the invasiveness of those factions which would preempt its agenda. After that, they can afford to be empathic.

The kind of "sensitivity" that leaders most require is a sensitivity to the degree of chronic anxiety and the lack of self-differentiation in the system that surrounds them. The development of that ability requires that they focus primarily on maintaining a self-regulation of their own reactive mechanisms, and that they muster up the stamina to define themselves continually to those who lack such self-regulation.

This is not merely a matter of putting one's own oxygen mask on first. It has to do with leaders (or parents or healers) putting their primary emphasis on their own continual growth and maturity. As with the focus on data and technique, the focus on empathy, because it encourages primary emphasis on others, subverts the nature of that self-differentiating process.

◆ THE NATURE OF HOSTILE ENVIRONMENTS

All entities that are destructive to other entities share one major characteristic that is totally unresponsive to empathy: *they are not capable of self-regulation.* This is an absolutely universal rule of life in this galaxy. This principle of self-regulation goes back to the origins of life on this planet, part of the ongoing natural processes of creation, and it may be the context of all evolutionary advances. It holds true for viruses, malignant cells, and abusers of substances or people, whether the latter are chronically troublemaking members of families or institutions or make up an entire totalitarian nation.

Equally significant for the functioning of parents and presidents is the fact that this fundamental characteristic of regressive entities is the basis for two derivative attributes that all pathogenic forces or entities also have in common, whether they are the cells of an organism, the individuals in an organization, or the members of a family. One attribute is this: all organisms that lack self-regulation will be *perpetually invading the space of their neighbors.* (Their relentlessness seems to give them a resolute stamina that the "good guys" can rarely muster.) The second attribute is: organisms that are unable to self-regulate *cannot learn from their experience,* which is why the unmotivated are invulnerable to insight.

Not only do these derivative principles hold true at every level of life's organization, from the viral to the human, and transcend the social science construction of reality, but when it comes to human beings, these principles are not amenable to empathy. If anything, they are strengthened by a focus on others rather than focus on the self. Recognizing the universality of these principles can create a major reorientation for understanding and dealing with many of the dilemmas of leadership in families and institutions, particularly resistance, sabotage, perversity, and madness. We will go step-by-step up the ladder of life's organization in order to describe these basic life principles about the importance of self-regulation and of promoting accountability over feeling for others.

Viruses

One of the smallest forms of "life," these partial beings do not easily fit into the conventional categories of animal, vegetable, or mineral. On the one hand, viruses reproduce, so they might at first appear to be animate; on the other hand, they are not self-sufficient. They have no inherent means of propelling themselves, and they lack the animus common to animals, so they can also appear to be mineral. In order to travel, they must enter a stream, or forge a tail from material co-opted from their host. This failure to have meaningful intent is in part due to the fact that viruses have no nucleus to organize their being (or their experience), and in part because often they have no surrounding membrane (a cell wall or skin) that helps them differentiate their own being from other entities in their environment. Viruses, in short, have no *self* in any meaningful sense of that word. They are in many ways the ultimate in reactivity, and they are the very essence of parasitic dependency. Lacking a means of creating their own energy, unlike cells or bacteria, both their behavior and their direction are determined by what is outside rather than what is within.

But if they are not animal, they also are not vegetable. The way viruses propagate demonstrates that, for they could not reproduce on their own even if they had the aid of a germinating agent. To multiply, viruses must infiltrate a host (either a cell or a bacterium), take over their host's DNA machinery, and turn it into a factory for themselves. The newly formed viruses then burst through their host cell's membrane, disperse, and invade other hosts. It is this random process that we call infection.

Critical for our discussion of the importance of self-regulation, however, is the fact that viruses do not regulate their own behavior at any stage in this process. Their invasiveness is not symptomatic of an attribute they possess. It is due, rather, to what they do not possess: the ability to be self-determined in any purposeful way. In addition, lacking both a nucleus and in many cases a self-defining wall, they have no way to learn from previous experience. They can change, but generally speaking, they do not evolve.

Malignant Cells

If we go up a step to the next level of life's organization, the cell, we find that on this level also, self-regulation is critical to the difference between life-sustaining cells and the destructive cells we call malignant. Here, both types of organisms do have a nucleus. Both types of cells have the same components, but malignant cells differ from normal cells in at least five other respects, all of which are connected by the issue of self-definition and self-regulation.

◆ Normal cells differentiate from their parent cell and gain a specific identity that imbues them with purpose. Depending on their position, specific genes turn on in ways that cause them to gravitate toward other cells that have a similar function.

◆ They develop to a stage called *specialization* in which they become somatically determined, congregating to form a colony with a particular life function that contributes to the overall functioning of the larger society.

◆ They communicate with one another and become part of a mutually reciprocal network that regulates each one's growth, behavior, and to some extent survival.

◆ During the process of specialization, normal cells cease to proliferate indiscriminately and propagate only offspring that have the same function as themselves. This not only means they organize their life in a new, meaningful way; it also ensures their becoming cooperative rather than competitive with the larger society of which they are a part and which gave them their life to begin with.

◆ They know when to quit. Normal cells have a gene for self-destruction. Under certain circumstances, when cells contain entities that are dangerous to the larger society to which they belong, that gene can be activated, thus robbing the potentially harmful force that has taken refuge within it of a base from which to operate. The process, called *apoptosis*, or programmed cell death, even though it has to do with self-destruction, is an evolutionary, altruistic phenomenon, not a regressive one.

This relationship between purpose and proliferation is far more basic to the evolution of a society than might at first appear, and it has important ramifications for the formation of any "colony." Once cells differentiate, they cannot just go off "half-cocked" in their own selfish way either to form new organisms or to transmit to the next generation characteristics they acquired during their own lifetime. Cancer (like all forms of anarchy), of course, is the subversion of that process. In the origins of multicellular life, a crucial evolutionary transition was that once an organism began to form, it had to find a means of preserving that form. Life in its earliest stages had to come to grips with the issue of how to prevent cell lineages from forming new, competing, and sometimes subversive organisms— which is, of course, exactly what tumors are.

Malignant cells differ from normal cells in all five of the following respects, and in every case the differences and their pathogenic potential are connected through the issues of self-regulation and self-definition.

- ◆ They either fail to develop or lose the capacity for self-definition that can enable them to become well-differentiated, with the result that they remain permanently immature. They do not evolve.
- ◆ They do not specialize. They do not colonize with a purpose that contributes to the organization of the larger community of which they are a part, and the colonies (tumors) they do form are totally un-self-regulating.
- ◆ They are rogue cells, unconnected through reciprocal networks with other cells that might influence their growth and behavior.
- ◆ They reproduce uncontrollably even after they colonize. There is no transfer of energy from reproduction to some higher purpose. In fact, they are guilty of treason, competing with or subverting the body that first gives them life.
- ◆ They do not know when to quit. Once taken out of a human organism and allowed to reproduce in a laboratory, they seem to be capable of purposeless immortality. The

only way malignant cells self-destruct is by taking their host
with them.

Malignant cells, like viruses, are the essence of selfishness. With no
sense of connectedness, they operate without any responsiveness to
a larger association. Since altruism is connected to connectedness, it
is, therefore, out of the question. At no time, however, can their selfishness be attributed to intent; as with viruses, their selfishness has
to do with lack of self.

It is precisely the combination of these five interconnected characteristics of malignant cells that creates the regressive process we
have come to call cancer. And it is these same five factors among
human organisms in any family or institution that create the
emotional processes that are also malignant. Furthermore, in neither
case can health be restored by a quick fix or through understanding.
The understanding that is needed is how to prevent the progression
of their invasiveness. For malignant processes at any level of life's
organization are not simply the presence of a noxious force; they are
rather an essential life process that has been perverted. The ultimate
similarity between organisms and organizations (between bodies and
bodies politic) is that, unlike diseases "caused" by the continued
presence of some chronically troublemaking noxious agent, as in the
case of a virus or bacterium, malignant processes continue to subvert
even though the toxic agent that initiated the original misdirection is
no longer around to continue energizing the pathology.

Organisms
Let us now go up a step to the level of the pathogenic human
organism. The behavior of substance abusers, chronically abusive
family members, members of institutions who never quit being difficult, and so on—do they not behave like viruses or malignant cells?
As with viruses, do they not function as though they had no nucleus,
as though they were more reactive than inner-directed? Are they not
more parasitic (prone to take advantage of) than symbiotic (mutual-
istic)? Do they not appear to lack the outer membrane that would
make them self-contained, and draw energy from what is around
them rather than from their own internal resources? Do they not
function as though they were isolated from the influences of others
around them, and do they not seem to be infectious as well as inca-

pable of modifying their own behavior? And, as with both cancer cells and viruses, does not their un-self-regulating invasiveness contaminate the larger colony (family or institution) of which they are a part? Do they not seem to possess a stamina that is wearying for the larger organism? Is it not true that they only seem to go away when they bring the institution down with them? Will being sensitive to their needs regulate their invasiveness or instill greater self-definition?

Do cells and the colonies of cells we call "individuals" function and relate in similar ways because humans consist of cells? Or is the similarity due to the fact that, at any level of life's organization, these are the only choices the natural processes of life give to us?

Over the years, I have been particularly struck by the inability of well-meaning parents to maintain consistent stands with their chronically troubling children. Admonitions to parents to be "consistent" consistently fail, even with the most concerned (read *empathic*) mother and father. One can only be consistent when one is focused on oneself, not on the random perturbations of the un-self-regulating other. The former is what leadership is about; the latter allows followers to set the agendas. That is why such parents, no matter what techniques they are taught, from being "available" and "understanding" to "tough love," almost always seem to be worn down by the repetitiveness of the child's unregulated behavior or their own treadmill efforts to modify their child's responses. I have found that parents are far better able to sustain a growth-producing attitude toward their children if, instead of seeking new answers and methods, it is the question that is reframed. Instead of trying to mobilize their empathy by showing them what child-rearing techniques will "benefit" their children, I have tried to challenge an immune (that is, self-defined) response in them by demonstrating how their children are viruses that are taking over their host, or even malignant cells that are destroying their "colony." In order to adopt this perspective, however, parents must be able to concentrate on the preservation of their own integrity (again, an immune phenomenon) rather than on the effort to "mutate" their child.

This shift in parental focus from the child to their own self also affects their stamina. For as long as a parent's focus is on the "other," the unremitting lack of self-regulation in the troublesome child gives it a never-ending, relentless strength that is hard for parents to resist as long as they are trying to be empathic. But once parents are reoriented toward their own welfare, their stamina begins to increase in the most natural way. And it is no different with teachers, therapists, professional people, and CEOs.

Nurturing growth always follows two principles. One is: Stay out of its way; you cannot "grow" another by will or technique. But the second is: Do not let it "overgrow" you. I have continually found that when parents can make the transition in their orientation from focusing on how to grow their children to how to prevent their children from overgrowing them, their children do begin to grow—that is, grow up—and so do the parents. In other words, there must be self-differentiation in the parent before there can be self-differentiation in the child. There are, of course, parents who seem totally incapable of separating their own welfare from their child's, because they cannot separate (that is, differentiate) their own self from their child's. These are parents who have become so emotionally fused with their child that the child's being is part of their being.

This comparison to viruses, malignant cells, and other cul-de-sacs in evolution is not limited to family relationships. It extends to all forms of organized life, and once again, it totally transcends the categories of social science virtual reality. Listed below are ten interrelated characteristics of potentially pathogenic "viral" or "malignant" members of institutions that are particularly troublesome to leaders. What links their potential for being toxic is that they are all attributes of "organisms" that lack the motivation to self-define or self-regulate and have remained in a primitive state. They are therefore, by nature, both invasive of the space of others and unable to learn from their own experience. Primitive organisms remain primitive, that is, they do not evolve because of the narrowness of their response repertoire and, therefore, the narrowness of their capacity to adapt to changes in their environment. On the human level of life's organization, such creatures always expect others to adapt to them.

◆ They tend to be easily hurt "injustice-collectors," slow healers who are given to victim attitudes. (It is as if they had no outer membrane to ensure their integrity.)

◆ They tend to idolize their leaders until their unrealistic expectations fail, whereupon they are quick to crucify their "gods." (There is a parasitic quality to their bonding.)

◆ Their intent is often "innocently provocative"; they do not see themselves as bent on destruction. The pathology they promote is rather a byproduct of their doing what comes naturally, so they never see how they contribute to the condition they complain about.

◆ Their repertoire of responses, as with the most primitive forms of life, is limited to being "on" or "off." This manifests itself in their linear, black-and-white formulations of life; their unconditional, with-us-or-against-us attitudes; and their inability to tolerate differences or dissent.

◆ They tend to focus on procedure and on rituals, and, as if their heads did not swivel, they get stuck on the content of issues rather than being able to view the surrounding emotional processes that are spawning the issues.

◆ They find that light and truth, the element that is most healthy to other forms of life, is toxic to their nature. They thrive in the darkness of conspiracy like anaerobic bacteria, such as botulism, which are hangovers from a very early stage of life.

◆ They seem to be driven by their reptilian brains rather than their cortex and thus manifest three basic characteristics of the reptilian way of life: they have a high degree of reactivity, a narrow range of responses, and of course they are always serious—deadly serious.

◆ As with all organisms that lack self-definition and self-regulation, they tend to ooze into, if not directly interfere in, the relationships of others. Thus they wreck staff communication and connections, and bypass, if not subvert, democratic processes.

◆ They tend to be easily stampeded and panicked into group-think, thus fusing with others like them into an undifferentiated mass (like a tumor).

◆ They are unforgivingly relentless and totally invulnerable to insight. Unless walled off or totally defeated, they tend to come back with a vengeance, as when an antibiotic is not taken for the fully prescribed period.

Leaders have to deal with such pathogens to the same extent, no matter what the structure or purpose of the (host) institution, or the gender, race, and ethnic background of the un-self-regulating pathogenic organism. Leaders, in fact, will find that these entities are interchangeable from church to synagogue, from profit to non-profit institution, from school to health care practice, from small business to large corporation. Wherever they are located, their presence and their outlook are regressive. In addition, these kinds of people share a natural affinity, as if they sense their commonality from the first time they meet, almost as though the signal were olfactory—one of our most primitive ways of sensing information. What was said about the deceptiveness of values in the previous chapter particularly applies here. These kinds of "organisms" often express themselves with beautiful "values." The problem is not in their beliefs; it is in how they function with those beliefs.

Still, no matter what their makeup or nature (personality), they are little more than annoying and cannot do much harm alone. And even when they join with similar others and form "tumors" that are often metastatic, they only have power in the face of a failed immune response in the body politic. But leaders could no more create a "mutation" in such human organisms through empathy than they could stop cancer or viral invasiveness by trying to be more "understanding" of those agents or more sensitive to their plight. For these ten characteristics are also descriptive of a chronically litigious person or of an assassin. And, reversing the perspective, it would not be so far off base to think of a cancer cell or a virus as a terrorist. If interviewed, the terrorist undoubtedly would complain that he or she had been isolated, ignored, victimized, abused, unrecognized, and alienated by the larger community. I once asked an attorney who represented "white collar" criminals why these individuals, who often developed brilliant schemes, did not just go straight, given the likelihood that their ingenuity would profit them in that direction also. And he replied, "They just don't seem to be able to get energized unless they are bypassing the law."

But perhaps the ultimate evidence for the fact that these characteristics are universal and transcend all social science categories is

that one could create a troupe of mummers who went from institution to institution and said, "Allow us to be the disruptive element
in your organization, and we can release all of you to put your ener-
gies into being creative. You don't have to tell us anything about your
place or the makeup of its members. We know exactly what to do."

This is not to say that for such individuals there is no hope for
rehabilitation, reconciliation, recovery, or recuperation. But empathy
alone will never promote the self-organization necessary for learning
from experience; that can only come about when they are told that
if they want to be a part of the community, they have to adapt to it,
and not the other way around. I recognize that this approach could
sound dictatorial; the emphasis here, however, is not on conformity
of thought but on conformity of behavior to the democratic
process. It is in this sense that promoting in others the initiative to
be accountable is far more critical to the health of an institution
than trying to be understanding or insightful.

Institutions

Everything that has been said thus far about self-regulation and
empathy is just as applicable to the next level of life's organization,
the human colonies that we call families, institutions, or nations.
And here again—or better, here especially—empathy is totally irrelevant to creating a more responsible unit. On the institutional level,
this principle is exemplified to the same extent by chronically
anxious families, by the functioning of organized crime (which often
colonizes in "families") and politically subversive groups in
American society, and by totalitarian nations.

On this level of life's organization, the entities that are most pathogenic lack self-regulation and self-definition. They always invade
the space of others; they always move to take over their environment
or their neighbors, and both their poorly defined boundaries and
their lack of integrity give them a parasitic quality that is ultimately
immoral. Both organized crime and subversive organizations are like
viruses in the sense that they do not develop out of their own structure but are dependent on others, which they must infect in order to
propagate. In fact, they thrive on taking over a "host." Similarly,
though they seem to have direction, it is not from some nucleus that
supplies them with self-organization, but rather as a reaction to the

environment that surrounds them. It is as if they had no membrane to define where they end and their neighbors begin.

Moreover, it goes without saying that such institutions are almost never able, or willing, to integrate their experience in a way that enables them to develop a more enriched individuality. They might get larger, but they do not "grow." Once again, like the undifferentiated mass of tumors, they do not evolve.

The five characteristics mentioned above that distinguish malignant cells from normal cells also may be used to distinguish normal—that is healthy—institutions from criminal or subversive ones. For the latter are totally disrespectful of boundaries and of the life of the larger organism (society) which gave them life, and they replicate without limits. In addition, they are not connected in any reciprocal way to other institutions, and they certainly do not know when to quit, much less die.

The form of human colonization that functions most similarly to a virus or a malignant cell is the totalitarian nation. No human entity is more invasive. The totalitarian nation is equally invasive of the lives of its citizens and the space of its neighbors. Those nations that tend to be invasive of other nations are almost always also invasive of the lives of their own citizens. The two are linked, once again, by the absence of self-regulation; they make no attempt to regulate their drive in either direction. They infect what they touch, and they seek to replicate their own being by taking over any host they "occupy." They certainly do not know when to quit. It is this same lack of self-regulation and the inner integrity required for self-definition that makes totalitarian nations as notoriously untrustworthy of agreements and treaties as a crime syndicate. Yet they may be no more immoral than a virus, for their perpetual immorality may stem less from evil intention than from the fact that they are incapable, constitutionally, of the self-regulation required to abide by an agreement. And this brings us back, full circle, to the irrelevance of empathy in the face of a relentless force.

There is, for example, almost no example in history of a sensitive or understanding approach to an invasive nation that successfully staved off a war in the long run. This seems to have been as true for Rome and Carthage, Athens and Sparta, the Allied Powers and the Central Powers of World War I, or the Allied Powers and the Axis

Powers of World War II. On the contrary, history is filled with examples of democratic countries trying unsuccessfully to stave off conflict with invasive nations by trying to appease them. Furthermore, this reluctance of democracies to go to war against totalitarian nations is identical to the reluctance of members of any family, marriage, partnership, or institution to stand up to the "troublemaker." And in institution after institution the invasive forces get their way because of a lack of "stamina" that is hard to muster up in the "peace-loving." The institution can be a church or synagogue, a stock market firm, a privately owned business, psychotherapy, the courts, or an academic institution.

Here is an example from academia. One month before an invited speaker was to lecture at an academic institution on an issue that had become intensely polarizing in her field (epidemiology), a chapter from her best-known work was sent out in an advance mailing to those who would attend in order to acquaint them with her thinking. Then, a tenured faculty member who was vehemently opposed to her ideas organized a rump committee that gave him permission to send out an article he had written that "refuted" what she was going to say, before she even had the opportunity to present her lecture. The faculty member did not attend the lecture but two of his disciples did, and they kept interrupting her comments during the question period in the midst of her answers, clearly more to take issue with what she was saying than to inquire further about the meaning of her remarks.

Furious, she wrote a letter to the president of the university saying that she thought the faculty member's behavior was not only uncouth, indecent, and disingenuous, but a subversion of the canons of academic freedom. She received no reply for months. When she finally heard from the president, he told her she was being unnecessarily defensive, that she knew her ideas were controversial, and that the faculty member, while sometimes gruff, was known for his keen intellect and famous for bringing out the best in people through his challenging confrontations. He was simply exercising his right to disagree. Later she found out that the president had been on sabbatical most of the year, and that there had been no one really running the show. Actually, the president was even more absent than that: he had been secretly interviewing for other jobs.

As mentioned earlier, what appears to be stamina and determination in a pathogen is really lack of self-regulation. It is not the presence of a characteristic that makes pathogens relentless but the absence of one. The stamina of pathogenic forces comes not from the fact that they are organized around some resolute purpose, but from the exact opposite: the unwillingness to define a purpose beyond invading and taking over. For pathogens, self-regulation is not a matter of choice; they can't help it. But the host can.

Self-Regulation in the Host
Despite their potential to create pathology, pathogens do not have the power to create pathology on their own. There must also be a lack of self-regulation in the host. Oncogenesis does not always lead to cancer; not everyone gets sick because of what they breathe in from the surrounding air. The fact that some people seem to be untouched by a surrounding epidemic is not due to the fact that they were lucky enough not to "catch" a cold. In fact, it is well known that every human organism contains "opportunistic infections" that are kept in check by their own immune system. In other words, it is not merely the presence of the pathogen that causes pathology, but also the response of the organism that "hosts" it.

It was mentioned above that Chamberlain, in effect, tried to reason with a "virus," that is, with a totally un-self-regulating organism. But, as Churchill later declared in contrast, World War II came about "because the malice of the wicked was reinforced by the weakness of the virtuous." The biological equivalent of Churchill's statement came several years ago when society's chronic anxiety became focused on recombinant DNA and there was great worry over the possibility that an organism might accidentally be created that would be toxic to humankind. At that time, several Nobel-level scientists pointed out that toxicity was not enough; to complete its pathogenic mission it also had to be able to bind itself to the cell wall and defeat the immune response.

Imagine that the cells of an organ receive an early warning signal that a rogue cancer cell is coming down the pike. Knowing that metastasis can only occur if the healthy cells allow the malignant cells to puncture their own membranes, they huddle together and agree it's all for one and one for all; no one is to allow this thing in where it might metastasize into a colony of similarly lethal offspring. But after a while some of the cells at one end of the organ realize that the metastasis has begun. They look at the other cells, now dying, and say, "What's the matter with you? What have you done? Why did you let it invade our space? We all agreed to keep that troublemaker out." And the cells that let the cancer cell in say helplessly, "We were watching it swim all alone out there. It just seemed so lonely, and well—we just started to feel sorry for it."

◆ SURVIVAL IN A HOSTILE ENVIRONMENT

Whether we are considering the self-defense of a nation, the preservation of a family's integrity, or the cohesiveness of an organization, the key to survival is the ability of the "host" to recognize and limit the invasiveness of its viral or malignant components. If lack of self-regulation is the essential characteristic of organisms that are destructive, it is precisely the presence of self-regulatory capacity that is critical to the health, survival, and evolution of an organism or an organization.

That is precisely the function of a leader within any institution: to provide that regulation through his or her non-anxious, self-defined presence. Whether we are considering an organism or an organization, pathology is always an interrelational phenomenon, and the determining variable is usually the integrity of the host. For the immune response, as I shall elaborate in the next chapter, is about integrity, not merely self-defense or hawkish retaliation. It both depends upon, and contributes to, the self-defining nature of an organism. Not only is this another principle that totally transcends the categories of social science; it is totally independent of empathic initiatives.

The previous section was about the irrelevance of empathy to appreciating what is toxic to life; this section will demonstrate that the capacity for, or the demonstration of, empathy is also irrelevant to, and often distracting from, the resources that go into survival. And those resources—a healthy dose of self, the capacity to take responsibility for one's condition, resiliency, self-regulation of anxious reactivity, a varied repertoire of responses—are applicable to all human organisms and organizations irrespective of gender, race, class, and age.

Several years ago, I was counseling a rather unsophisticated man who had endured an operation with a twenty-percent chance of survival. When told about his condition and the odds that were against him, he engaged in no calculations about his chances, nor did he even wait to consult with his physician brother. He said simply, "I want to be one of the twenty percent." When I saw him a year later, he had cut his work week down to forty hours so that he could travel several times a week, fifty miles each way, for radiation, and was in fact inquiring whether they could increase his dosage so that he could heal faster. Intrigued by his capacity to take charge of his life and his persistent drive in the midst of his toxic environment (and the expertise of experts), I presented the following scenario to him, along with a question that I had long pondered.

Toward the end of World War II, after delivering parts of the first atomic bomb to the Marianas, the USS *Indianapolis* was torpedoed suddenly by a Japanese submarine in the middle of the Japan Sea. The ship went down quickly before a mayday message could be sent out, and eight hundred men were left helpless in the hostile environment of a salty sea, man-eating sharks, and a scorching sun. Although they knew it was to their advantage to stay close to one another, some of the men swam away from the safety of the group and, either willingly or out of madness, gave themselves up to the sharks. "How do you explain that?" I asked my client. "Unless you assume they were exhibiting extraordinary altruism, those men who swam away functioned in exactly the opposite direction from the one you have followed with regard to the dangers to your own life. You have responded with cool, with stamina, with perspective, and with courage."

Without much reflection, he answered immediately, "Those guys who swam away, they didn't have no future."

Moreover, the same lack of presence of the *Indianapolis*'s captain that led to his ship's being torpedoed—the ship was on a straight course rather than zigzagging—might have contributed to a lack of social cohesion of the men in the water and thereby robbed them of an integrating force that might have optimized their potential for survival. The captain was later court-martialed on what some have said was a trumped-up charge to make him a scapegoat for lack of communication in the Navy. It was the greatest loss of life on one ship since Pearl Harbor. On the other hand, certain facts of the captain's life after the trial, such as his wife's death and his own consequent suicide, suggest a very emotionally dependent man, certainly not the kind to take charge personally, but rather someone who would have been more or less a target. I believe it was that same passive attitude toward life, which failed him in crisis, that got him into the situation of being torpedoed in the first place.

Broadening that concept, it may be said unequivocally that whenever anyone is *in extremis* (whether it is a marital crisis, an economic crisis, a political crisis, or a health crisis), their chances of survival are far greater when their horizons are formed of projected images from their own imagination rather than being limited by what they can actually see. Or, to reverse it, to the extent the horizons of individuals *in extremis* are limited to what they can actually see, their chances of survival are far less than if their horizons include projected images from their own imagination. Actually, even the thinking processes that lead one to assume that one's life situation is *in extremis* are partially determined by the breadth of one's horizons at the time—which, of course, correlates with one's imaginative capacity and sense of adventure.

This principle of survival is supported by the experiences of many who survived the Nazi Holocaust, and perhaps is also indicative of many who were far-seeing enough to get out. Both those who have written about their survival and those who have researched the survivors consistently note a capacity to see beyond the barbed wire. Such vision obviously did not guarantee survival, but it does seem to have maximized the chances for it.

Other factors were involved, of course. One was dumb luck, referred to by concentration camp inmates as *selectzia*—as though someone were pulling cosmic strings. On a given day, you might have been selected for the gas chambers merely because of what stalag you were housed in and therefore where you were standing the day they selected your housing, or whether the number tattooed on your arm was odd or even. In addition, personal factors seemed to affect destiny: whether, for example, you were committed to endure and were constantly on the look-out for another piece of bread that might be clutched in an already dead person's hand, which is another way of saying whether you tried to be a leader in your own survival. Still, while it did not guarantee survival (it was not a matter of right thinking), what did seem to have mattered most among these factors was the will to survive, and that meant being able to project one's imagination beyond the stalag or even the gates.

There are always three factors involved in survival, no matter how toxic the environment—which could be the ghetto, an authoritarian government, a lousy boss, recalcitrant employees, a board of trustees, a "controlling" spouse, a "Jewish mother," an abusive father, an epidemic, a gasoline shortage, a birth defect, prejudice and discrimination, an automobile accident, a bad lawyer, a statistical profile of your condition, or a shark-infested ocean. One is the physical reality; the second is dumb luck; and the third is the response of the organism, which can often modify the influence of the first two. The relationship of these three factors can be imagined as dials on an amplifier, with survival depending on the overall mix. Whenever the first two dials—physical reality and dumb luck—are turned up to maximum volume, the third dial will not make any difference. That would be true in cases of being held under water, falling out of an airplane, exposure to radiation, and certain end-stage cases of terminal illness, although exceptions to the latter do exist. (In evolutionary time, if you hold a whole species under water, depending on the richness of its gene pool, you might get some amphibians.) In most crises, however, the first two dials are rarely going full blast— but when an individual's anxiety is high, he or she will tend to ignore the third dial and focus only on the first two. Similarly, when the anxiety in society is high, all research and healing will tend to concentrate on the first two dials and almost completely ignore the third—the organism's own response to the environment.

When life crises are viewed in terms of proportional or systems thinking rather than straight-line, linear thinking, then outcomes other than mere capitulation or escape become possible. One such outcome is the mobilization of an organism's resources such as resiliency, determination, self-regulation, and stamina. (Many battles can be won simply by not giving up; one does not have to conquer the other.) A second is transformation of the organism, which includes a higher capacity to deal with future crises. And a third is modification of the toxicity of the environment.

Here is an example of the third. An attractive young woman came to New York from the Midwest to try her luck on the stage. On her first payday in the city, she was mugged in the vestibule of her brownstone by a man who put a knife to her throat and demanded her money. She remembers saying to herself, "I'll have to say my lines and let him say his." Then, as though she were the producer, director, and star of her own play, she explained as calmly as she could that she had just arrived in New York that week and had not worked long enough to earn a biweekly paycheck. Then, as any good actress or acting coach would do, she shut her mouth and waited for his response. The hardened New York streetwise criminal snorted, paused, released her, grabbed her bag, dumped it on the floor, and, seeing nothing of value, ran off—leaving her trembling, perhaps, but triumphant. Her regulation of her own reactive mechanisms regulated the anxiety in "the hall." This modified the anxiety of the thief, who took his cue from her non-anxious presence and did her no harm. In addition, the experience emboldened her to try for parts she never thought she would get.

Will things always work out this way? Of course not. As mentioned, there are situations where our response is irrelevant, where the first two dials are turned too far up. But our response is always far more influential than our chronically anxious society leads us to believe, and it is sometimes the ultimately determinative variable, whether one is considering the loss of one's job or aging. Those who are less reactive are more self-contained, less blaming, more imaginative, less anxious, and more responsible. When they do seek help, they generally can hear suggestions well, offer less resistance to suggestions for change, and treat their consultant as a coach rather than a savior. Such an approach emphasizes strength rather than weakness, accountability rather than blame, taking responsibility for self rather than feeling for others.

Our potential response combines all those traits mentioned in previous chapters that enable self-definition and self-regulation: the richness of our repertoire of resources, including persistence, stamina, resiliency, hope (that is, broad horizons), and the capacity to think systemically in the first place. Changes in the toxicity of the environment that are not accompanied by changes in response are not likely to endure. Rather, it is the *problem* that is likely to endure and recycle. For all the good that comes from justly trying to improve people's environment, changes in the political realm do not bring about increased maturity. Neither greater economic opportunity nor equal rights guarantee an increase in people's capacity to handle crisis maturely.

There are, of course, those who have the worst of both worlds. These unfortunates in our society experience intense crisis combined with an inability to deal with crisis. They are more likely to be chronically institutionalized, or pariahs in society. Sometimes, however, they are free-roaming, even upstanding, members of society who deal with their troubles through serial marriages, serial jobs, serial neighborhoods, serial consultants, and serial churches or synagogues. When they colonize with others of the same bent, serial rejection and subversion of leaders soon follow.

One woman reported the following change in her thinking after great personal struggle to overcome her feelings that her background and family environment had determined her fate:

> I guess the one thing you have absolutely no influence over is where you appear on this planet. I might have been born in Vietnam with napalm raining all around, or to the wealthiest parents imaginable—but they and their own parents had so many unresolved issues between them that they were absolutely crazy-making. I used to think that if I had a choice, I'd take the napalm; at least you'd have a chance. But after what I have come to understand about the value of the organism's response, I think I'd take a chance with my parents.

For leaders, this is a way of thinking that reflects universal principles of life that are applicable to all institutions and societies. It offers a perspective that can help leaders in their evaluations of others by noting how they deal with their pain. And it can be useful both in making "tough" decisions and in dealing with reactivity to one's leadership.

There is one more aspect of this formula that is important for leaders and their consultants. An enormous number of problems that parents, marriage partners, and other leaders have to deal with are crises produced by their own differentiation. To the extent one focuses solely on how painful a situation is, there is no way to judge whether things are getting worse or really improving, fundamentally. Despite the fact that things seem to be getting worse, that is, more toxic, the entire system also may be adapting for the better. To recognize that fact can help keep anxiety down. If a leader who has sought help can be taught how to stay in touch with the reactive group without taking their issues so seriously that he or she is thrown off course, increased differentiation can become a form of leadership that, if sustained, often will result in the rest getting over what ails them. This can turn the pattern of adaptation toward the one who is becoming better differentiated, thus affecting the evolution of the entire "colony." Exclusive focus on pathology, on pain, and on empathy does not even allow that possibility to come into view. To the extent that those who specialize in conflict resolution focus primarily on empathy, their interventions will not really help the system mature. This is equally true for family and institutional relationships.

◆

The first half of this chapter was about the irrelevance of empathy in the face of un-self-regulating organisms that are by nature always invasive and cannot learn from their experience. The second half was about the inability of empathic initiatives to help people mature and take more responsibility for their own emotional being and destiny. These are opposite sides of the same coin of the realm of human experience. That coin is integrity—not integrity in the sense of morality, though it does include and lead to that, but integrity in the sense of wholeness and coherent organization. And not integrity in the sense of honesty, though it does include and lead to that, but integrity in the sense of immunity. For as I will show in the next chapter, everything that is true about immunity is true about self, as it is about all protoplasm.

It is in our understanding of the immune response that leadership and self come together. For, as I will elaborate in chapter 5, the immune response is not primarily about getting rid of enemies. That function is a byproduct of something far more essential: the preservation of an organism's integrity. The factors that promote such integrity in any human organism are exactly the same factors that, when they appear in a leader, promote the integrity of the organization he or she is leading.

If I am me because you are you,
and you are you because I am me,
then I am nothing, and you are nothing.
—Yiddish proverb

Chapter Five

◈ AUTOCRACY VERSUS INTEGRITY:

THE FALLACIES OF SELF

Half a billion years ago, life "exploded" on this planet into most of the bodily forms that exist today. Some have termed that period the "Big Bang" of evolution, thereby drawing a comparison between the diversification of species and the expanding galaxies of our universe. But a "bigger" evolutionary explosion took place on planet Earth a billion years prior to the formation of species, with enormous consequences for the eventual development of leadership and self. It occurred in the microcosm of life, not in the macrocosm, and, as with all fundamental shifts in emotional process, the extent of its influence is not quantifiable simply in terms of data.

The "Big Bang" of evolution was the arrival of the *eukaryotes,* the first cells to contain a nucleus. The possession of a nucleus enabled this "new kid on the block" to increase greatly its genetic content, eventually giving life a far richer complexity of choices. Prior to that evolutionary leap, reproduction was not in the service of diversity.

For two billion years before that transition, these cells' predecessors, *prokaryote* cells, lacked a nucleus and tended to clone life on this planet. With only one chromosome, attached to a rigid cell wall that minimized communication with the environment, variation from generation to generation was highly limited. The meaning of self was narrow, and leadership was an irrelevant proposition.

The "astronomical explosion" that followed the appearance of the eukaryotes was the opportunity for almost infinite variety. It was as though Creation was stuck in its own Dark Ages and had decided on a new route altogether (or at least "to shift the paradigm"). The expanded range of combinatorial possibilities enabled by a nucleus that could house a much larger volume and new arrangement of genes promoted an individuality in reproduction that had far more fundamental ramifications for the future direction of life everywhere than did the later diversification of species. Were it not for this "Big Bang" in the microcosm of cellular life, the later explosion in the macrocosm of multicellular organisms (and in our time of families, cultures, and societies) could not have taken place at all.

The arrival of the prokaryotes marked the true beginning of cellular life. For the first time, the three characteristics of all existing life forms came together: reproduction, metabolism (energy production), and heritability. But it was the arrival of the eukaryotes that marked the beginning of individuality, as well as the struggle to preserve it.

Imagine, therefore, the effect that the appearance of the first eukaryotes had on the balance between self and togetherness in the world of the prokaryotes:

Prokaryote: Let's get together.
Eukaryote: Not with you.
P: What's the problem?
E: I want to preserve my self.
P: What the hell is that?
E: Me.
P: But we're the same.
E: That's your perception.
P: It won't make any difference.
E: There's been a change.
P: You're a mutant form?

E: It's bigger than that.

P: I don't understand.

E: I'm not sure you ever could.

P: Something's gone wrong.

E: Joining you would be a regression.

P: I'm a cul-de-sac?

E: We're going to start a whole new tradition.

P: It won't last.

E: I'll take my chances.

P: Fusion is natural.

E: I want more definition.

P: But I'm very clearly defined.

E: I want more variety.

P: You're bored?

E: I have a nucleus.

P: What the hell is that?

E: It defines my potential.

P: Don't I have seniority?

E: You sure didn't go very far with it.

P: Take me along.

E: I'd rather join with others like me.

P: That's elitist.

E: I'm just organized differently.

P: You'll be sorry.

E: My integrity depends on preserving my self.

P: Wow, are you selfish.

All multicellular organisms that exist today (animal, vegetable, or fungal) are descended from the eukaryotes. Prokaryotes still exist in the form of bacteria and nitrogen-fixing blue-green algae, but they are extremely resistant to change. They have an uncanny ability to survive, but it takes them a long, long time to evolve.

To this day, wherever protoplasm colonizes, the basic tension between the lifestyles of the "prokaryotes" and the "eukaryotes" continues. The struggle between the forces for playing it safe and the forces for the preservation of individuality, between a creativity that adds new dimensions to life or a reproduction that simply reproduces, is omnipresent. Regression, therefore—any kind of regression—usually sides with the "prokaryotes": with those who compromise individuality by their narrow repertoire of responses; with those who have a limited capacity for complexity and creativity; with those whose approach to togetherness aims at fusion, not differentiation; and with those forces that focus on safety and survival rather than growth and change.

It is important to note, therefore, that when the first eukaryotes arrived, evolution leaped forward precisely because life decided to no longer play it safe. After all, the new, highly enriched, creative process engendered by dividing nuclei (mitosis) also created far more potential for "mistakes" (mutations) than the more predictable, straightforward "like father, like son" approach. But evidentially, as with Columbus and his fellow navigators, life decided right then and there that mistakes were a small price to pay for the rewards that novelty could bring. Venturing into harm's way is the "eukaryotic" tradition; regression, on the other hand, always sides with the "prokaryotes." And a failure of nerve among its leadership will allow any society to regress to its "prokaryotic" stage.

This chapter will explore the third "equator," or emotional barrier, that has to be crossed before leadership in America can be free to venture in "harm's way." That barrier is the association of self with autocracy and narcissism rather than with integrity and individuality. This negative orientation toward self is a natural spin-off of a chronically anxious society's focus on pathology rather than strength. Such a distorted focus contaminates all thinking about individuality in both families and other institutions, and eventually it extends to a counter-evolutionary perspective on leadership. That is because those who lack self-definition, whether they are children, marriage partners, employees, clients, therapists, or supervisors, will always perceive those who are well-defined to be "headstrong."

As with Columbus, they will describe well-differentiated leaders as compulsive rather than persistent, as obsessive rather than committed, as foolhardy rather than brave, as dreamers rather than imaginative, as single-minded rather than dedicated, as inflexible rather than principled, as hostile rather than aggressive, as bullheaded rather than resolute, as desperate rather than inspired, as autocratic rather than tough-minded, as ambitious rather than courageous, as domineering rather than self-confident, as egotistical rather than self-assured, as selfish rather than self-possessed—and as

insensitive, callous, and cold rather than determined. Such sabotage
will be cloaked by supposed virtues like safety and togetherness.

The illusion underlying this third emotional barrier to well-
differentiated leadership is the facile "peace over progress" assumption that communities will get along best when everyone stops being
"selfish." This pathologizing of individuality is an emotional process
that occurs equally in the profit or the non-profit world, once again
transcending the categories of the social science construction of
reality. For example, at a team-building seminar I attended for business executives, several experts kept using the word *aggression* as the
noun form of *aggressive*. Deciding that it was important to separate
initiative from hostile intent, I tried to point out that the noun form
of *aggressive* is not *aggression* but *aggressiveness*. *Aggressive* only means "to
move toward something" (from the Latin *gradior*, "to move"); *aggression*, while based on the same root, conveys invasiveness of another's
space. Sometimes moving forward is invasive, but sometimes it is just
self-expression. In the latter event, the person might be labeled
aggressive, but in the former case, the person should be labeled
aggressionistic. Many of those present, however, responded that I
was playing with words and they went right on confusing strength
with abuse.

At a national conference for rabbis, a psychoanalyst gave a major
presentation on the evils of narcissism, showing how most of the ills
of our society were due to this blight in which people of the "me
generation" were concerned only about themselves. Constant
applause punctuated every one of his remarks that urged thinking of
others first, and he received an enthusiastic, standing ovation at the
conclusion. But afterwards, one of the more experienced members of
the audience turned to his colleagues and said, "When you have to
go before your board of trustees and defend five thousand years of
tradition, all the while jeopardizing your job, your home, your health,
your kids' education, and perhaps even your marriage, you had better
have a good, strong dose of what he simplistically labels narcissism
or you won't survive the day."

Nor would the problem be different for any other parent or president trying to remain steadfast in the face of demands for quick-
relief change. Well-meaning efforts to eliminate the evils of
selfishness by eliminating self can have as regressive an effect on a

community as taking away self by force. Preserving community by eliminating self is as counterproductive as trying to prevent the scourge of fire by eliminating air. The "cloistered virtue" approach to life will support neither the growth of a society nor the development of the kind of leaders that a society requires in order to evolve.

Far from being antagonistic to the purposes of community, therefore, the expression of self in a leader is what makes the evolution of a community possible. This principle also transcends the virtual reality of social science categories. It applies equally well to cells, families, partnerships, institutions, corporations, or nations, irrespective of gender, race, culture, or era. Well-defined self in a leader—what I call self-differentiation—is not only critical to effective leadership, it is precisely the leadership characteristic that is most likely to promote the kind of community that preserves the self of its members. Lack of morality, as I suggested in the last chapter and as I will elaborate below, has to do with invasiveness, not with strength; with lack of integrity, not with power.

The twin problems confronting leadership in our society today, the failure of nerve and the desire for a quick fix, are not the result of overly strong self but of weak or no self. There certainly is reason to guard against capricious, irrational, autocratic, vainglorious leadership in any form of organized life. But democratic institutions have far more to fear from lack of self in their leaders and the license this gives to factionalism (which is not the same as dissent) than from too much strength in the executive power. Indeed, that is precisely one of the major advantages of democratically based institutions: they can reap the benefits of imaginative, aggressive, energetic leadership far less perilously than totalitarian societies driven by unbridled autocracy. As I shall elaborate below, this was precisely the view of both Alexander Hamilton and James Madison when they wrote the *Federalist Papers* to support the "colonization" of the thirteen colonies, arguing that the integrity of a community is assured only when it can preserve the integrity of its leader.

This chapter is divided into two sections. The first charts a new orientation for self by removing it from the abstractions of philosophy and psychology and rooting it instead in the natural history of life. I will describe how, as life has moved from simpler to more complex forms, it has continually been confronted by a tension between individuality and togetherness that is not dissimilar from the bonding problems of any relationship system today. But, as multicellular organisms became more complex, life has always resolved that tension in a way that preserved the drive for individuality, both with regard to the integrity of cell lineages and with regard to the organism itself. Far from being the root of pathology, therefore, the self is to be revered. Far from being merely a dimension of life, the differentiation of self is vital to life's survival and development.

There is a striking correspondence between the way life has resolved the tension between individuality and togetherness and the manner in which the framers of the American Constitution of 1789 dealt with the exact same relational problems between the "colonies." In fact, it might be stated that the American form of democracy, as structured by the Constitution of 1789, is that form of government which most corresponds to the way life itself worked out these essential tensions of existence. There, too, the togetherness advantages of a larger "organism" were brought about in a way that preserved the integrity of the "cell lineages" (states). Therefore, when leaders anywhere in America work to preserve individuality, their own or others', they stand on two traditions: the processes that gave rise to our nation and the processes that gave rise to our species.

In the second section of this chapter I will present a view of self, consistent with these biological and political perspectives, that is applicable to all personal relationships as well as essential to well-differentiated leadership. Far from juxtaposing self to community, I will suggest how parents and presidents can be self-"ish" without being selfish.

The issue of self touches on every single leadership issue discussed in the book thus far. It will lay the groundwork for the concept of self-differentiated leadership and show how the most critical issues of leadership have to do with the self-differentiation of a parent or a president. These issues include:

- ◆ the capacity to "go it alone";
- ◆ the ability to recognize and extricate oneself from relational binds (emotional triangles);
- ◆ the folly of trying to will others to change;
- ◆ the modifying potential of the non-anxious presence;

- ◆ the ramifying power of endurance in crisis;
- ◆ the self-regulation necessary for dealing with reactive sabotage; and
- ◆ the factors in the leader's own being that make for his or her own stress.

On the broadest scale, the preservation of self in its leaders is a society's greatest protection against descending into a counter-evolutionary mode. It is only the emergence of self in its leadership that can enable any society, family, institution, or nation to evolve out of a regression.

◈ A NATURAL HISTORY OF SELF

The notion of "self" has been pondered for centuries by philosophers, psychologists, theologians, and political theorists. This notion has, however, been primarily a cerebral tradition that associates self with consciousness and that tends to think about self as a concept that occupies our minds rather than as an entity that occupies space. We talk about a person's "self-concept" (or image); we wonder about a person's "self-confidence" or "self-esteem." When we talk about a person's ability to achieve "self-realization," it is understood in terms of their inner being or yearnings.

While this way of thinking about self is useful, it tends to lose touch with the fact that individuality is far more than a psychological state or a philosophical concept. It is basically a category of existence that has substantive reality and that has been an essential force in the natural processes of life since its beginnings. Maintaining, preserving, or expressing one's "self," therefore, is not simply a subject for self-help manuals or psychotherapy; the effort to be one's self, as I shall now demonstrate, lines one up with what has enabled life to develop and survive since creation.

Since its beginnings, life has gone through at least eight major transitions of complexity. During each of these transitions, a new form developed that became the basic unit that the selective forces in the environment acted upon. At every transition, however, life learned to benefit from the new, more complex unit without sacrificing the integrity of the previous unit that enabled the new form to come into being. If we trace the progression of complexity from the first self-replicating molecules to the individual organisms we know today as human beings, we find that the preservation of individuality (self) was as critical to the evolution of life as the forming of new "communities." These eight major transitions are:

◆ In a way not yet understood, some chemicals found a way of reproducing their own form, so we have the initial appearance of self-replicating molecules.

◆ Out of that set of self-reproducing molecules, those that consisted of what later came to be the base acids of DNA began to connect up in the strings we now call genes.

◆ Some of the genes themselves began to link together to produce the forms we know as chromosomes.

◆ Chromosomes began to become enclosed within membranes, thus forming the first prokaryote cells.

◆ Eukaryotes—cells with their genetic material segregated in a nucleus, which contained other organelles that provided energy, firmer internal structure, and more resiliency— arrived on the scene.

◆ Eukaryotic cells aggregated to form the first living communities, multicellular organisms.

◆ Various cells began to differentiate, with a division of labor, and then further aggregated into tissues and organs.

◆ Multicellular organisms diversified into species and the line of descent that eventually led to mammals, hominids, families, a larger brain, language, and ultimately the forms of colonized protoplasm we call societies, cultures, communities, institutions, and nations.

Although the progression is constantly to higher and higher orders of complexity, all along the line the principles life followed in its efforts to preserve individuality are characterized by simplicity.

As life forms became larger and more complex, a mutuality of self-interest arose in which both the smaller unit that had been incorporated and the more complex system into which it had been incorporated worked for the survival of one another. Within such "confederations," to the extent that the smaller unit helped the larger unit deal advantageously with the environment, the larger unit, by surviving, ensured the survival of the smaller unit. It was thus to the advantage of the smaller unit to work to preserve the larger unit's integrity. That is because those smaller units that worked for the survival of the larger unit were more likely to survive.

As previous, smaller units become incorporated into new, larger forms, they were willing to give up some control of their fate (sovereignty) in order to take advantage of a togetherness that optimized their struggle with the environment. In order "to form a more perfect union," they ceased propagating independently, and from that point on replicated only as part of the larger unit. This has held true whether we are considering genes, chromosomes, cells, or organisms. And in the case of the last, it holds true irrespective of that "organism's" culture.

At each transition to a higher order of complexity, a process occurred that could be called "out of many, one." However, since the larger unit's capacity for survival benefited from the richness (variability) it obtained by incorporating the smaller units, life did not violate the integrity of the previous form. At each transition, as more complex forms of togetherness replaced previous forms as the basic entity around which life organized itself, the new form always preserved the integrity of the previous form so long as the previous form did not do violence to the integrity of its own individuality.

At every transition, both the capacity for joining and the capacity for self-differentiation were deeply influenced by the way those processes were handled in previous generations. The functioning of each unit was to a large extent shaped and limited by its own multi-generational past as it, in turn, shaped and limited the functioning of the next, larger unit that succeeded it. Life's connection between generations, therefore, is not a rebounding, linear, billiard-ball phenomenon but more like an infinitely long collapsing telescope in which each generation overlaps and to some extent shapes the next "cylinder of time." Life has evolved not in terms of the ways the past has an impact on the present, but in terms of the ways the past is present in the present.

After the fifth transition, with the arrival of the eukaryote (nucleus-bearing) cell, the struggle for the preservation of individuality intensified. This occurred in two dimensions, internally and externally. As multicellular organisms arose, it was necessary to keep various cell lineages within them from competing with the larger organism that had incorporated them by going off in their own direction and forming another (competitive) organism within. Second, it was necessary for individual cells, as well as multicellular units, to defend themselves from being taken over (parasitized) by other, competing cells and organisms. The preservation of individuality, therefore, also required the development of a system of recognition, a means of knowing self from non-self.

The first problem, basically the problem of "liberty and order," was solved through what has come to be called "somatic determinism." All the cells within an organism contain the same genes, but only a few genes within its gene pool turn on. Which specific genes turn on is determined by the cell's relationship to other cells, not by the nature of the genes themselves. Those genes that do turn on determine its fate, its ultimate position within the larger organism. Similarly, the functioning of individuals in any institution is not determined by their nature (personality) but by their position within a relationship system, as well as by what other "cells" will permit them to do.

Once that has occurred, the cell is said to have *differentiated*. It now has individuality. But to prevent its individuality from leading to chaos or anarchy, once that cell has differentiated to a specific function it can only produce cells with the same function. It can no longer produce offspring (germ or stem cells) that have the capacity to produce a competing organism. As mentioned in the previous chapter, there is thus a relationship between purposiveness and harmony. Cancer cells that form competing organisms, such as tumors, do not differentiate.

The second problem for the preservation of individuality—being invaded or parasitized by another organism—was solved with the development of the capacity of cells and organisms to mount a defense against what is "not-self." But a system of recognition had to come first. This capacity to "avoid foreign entanglements" evolved into the immune response and perhaps also consciousness. This capacity aided in the formation of species, families, and communities.

An Example from American History
Each of the following five principles guided the framers of the American Constitution of 1789 as they endeavored to accomplish

what is enshrined in the motto on the back of our coinage—*E Pluribus Unum,* "Out of many, one." These principles are:

◆ mutuality of self-interest between smaller and larger units;
◆ a surrender of fate (sovereignty) among the smaller units in a bargain that guarantees advantages;
◆ the formation of a new, more complex union;
◆ multigenerational influence; and
◆ limitations that create checks and balances on the power of the various entities.

And in both cases—biologically and politically—this principle was overriding:

◆ For life to continue to evolve, all newly developed forms of togetherness ultimately must be in the service of a more enriched individuality, and not the other way around.

This is, after all, the essential difference between democracy and autocracy. The process of creating one country out of different colonies is not just similar to the way life has developed, it is identical. In political terms it is the problem of liberty and order, but it can also be understood more fundamentally as the problem of individuality and togetherness, and the founding fathers solved it as though they had received the blueprint from life itself. (Hamilton in one of the *Federalist Papers* actually compares anarchy to tumors.)

The problems confronting the various cell lineages (states) are well known. They had fought a long and bitter battle for "independence." But now to ensure that independence they, ironically, had to increase their dependence on one another. They had already made one effort under the Articles of Confederation but that had failed, because in their concern to preserve their hard-won individuality they had created a very weak form of togetherness. The authority of the supra-organism (central government) was not directly over the people. It was mediated by the individual states. Any given "cell lineage," therefore, might choose not to enforce the laws passed by the incorporating larger organism. In addition, there was no immune system. A strong, central executive power that could suppress rebellion within any state, invasion of one state by another, or any cell lineage from joining a competing organism was missing.

Furthermore, in their concern to preserve individual cell lineages, they had given each lineage power over the destiny of the others; in order to change the original compact, complete consensus was needed. Under the Articles of Confederation, the concern to protect individuality thus triumphed over the concern to gain benefits from union. No cell lineage wanted to surrender its sovereignty. As with a couple afraid to "tie the knot," the thirteen colonies were "living together" rather than getting married. After 1789, they got "hitched."

Also similar to the problems of most couples who have difficulty joining in matrimony (either before the wedding or after), multigenerational factors were involved. As with the first cells that formed multicellular organisms, these various cell lineages, too, had been brought together more by a common enemy than by an inherent similarity. Aside from a common language, they represented disparate groups that had come for reasons as diverse as solving debts, seeking religious freedom, or entrepreneurial desires. The original colonization might have begun as land grants from a king or as a private corporation. Their traditions could have been French, English, Spanish, or Dutch. Also, their physical location affected their different characters. The various "cell lineages," therefore, had different multigenerational traditions going back as much as one hundred or one hundred fifty years, making each unique.

But in the end, they decided to make the "transition." The loss of some sovereignty was deemed a price worth paying in order to optimize their chance of survival. The reasons were the same ones that had driven life to make similar decisions billions of years earlier. As individual units, the states were more vulnerable to the environment or to being "parasitized" by other (foreign) "organisms." They decreased their competitiveness with one another in order to be safe from the competitiveness of other predators.

A means also had to be found, however, to protect the cell lineages from their protector, the incorporating organism. Such fear might be normal in any case, but the experience of previous generations with England's interference in their lives had intensified their concerns about a strong central authority.

During the constitutional debates, some were concerned that the larger states might gang up on the smaller ones. The compromise that ensured the integrity of the smaller cell lineages was *bicameralism:* in addition to a House of Representatives apportioned by the number of people in each state, they created a Senate in which each state had the same number of senators (two) no matter what its size. But Madison made the point (and it is true to this day) that the alliances were far more likely to be by section (sectionalism) than by size. Interestingly, this too is how biological organisms work, both in the embryonic stage where "positional influence" determines fate, and in the developed organism where power is more likely to reside in location than in size.

Political theorists are fond of showing how the writers of the French Enlightenment—Voltaire, Diderot, and particularly Montesquieu—influenced the thinking of the constitutional framers, especially their understanding of the distribution of power. Montesquieu's views on government are quoted several times in the *Federalist Papers.* But the framers also were familiar with the attempts at confederational togetherness that were made in Athens, Sparta, and Rome two thousand years before, as well as the more recent efforts in "modern" Europe. They did not have to know about cell lineages to see what works. They were observers of life and so they wound up with life's solutions. In other words, the American Constitution was not merely an accidental bundle of compromises but rather a "natural" solution to the tensions of individuality and togetherness.

As anyone who has taken Political Science 101 knows, the solution was a set of checks and balances delineated primarily in three major principles: federalism, separation of powers, and supreme law of the land. Each has its evolutionary parallel.

First, the institution of federalism guaranteed the various cell lineages their individuality. While the incorporating organism was given strong economic and police power, its power was limited to what was specifically delegated in the Constitution. In other words, the incorporating organism did not have a right to say, "We have the power because the Constitution does not say we do not have the power." Only what is delegated (or implied) is permissible, and all which is not stated is *reserved* to the cell lineages. The "reserve clause," as it is called, is the key to preserving the integrity of the cell lineages, both because it gives them some autonomy and because in so doing, it allows them to differentiate from one another.

Second, the fact that the incorporating organism is not plenipotentiary (all powerful in all spheres) is not enough to guarantee that it will not use its power to do away with the smaller cell lineages. In order to give the central government the power it needed, both internally and externally, but at the same time to limit its ability to use that power capriciously, the government was divided into three distinct sections, each with some check on the other. Thus—unlike other nations, and England in particular—the legislature which made the laws was separated from the executive charged with carrying out the laws, and both were separated from the judiciary, which interpreted their administration. This division of labor is not unlike life's solution of somatic determinism, which confines each part of an organism to a specific purpose.

Third and last, to ensure that no cell lineage would go off on its own and become a competing organism, or subvert the overall purposes of the superorganism by not following, enforcing, or obeying the national laws (or try to nullify them by its own authority), the Constitution of 1789 specifically calls itself "the supreme law of the land." All conflicting laws are subject to its authority. This clause thus gave the country an integrating instrument for "union." While at the time of the Civil War some cell lineages sought to gain back their sovereignty and form a different kind of confederation, it was the existence of this concept that gave those who wished to preserve the "supra-organism" a well-founded rationale for doing so.

◆ THE POLITICS OF SELF

The struggle between individuality and togetherness exists in every relationship system, and is a far more basic issue for compatability in relationships than any other (social science) difference. It surfaces in every marriage and family relationship when one member wants more closeness and one wants more space, and it is often the key to understanding local, national, or international issues when one group presses for alliance and another's concern is sovereignty. It is the essence of all business agreements that appropriate or classify "shares." It is part and parcel of the structuring and restructuring of organizations and institutions in their endeavor to define individual job descriptions and then link them with flow charts. Not only was it the critical issue between the original thirteen colonies, but it may even be the key to many illnesses, including cancer, AIDS, allergies, and a host of autoimmune diseases, since unregulated growth, reactivity, and the immune response are the quintessential battles of self. And it is the critical component in leadership if leaders are to be leaders.

Yet despite the fact that the preservation of self has proved vital to the preservation of life both biologically and politically, the force for individuality is suspect when it comes to human institutions. As I have tried to demonstrate, it is not necessary to have authoritarian dictators to destroy the integrity of a democratic society's citizens. One only has to keep escalating the togetherness-promoting anxiety so that individuality is not only squelched, it becomes instinctively feared. This is true generally, and all the more so in chronically anxious societies. The emphasis on family togetherness and team-building in our culture has value, but that is not what is needed.

Normally, as we have seen, at every level of life's organization from the cellular level on up, the evolution of a society requires that this universal tension between the forces for individuality and the forces for togetherness must be kept within some balancing range. But when that balance goes beyond certain thresholds, as occurs in periods of chronic anxiety, then—whether we are considering an individual organism, a specific institution, or society itself—we wind up not with evolutionary processes but with the *devolutionary* extremes of totalitarianism or anarchy, tyranny or tumors. (Had Hamilton and Madison been writing with today's knowledge of viruses and the immune response, they might easily have employed a biological metaphor.)

How, therefore, are leaders to get past this third emotional barrier, the pathologizing of self? For success here is basic to the capacity to cross the other barriers of data and empathy. It is only when self is valued that leaders can be less at the mercy of the data/technique deluge, no less its addictive properties. It is only when leaders value self that their cortex can be kept from the service of the reptilian brain and their cerebration can be true thinking. It is only when leaders value self that they can recognize the importance of making their own self-definition more crucial than feeling for others. It is only when leaders value self that in times of crisis they can emphasize the response of the organism rather than the conditions of the environment. It is only when leaders value self that they can prevent it from being eroded by the chronic anxiety of a society in regression. It is only when leaders value self that they can muster the self-regulation necessary for countering the sabotage that will greet them, ironically, in direct relation to the extent that they value and express their self. It is this latter conundrum that so often takes leaders unawares and throws them off course, just when they are functioning best.

How are parents and presidents to value, indeed treasure and preserve, self without worrying that they are being narcissistic or autocratic? To resort to being only an "enabler" for others or to try to concentrate on building teams instead simply fudges the issue. *Someone still has to go first!*

It is interesting to note that the word *self* did not have any "self" in the English language until 1570. It was not until after the Protestant Reformation had became a force for individuality, somewhere around the time of Drake and Shakespeare, that the word *self* first began to be used as an independent noun. Prior to that, it was only used to modify or amplify other words, as an adjective (*selfsame*, for example), or as a pronoun (*himself, herself*). There are less than a dozen compounds incorporating the word *self* in Middle English. Yet if we go back two thousand years, Socrates was saying it was important to "know thy self."

Given the obvious and crucial value of self to the evolution of our species, how shall we explain the fact that the word *selfish* is almost the only word in the English language where the addition of the suffix "-ish" turns an otherwise neutral noun, self, into a pejorative label, "selfish"? Normally, adding "-ish" to a word only means "having the quality of." *Bookish* is not necessarily negative; nor is *blueish, reddish, grayish, greenish, pinkish, faddish,* or *Jewish.* Even *childish* or *clannish*, while often used judgmentally, merely mean behaving like a child or a clan. Why does not selfish mean "behaving like, or having the character of, a self"? Why does it not mean simply "self-y"?

The grammatical uniqueness of *selfish* reflects the ambivalence inherent in the reality of self. Whether we are considering families, institutions, or whole nations, self is both desired and feared, praised and denigrated, stolen and surrendered.

The ambiguity and ambivalence associated with self is evident from the varied and contradictory ways in which it is used in the English language. It can be simply descriptive or it can, by its mere connectedness to another word, modify its meaning positively or negatively. For example, the word *self* can be used in a purely reflexive mode, as in terms like *self-explanatory, self-evident, self-expression, self-taught, self-defense,* and *self-service.* The addition of *self* to these words simply states an objective fact about a process that relies on its self. No additional meaning is added to the original word merely by the addition of *self.* But when *self* is added to the following list of words, in every single case a word that was otherwise neutral suddenly takes on a pejorative connotation: *self-centered, self-justified, self-congratulatory, self-glorification, self-conscious, self-admiration, self-appointed, self-seeking, self-important, self-serving, self-righteous, self-absorbed, self-satisfied,* and *self-pity.* These compounds all suggest that self-focus is prideful, egotistical, narcissistic, and perhaps immoral.

Yet the exact opposite occurs in the following words. The addition of *self* to the words in the next group gives an otherwise neutral word a positive connotation, or it intensifies the root in a more positive way: *self-assertive, self-possessed, self-assured, self-actualization, self-made, self-control, self-determination, self-starter,* and *self-supporting.* These compounds suggest that having self is good, laudable, and noble.

The ambiguity and ambivalence of *self* becomes even more complicated when one realizes that while the compounds listed above are positive because they suggest a person *possesses* self, the following qualities are also considered positive because of the *absence* of self: *self-denial, self-sacrifice, self-effacement, self-abnegation, self-renunciation, self-less, unselfish,* and *self-negating.* On the other hand, the following have negative connotations because the person did not respect himself or herself: *self-destructive, self-condemning, self-abasement, self-hatred,* and *self-deceptive.*

How can it be good to be both self-sufficient and self-less, self-made and self-effacing, self-respectful and self-denying, self-possessed and self-sacrificing, self-assertive and self-renouncing? Actually, the word *self* has trouble retaining its self. It is far more likely to be fused into an adjective, as with the above lists, or a pronoun, as in *himself, herself, myself.* But suppose we began to think of self as an entity that we possessed, like a book or a car? And then suppose we freed *self* from the possessive pronoun and began to write *my self* or *her self* or *him self,* as we might say *my book* or *his car* or *her job*?

The ease with which we fuse *ourselves* with *our selves* can be seen from the following exercise. Below are some of the most common uses of the pronoun *self,* but here the word *self* has been separated from the person who possesses it. (It helps to think of your self as a little cartoon character standing alongside you, perhaps holding your hand, and smiling, always smiling.)

- I lied to my self.
- I embarrassed my self.
- Excuse your self.
- Contain your self.
- Explain your self.
- Sacrifice your self.
- I lost my self in my work.
- Stand up for your self.
- I came to terms with my self.

- Limit your self.
- I thought to my self....
- I made my self angry.
- I'm all by my self.
- I gave my self permission.
- Do your self a favor.
- You're destroying your self.
- Get out of your self.
- Help your self to another portion.

The Impact of Togetherness on Self

The emphasis on togetherness is not something that can be willed. It isn't even necessary to will it. It will work for leaders to the extent that the system remains well-differentiated. The stress for leaders lies in their efforts to will togetherness—which is equally true in marriage, partnerships, and business institutions. People need one another, and that can be made to work for leaders.

One problem is that the togetherness force has been equated with morality. This is the "selfishness" confusion again. Yet it is precisely the togetherness force that leads to the kinds of intractable problems we see in totalitarian nations and the most impaired families. The social science construction of reality focuses on divorce, drinking, abuse, and so on as critical symptoms in a family. However, it is the *lack* of differentiation in families that leads to symptoms rather than too much of "self." It is important here to distinguish between the apparent individuality that is really reactivity to the other (and thus a manifestation of fused togetherness) and the genuine acceptance of difference.

It would at first seem that the opposing forces of individuality and togetherness both are necessary for life and must be balanced in such a way that each serves as a check on the excesses of the other. But there is, I believe, a difference between them. The two forces are not mutually respectful. While I cannot prove the following in any substantive way, it is my perception that the togetherness force is blinder to the value of the individuality force than the individuality force is to the value of joining. By this I mean that the move toward togetherness is in some way more natural; that protoplasm at any level seems naturally to join with other protoplasm, with little concern for the preservation of individuality. And precisely because of that fact, the forces for individuality must be more vigilant.

What is self? Is it a concept or a fact of existence? Does the self-promoting "glad-hander" possess a great deal of self or a great deal of emptiness? In any marriage where one partner is chronically abusing the other, physically or verbally, which partner can be said to have less of a sense of self? Do hard bargainers show a stronger sense of self than compromisers? Who had more of a sense of self, Hitler or Chamberlain? Both were convinced they were right, both had ideals, both saw themselves as acting for the good of others, both acted with conviction and persistence.

What goes into a sense of self—principles? flexibility? individuality? And how does one know when another person is rigid or principled, flexible or wishy-washy, zany or nuts? Is the difference between genius and madness whether or not you turn out to be correct? How does one judge the sense of self in any team manager when some are said to have been successful because they tolerated no nonsense and some because they were understanding? Do parents who make sure to be "available" display more of it than those who concentrate on tough love? Do people who "go into therapy" have less of a sense of self than those who do not, or are they by selection more motivated to get past their denial? And do therapists have more self than their clients, or did God put troubled people on earth to give helpers something to do? Whether we are talking about eukaryotes or marriage relationships, the pressures and the tendencies to lose one's sense of self are great, and all the more so in a regressed society.

Perhaps the most significant shift in twentieth-century medicine was the focus on stimulating the body's own natural defenses to toxic forces in the environment rather than trying to eradicate those hostile entities directly. Indeed, by shifting the focus to an organism's response, a new understanding of their relationship emerges, one that is consistent with what was said in the previous chapter about invasiveness and the response of the organism. Herein lies the rub, the complication, the conundrum. Anyone who wishes to advance our species or an institution must possess those qualities which those who have little sense of self will perceive as narcissistic. All this besides the fact that "arrogant," "headstrong," "narcissistic," and "cold" will be the terms used against any person who tries to be more himself or herself.

This point is illustrated by the following tale. A woman found her husband to be passive and recalcitrant about every suggestion she made. Energetic herself, she wanted to have adventures and to meet people, but she wound up in constant conflict precisely because she made her functioning dependent on his. It was suggested to her that instead of trying to coerce her husband or allow herself to be seduced into arguments about right/wrong or control, she should simply start making plans for her self and invite him to join her if he wished, but go in her own direction when he did not. Trying to put this suggestion to work, she said to her husband, "They have invited us to dinner and I have decided to go." Whereupon he responded, "Why do you force me to do things like this?"

It was the inability of either one to differentiate and thus separate one self from the other that put her into a bind and made him respond as he did. In such a personal relationship, if the wife will take responsibility for herself, often the husband will begin to function in the marriage at a higher level. In fact, the well-differentiated partner will probably always have to be the one to take the initiative to enhance the functioning of the togetherness. Societal regression reinforces the dysfunction of the togetherness or immaturity.

To be a leader, one must both have and embody a vision of where one wants to go. It is not a matter of knowing or believing one is right; it is a matter of taking the first step.

There is a way of understanding the self that leads to integrity and well-differentiated community rather than narcissism, isolation, and lack of feeling. It is to be found in the latest understanding of the immune system, which turns out to be far less connected to self-defense than to integrity. This change in thinking is also a good example of the kind of paradigm shift that has been occurring in the hard sciences. Up until the mid-1960s, immunity had been thought of primarily in terms of a system of defenses that the body mobilized against foreign invaders. This way of thinking goes back to microbiologists of the late nineteenth century such as Pasteur and Ehrlich. More recently, however, the immune system has come to be seen primarily as the source of an organism's integrity, developed out of the organism's need to distinguish self from non-self.

This increased understanding of the immune system (which involves many different subsystems of the body, including the bloodstream) changed other notions as well, so that the destruction of what is not self was seen to be a byproduct of the capacity to recognize what in effect is toxic. So crucial is this seemingly elementary concept to the development of organized protoplasm that it might even be stated this way: were it not for the rise of the immune response, most matter on this planet would be one huge fused mass. In other words, the very possibility of the existential category of self may have been made possible only with the rise of an immune response, which is the capacity to recognize and distinguish what is foreign.

There are four characteristics of the immune response that have parallels for human relationships. It is almost as though the Creator put into the human body (protoplasm) the basic lessons of life. The four characteristics (each of which can be understood in terms of self and human relationships) are:

◆ The immune system makes possible the category of self.
◆ It does not come full-blown at birth, but grows from response to challenge.
◆ It is necessary for closeness, proximity, and love.
◆ It can be perverted to attack the host.

In 1970, an experiment was conducted in a French laboratory in which two organisms from the same species that had not developed immune systems were moved closer and closer toward one another. At a certain threshold of proximity, the smaller one began to disintegrate, and within twenty-four hours it had lost all the principles of its organization. The researchers tried to ascertain what the larger one had done to the smaller one, but in the end found that it had done nothing at all except exist; it had not secreted some substance, nor destroyed it in any hostile way. The smaller one simply began to disintegrate in response to the *loss of distance*; its disintegration was brought about through internal mechanisms triggered by the closeness of the other. The researchers concluded with the simple statement that they had induced auto-destruction in one member of a species by bringing it into proximity with a larger member of the same species. They suggested (with eye-popping consequences for chronic illness in a family) that this could be viewed as an adaptation to their relationship.

It is possible to blame the larger one for getting so close. But it is also possible to say to the smaller one, "You should not have let the other's mere presence overwhelm you." The smaller one could never have heard the advice, however, since it had no mechanism for preserving its self. In fact, neither could the larger one, in a situation where the tables were turned.

It has always been known that when organisms of the same species that lack immune systems touch, they fuse as one. That is why the immune system is considered to have a more fundamental role than protection: namely, providing an organism with integrity. In fact, within medicine the immune system today is defined as the capacity to distinguish self from non-self. It is its dedication to this principle that sometimes makes it reject transplants even when they are in the service of the organism. But if its main activity appears to be protection, the immune system is also essential to love, since without "immunity" not only would we never dare touch, but many of us would lose self if we got too close because of emotional fusion.

And many of us do "lose it." Indeed, it may be stated that the major relational problem for our species is not getting together;

protoplasm loves to join. The problem is preserving self in a close relationship. No human on planet Earth does that well.

With our species, however, "the bigger one" and "the smaller one" are not to be measured in terms of size or weight; that is not the issue. Similarly, space is to be understood not simply as a physical category but as an emotional category. I know how to teach any family or organizational member, regardless of size, how to make another member of that system dysfunctional. I would simply teach them how to overfunction in the other's space. While terms such as *codependency* and *enabling* suggest something similar, they focus on behavior or perhaps adaptation to another's behavior. When one overfunctions in another's space, the existential reality is much deeper: it can cause another's being to disintegrate. That emotional phenomenon occurs daily across our planet, in parent-child relationships, marriage relationships, supervisory relationships, and physical or mental health care relationships. Chronic illness is an adaptation to a relationship.

Self is not merely *analogous* to immunity; it *is* immunity. And from now on, whenever new understandings are gleaned in this field, whatever is found to be accurate about the immune response will also be true about self.

Another lesson about self to be learned from immunology concerns inner consistency. The immune system does not reside in one organ. It is not positioned in some advantageous location. The importance of this evolutionary development is connection. Neurotransmitters are chemicals which communicate throughout the neural network, communicating information and emotions throughout the self.

A human organism's immune system is not a given at birth. Unlike a woman's ovaries—where the number of eggs is determined in her own sixth fetal week and are not replenished as eggs are used up—people are initially without an immune response other than the antibodies they receive through their mother's placenta. The immune system develops in response to challenge. The various components have an almost infinite capacity to combine and recombine to produce molecules (antibodies) that meet. These have the capacity to discriminate what is non-self and potentially threatening to an organism from that which is. The process of distinction is still open to various theoretical speculations, but once set in place it generally performs.

For all its efficiency and good purpose, however, sometimes things go wrong. Under certain conditions the immune system makes a mistake. It fails to distinguish friend from foe and attacks the self of the body instead. More and more diseases have been implicated in this hawkish response. It has been suggested, however, that this autoimmune response only occurs in the presence of a threat. In other words, things do not "just go wrong." The immune system does not on its own simply go out and attack the self of the organism it is supposed to integrate and defend. It is only after it has been aroused by a warning signal that it will make this error as part of its self-defense. The immune response is the capacity to distinguish self from non-self. While that might not seem hard to do intellectually, it is not always easy to do emotionally, as any mother knows. Knowing where one begins and another ends is a fundamental human problem.

There is no better example of anxiety's effects on leadership. The nature of the human organism itself can be a model for self and a model for leadership of an organization.

Perhaps the most important lesson from our immune systems is this: the major purpose of the immune system is to *preserve the integrity of the organism.* Previously it was conceived of as a system of defenses, an armamentarium of weapons for dealing with different invaders— and to this day the metaphors of immunology are often warlike. But microbiology has revealed the enormous complexity of this system, which involves several different organs, the bloodstream itself, and an array of different entities that have specialized roles, from signaling one another to completing one another's work. When this is combined with new understanding of the brain and its release of neurotransmitters, a more organic or systemic notion of the immune system has evolved.

The ramifications for self-differentiated leadership of that one concept (that survival is related to integrity) are far-ranging, and open major new vistas for understanding the place of leaders in a "body" politic. In fact, as I will show, a leader functions as the immune system of the institution or organization he or she "heads."

Differentiation

Differentiation is the lifelong process of striving to keep one's being in balance through the reciprocal external and internal processes of self-definition and self-regulation. It is a concept that can sometimes be difficult to focus on objectively, for *differentiation* means the capacity to become oneself out of one's self, with minimum reactivity to the positions or reactivity of others. Differentiation is charting one's own way by means of one's own internal guidance system, rather than perpetually eyeing the "scope" to see where others are at. Differentiation refers more to a process than a goal that can ever be achieved. When people say, "I differentiated from my wife, my child, my parent," that proves they do not understand the concept.

Differentiation refers to a direction in life rather than a state of being:

- ◆ Differentiation is the capacity to take a stand in an intense emotional system.
- ◆ Differentiation is saying "I" when others are demanding "we."
- ◆ Differentiation is containing one's reactivity to the reactivity of others, which includes the ability to avoid being polarized.
- ◆ Differentiation is maintaining a non-anxious presence in the face of anxious others.
- ◆ Differentiation is knowing where one ends and another begins.
- ◆ Differentiation is being able to cease automatically being one of the system's emotional dominoes.
- ◆ Differentiation is being clear about one's own personal values and goals.
- ◆ Differentiation is taking maximum responsibility for one's own emotional being and destiny rather than blaming others or the context.

Differentiation is an emotional concept, not a cerebral one; but it does require clear-headedness. And it has enormous consequence for new ways of thinking about leadership. As Dr. Murray Bowen liked to say, it is a lifetime project with no one ever getting more than seventy percent there.

Differentiation is not to be equated, however, with similar-sounding ideas such as individuation, autonomy, or independence. First of all, it has less to do with a person's behavior than with his or her emotional being. Second, there is a sense of connectedness to the concept that prevents the mere gaining of distance, leaving, or cutting-off as ways to achieve it. Third, as stated above, it has to do with the fabric of one's existence, one's integrity.

Obviously, differentiation has its origin in the biological notion that cells can have no identity, purpose, or distinctiveness until they have separated from (that is, left behind) their progenitors. Differentiation is a prerequisite to specialization, even if one is ultimately going to fuse to accomplish one's purpose.

But also implicit in this biological metaphor or homology is the idea that such self has little meaning if the cell cannot connect. In its simplest terms, therefore, differentiation is the capacity to be one's own integrated aggregate-of-cells person while still belonging to, or being able to relate to, a larger colony. As already indicated, such a biological metaphor also has ramifications for thinking and the conduct of therapy, since the incapacity to achieve some balance in the self/togetherness struggle will tend to create a style of thinking that shows up in either/or, all-or-nothing, black-and-white conceptualizations and, eventually, family cut-offs. Conversely, the capacity to think systemically and avoid the polarizations characteristic of reactivity seems to go along with the emotional growth associated with differentiation.

A problem common to all social science theorizing is that the more accurately any system of thought can make predictions, the less room it allows for free will. It is one thing to develop a theory about subatomic particles, plate tectonics, or black holes and, without any conflict at all, to use the theory's power for prediction as a criterion of its validity. When the subject matter is the human animal, however, then the more elegant the theory, the less dignity is left for the human. It is, after all, precisely because the human is not a soulless star or particle that social science theory always fails to gain the measure of certainty found in the "hard" sciences. It may be the awareness of this dilemma that has led many family therapists to try to synthesize family and individual model thinking.

Family systems practitioner Murray Bowen handled the problem by developing his systems theory in a way that is consistent with natural systemic concepts, despite the uncontrollable or unknowable element in the human animal, while still leaving room for a variable that could account for the differences, inconsistencies, and mysteries that result from human will. What the Bowenian concept of differentiation does is to supply a variable that allows the rest of the theory to be developed in a systematic, consistent manner. But it keeps the theory honest by allowing for exceptions.

In addition, the variable provided by differentiation helps Bowen's theory deal with a problem common to all systems theory: how to account for change at all if systems are perpetually kept in balance by their own homeostatic forces. Why, for example, do some identified patients improve despite the system? Why, despite the impeccable logic of systemic thinking, do things sometimes just not turn out the way they are supposed to? And why do the elements that we assume to have caused pathology in one system not have the same effects in another?

It is perhaps in this context that Bowen's scale of differentiation can best be understood. The scale is an effort to say that despite the universality of systems concepts, people are different. But, the scale also suggests, the differences that count are not to be found in the traditional categories of sociology or of psychodynamics. What counts, rather, according to the scale, is a person's capacity to function in a differentiated manner, as that term is defined above. And that is more a function of sibling position, emotional triangles, and multigenerational processes than gender, culture, or environmental conditioning.

As I have said before, this concept of differentiation is a focus on strength rather than pathology. It comes up fully on the side of personal responsibility rather than faulting the stars, society, the environment, or one's parents. Despite the tinge of predestination associated with multigenerational transmission, differentiation is inherently an anti-victim, anti-blaming focus. Just as it is a variable that prevents systemic concepts from "blowing away" individual dignity, so too, when it comes to change, precisely because differentiation is a focus on the individual's response, it refuses to allow the system to take all the responsibility. For example, for years I have told women who were trying to maintain a differentiation position in their marriage, "Whenever your husband calls you a bitch you are probably going in the right direction. See if you can get him to say that more often." For when one individual in a marriage stands up to another, while the other will not like it at first, he or she generally will begin to find the person more attractive.

Two final questions are worth mentioning here, one relating to morality and the other to what I shall call sabotage. Much of the concern about strong leadership stems from a concern with morality. There can be no question that strong leadership will show, however, that morality has more to do with space than with values, with dependency than with power. Second, although I will be emphasizing the importance of a leader's own self, it can never be obtained without a reaction in the form of the automatic, mindless sabotage that always responds to well-differentiated self in a leader. Most theories of leadership recognize the problems of resistance, but there is a deeper systemic phenomenon that occurs when leaders do precisely what they are supposed to do—lead. The very presence of differentiation in a leader will stir up anxious response. Yet staying in touch with the capacity to understand and deal effectively with this system is—beyond vision, beyond perspicacity, beyond stamina—the key to the kingdom.

Final Exam Question, Music Appreciation 101:
What would have been the reactions of Vivaldi, Bach,
Mozart, and Beethoven to Dave Brubeck's 1959
"off-beat" composition "Take Five," which
revolutionized tempos and time signatures
in the world of jazz? Would they have
been mystified, aghast, or just said,
"Wow, what I could have done with that freedom!"?

Chapter Six *

◈ TAKE FIVE

n the final analysis, the relationship between risk and reality is
about leadership. The Old World's process of reorientation
could never have come about if that civilization had not
produced individuals who were willing to go first. These "captains
courageous" were not necessarily brilliant, learned, or noble.
Verrazano and Vespucci came from a high social class, and
Columbus possessed one of the major libraries of his time. But for
the most part what united those who went first was desire, the
capacity to be decisive, and just plain "nerve" rather than knowledge
of data or technique, despite the fact that such knowledge was also
useful. Unlike the astronauts of our time, for example, the navigators of this period did not have the advantage of advanced probes.
They had no way of staying in touch with their home port and
could never be positive about their position while at sea.

To attribute these explorers' feats simply to a desire for fame and
fortune not only denigrates their passion and resolve; it also leaves

* *Here begins the portion that remained unfinished at the author's death in 1996.—Eds.*

out the fact that they were hardly alone among their contemporaries in those desires. Moreover, the technology that did exist in those days was available to others as well. China, for example, had four major ingredients for expanding its civilization: sailing technology, plentiful commodities, advanced culture, and gunpowder. What differentiates the great explorers is their "self-differentiation"— which is a universal emotional phenomenon, not a social science category.

There are five aspects of their functioning that enabled these explorers to lead an entire civilization into a New World; and they are the very same factors that must be present in the leaders of any social system if it is to have a renaissance.

◆ *A capacity to get outside the emotional climate of the day.* Vision is generally thought of as a cerebral event. But the ability to see things differently and the effect of that ability on one's functioning—whether in art, science, exploration, or the concentration camps—is an emotional phenomenon. It is having some sense of where you begin and end, and where others in your life end.

◆ *A willingness to be exposed and vulnerable.* One of the major limitations of imagination's fruits is the fear of standing out. It is more than a fear of criticism. It is anxiety at being alone, of being in a position where one can rely little on others, a position that puts one's own resources to the test, a position where one will have to take total responsibility for one's own response to the environment. Leaders must not only not be afraid of that position; they must come to love it.

◆ *Persistence in the face of resistance and downright rejection.* To succeed at a new venture requires a kind of relentless drive that sometimes may seem to border on the demonic. But no one has ever gone from slavery to freedom with the slaveholders cheering them on, nor contributed significantly to the evolution of our species by working a forty-hour week, nor achieved any significant accomplishment by taking refuge in cynicism. The resistance leaders meet also comes from inside, the voice that constantly asks, "How can *you* have it right and everyone *else* be crazy?"

◆ *Stamina in the face of sabotage along the way.* As the saying goes, no good deed goes unpunished. A major difficulty in sustaining one's mission is that others who start out with the same enthusiasm will come to lose their nerve. Mutiny and sabotage came not from enemies who opposed the initial idea, but rather from colleagues whose will was sapped by unexpected hardships along the way.

◆ *Being "headstrong" and "ruthless"*—at least in the eyes of others. These explorers did not allow relationships to get in the way of their vision. They did not use and manipulate others, but in binds where they had to choose between continuing a relationship and giving up their goals, they stuck to their goals over "team-building," consensus, and camaraderie.

What makes these attributes universal is that they are not necessarily connected to personality traits, cultural factors, or anything that can be labeled gender-specific. They are rather qualities that have to do with the capacity to function well when the world about you is disoriented and stuck in a certain way of thinking. Nothing could be more universal. They apply equally to marriage, family life, and the corporate "world."

While the early navigators had their tragic flaws, the likes of Prince Henry the Navigator, Bartolomeu Dias, Columbus, da Gama, the Cabots, Cartier, Magellan, Frobisher, and Drake had much in common. But there are also enlightening differences among these leaders, particularly in terms of their ability to handle sabotage and seduction, the real Scylla and Charybdis that endanger any adventurer's journey. A brief comparison between Verrazano, Magellan, and Columbus will illustrate the balance that is required.

In exploring the Atlantic coast between Florida and Labrador, Verrazano was overly cautious and perhaps a little naïve. With no towing service around for miles, he was petrified of going aground, and his cautiousness ironically cost him not only discoveries but eventually his life. When drawing near to an island in the Caribbean, he followed his usual habit of not getting too close to shore and instead rowed in with his brother. He was promptly killed by the cannibal inhabitants before the eyes of his shipmates because, having anchored so far out, his party was out of the range of the longbows on their ship.

Magellan, on the other hand, was fearless beyond belief. An episode in his life that foreshadowed his stamina is a "PT 109 experience" similar to John F. Kennedy's. Early in his career, when one of his ships went aground, Magellan sent another one for help but remained with his crew, staying in charge, keeping them disciplined, and maintaining the oversight necessary for the survival of their cargo and their lives. The tenacity that enabled him to accomplish one of the great sailing feats in history was also his downfall, however. For after crossing the Pacific and overcoming the difficulties of constant hunger, thirst, and scurvy to reach the Philippines, he was done in by that same bravado. Magellan became more invested in his fire-power than his mission, which was to circumnavigate the planet. He allowed himself to become involved in an internecine struggle between two factions on the island, when he should have stayed above it and left them to their own devices. He thus forgot his goal and purpose, and was killed when he interfered in the midst of a fight, the outcome of which was totally irrelevant to his mission.

Columbus, in contrast, always seemed to know "where he's at." Not reputed to be a great chartist, he was, on the other hand, superb at "dead reckoning," the capacity to chart a course through one's own constant measurements rather than relying on the use of someone else's map—a kind of biofeedback with one's environment. Because he was so decisive, it is not surprising that Columbus responded as he did in a situation that easily could have thrown him off course, if not led to a complete aborting of his mission. As the (probably apocryphal) story goes, upon arriving at the Canary Islands on his first voyage, the reigning queen begged him to stay and be her navy so that she could get back at Isabella for exiling her there, presumably for flirting with King Ferdinand. But Columbus had read *The Aeneid* and knew about Dido; more importantly, he had read *The Odyssey* and knew about the Sirens. He bound himself to his mast, metaphorically speaking, and responded, in effect, "Not me; I've got a job to do."

While the five characteristics of leadership mentioned above apply, to a greater or lesser extent, to all of these navigators, Columbus is the very embodiment of them all. Not only was he one of the most imaginative men of all time, he was also one of the most determined, as well as the great example of the principle that *vision is not enough.* Almost two millennia previously the Greeks also knew the world was round, but Columbus was the first to say, "Follow me westward as a way to go east." To be determined, decisive, visionary, and still keep your wits about you may be what it takes to reorient any marriage, family, organization, society, or civilization.

First of all, Columbus was no ordinary deck-swab. He had one of the finest libraries of his time. With one foot in the medieval world and one in the Renaissance, he had read the famous sea stories, the classics, the *mappamundi*, the esoteric Christian literature about the fabled Prester John and others. Some of his books survive, showing that he often wrote notes in the margins of what he was reading in the language in which they were written. While he had some of the mystic in him, he was also a student, and his imagination was rooted in the experience of history as known at that time.

Second, he was excited by life. Adventure was his natural environment. His log of the first voyage reveals not a man bent on conquest but a man excited by discovery. He was an (amateur) biologist, botanist, geologist, sociologist, psychologist, and ichthyologist. In his log of November 1492, Columbus writes, "I am detained by sheer pleasure and delight as I see and marvel at the beauty and freshness of these countries." He took notes about birds, flowers, mountains, animals, and sea creatures with a sense of wonder.

Third, while Columbus did not do well as a land-based governor in charge of his own command, he was a man with some savvy of how relationship systems function. Over and over he records how he warned his men not to interfere in the way of life of the natives they encountered, either by hurting them personally or by taking their things. But it is at the very beginning of the journey that we get a hint of his capacity for understanding both the problems of leadership and the importance of self-differentiation in the leader. On the way to the Canaries, the *Pinta*'s rudder broke down and the crew seemed to have trouble fixing it. After several becalmed days, Columbus began to sense that this might be an effort to sabotage his whole venture; his colleagues' will had already waned. Displaying an unusual awareness of the value of self-definition over efforts to coerce another, he signaled that he was going on to the Canaries by himself and would wait for them there, prepared to go on alone if he had to. He jots in his log, "I see that I'm going to have to accept what I cannot control." The *Pinta* arrived two days later.

Columbus was probably not the first member of his civilization to try to push out the end of its envelope. Others also ventured past Gibraltar into the Atlantic, but all went the northern route. Because they knew of the strength and danger of westerly winds, the way to play it safe was to stay in northern latitudes and thus be assured that those winds would eventually ensure one's return. But the cost of safety was great. It meant beating against those same winds on the way out, and that took its toll in terms of time, energy, supplies, and progress. What most differentiates Columbus is that he says in effect, "I'll worry about returning after I get there," drives south below the westerlies to the launching pad of the Canaries, and substantiates the relationship between risk and reality.

The rest of this book will take up Columbus's challenge. Earlier chapters were devoted to showing the emotional barriers to new thinking about relationships that keep leaders imaginatively stuck: specifically, the reliance on data, empathy, and togetherness. Now we will cross those barriers in order to help leaders out of the imaginative gridlock that characterizes the individual-model orientation of the social sciences. To return to the metaphors of chapter 1, the remainder of this work will offer a new orientation to reality based on natural systems principles. It will go another way. It will present a view of relationships, and therefore of leadership, that goes in a direction that is not only different from but sometimes opposite to the direction of traditional pathways. It will suggest that the treadmill upon which many parents, healers, mentors, and managers find themselves, along with most leadership training programs, has less to do with problems of methodology and data than with a flaw in the basic model. And it will suggest that rather than finding new answers to established questions about leadership, it is the basic questions themselves that must be reframed. As with any major shift in paradigms, such a change of direction will inevitably have important ramifications for what information is worth gathering.

Rather than simply telling it like it is, the social science (Old World) construction of the reality of relationships is virtual reality. Psychodynamics is a model, culture is a perspective, gender is a dimension. They are angles of entry into human problems, ways of organizing our minds, and they should not be confused with "the truth," much less the whole truth. The conventions through which we try to understand human relationships today may be as misoriented as was the medieval view of heaven and earth. Thus to suggest that gender, ethnicity, and psychological profiles are not the stuff of human relationships, or that the concentrated focus on data, method, feelings, and togetherness is misguided, can sound as counterintuitive today as it would have been in Columbus's time to say that the Earth revolves around the Sun. On the other hand, from the perspective of the emotional process view of reality that I shall develop here, the way most leadership programs understand the human phenomenon is tantamount to still assuming that the world is flat.

In making this conceptual leap, I will offer a fresh way of seeing relationships and thinking about institutions that can free leaders from ideas and assumptions that have become so unquestioningly accepted that, as learned as they may be, they have the same hold on our imaginations as superstitions. It is also useful to keep in mind, though, that even when a radically new hypothesis turns out to be wrong it can lead to ways of functioning that serendipitously stumble on the unimaginable. After all, Columbus's hypothesis that it was three thousand miles to Japan was not exactly correct.

More than a view of reality is at stake here, of course. The emphasis in our civilization on data, on method, on technique, and on social science categories misdirects leaders in two ways. First, it directs them away from the reality of underlying emotional processes. Second, as long as emotional process is ignored, so is the sense of self, which will then undercut a leader's confidence in the uniqueness of his or her own personal being. All this when what our civilization needs most is leaders with a bold sense of adventure. As I noted earlier, our nation's obsession with safety ignores the fact that every American alive today benefits from centuries of risk-taking by previous generations. While not all Americans share equally in that heritage, to the extent anyone does, it is because every modern benefit from health to enjoyment to production has come about because Americans in previous generations put adventure before safety. We run the risk of becoming a nation of "skimmers" who constantly take from the top without adding significantly to its essence.

For both families and institutions, if not our nation itself, our chronically anxious civilization inhibits well-differentiated leaders from emerging and wears down those who do. Among our reigning "Old World" superstitions are the following notions:

◆ Leaders influence their followers by the model they establish for identification or emulation.
◆ The key to successful leadership is understanding the needs of their followers.
◆ Communication depends on one's choice of words and how one articulates them.
◆ Consensus is best achieved by striving for consensus.
◆ Stress is due to hard work.
◆ Hierarchy is about power.

Instead, the "New World" orientation to relationships will produce a view of leadership that says the following:

◆ A leader's major effect on his or her followers has to do with the way his or her presence (emotional being) affects the emotional processes in the relationship system.
◆ A leader's major job is to understand his or her self.
◆ Communication depends on emotional variables such as direction, distance, and anxiety.
◆ Stress is due to becoming responsible for the relationships of others.
◆ Hierarchy is a natural systems phenomenon rooted in the nature of protoplasm.

◈ INNOVATIONS AND PARADIGM SHIFTS

The twentieth century was one of continuous surprise. This has been equally true from the points of view of science, politics, and society. The rate of change itself has seemed to change. Some of these changes have altered views that have been preserved for centuries; some have reversed radical changes that began within this century itself. In physics, quantum theory, relativity, and superstring theory have exceeded the realms of human thought in those areas for several millennia. In cosmology, the concept of the "Big Bang" has offered a far different conception of the universe.

In contrast, the social sciences (with the exception of economics) have stayed true to their original concepts. Generally, the same sort of basic shift has not occurred in the "soft" sciences. Of innovative methods for gathering data, there have been plenty; nor have the social sciences lacked imaginative new hypotheses or internecine struggles. But the type of shift that enables one to see reality itself in a new dimension has not occurred. Almost all views of psychology, for example, whether they tend toward Freud's understanding of psychodynamics or Skinner's notions of behaviorism, fall within that traditional range. Similarly, efforts to understand society focus primarily on customs, ceremonies, and values, and often go back to framing attitudes in terms of the psychological. There have been many innovations in psychotherapy, much clever research, unending amounts of data. But there has been no shift in understanding the reality of relationships that is at all equivalent to what has occurred in physics, biology, or astronomy.

It is possible to explain this by saying that the "hard" sciences are more open to verification. "Soft" science has become engulfed by societal regression and gridlock to the point of becoming a faith system—that is, a system of salvation. One major exception to this gridlock, however, is the family systems model, developed by several who were influenced by systems thinking elsewhere. The family systems model turned out to be not just a new technique for addressing family problems, but a different way of conceptualizing the human phenomenon, a new paradigm for understanding relationships. What the family systems model did was to shift the unity of observation from a person to a network, and to focus on the network principles that were universal rather than specific to culture. Such thinking opens the door for a major reconceptualization of leadership.

The family systems model turns out to be about more than families. Thus when a church, an organization, or a sports teams says, "We are like a family," more is involved here than closeness, togetherness, or emotional distance. Similarly, when efforts are made to distinguish how families are different from other institutions, the difference is one of intensity or degree rather than of kind. For despite the urgings of therapists, clergy, and other well-meaning professionals for people to come together, it is a far less important maneuver than for people to retain their own individuality. Coming together is a natural process, and while evolution requires coming together as much as it requires preservation of individuality, the two forces are not equally respectful of one another. While individuality can lead to chaos, anarchy for the most part does not, and the natural forces for togetherness create a check. On the other hand, there is nothing inherent in life itself that checks the togetherness forces from snuffing out individuality, except the vigilance of individuality to protect itself.

That differentiation is not a function of intelligence, power, good will, or industriousness is exemplified by the following clinical case. Many years ago a high-ranking member of government came to see me about his marriage problems. Very experienced, hard-working, nationally known, extremely knowledgeable in his field, and a significant contributor to the passage of several major bills, he was thinking of throwing his hat in the ring for the presidency. But, he complained, his wife was "terribly dependent and unsupportive." However, after she called for some sessions of her own, it was his lack of differentiation that began to surface. He started to call me the moment he had calculated she would have finished each appointment, to find out what had transpired. At her very first session she had begun, "I want you to know that I love my husband very much, and I want to save our marriage. But I also love my country very much, and there's no way I want to see him become President."

◆ SYSTEMS THINKING

The word *system* is used so often today that, like the phrase *paradigm shift*, it has lost the distinctiveness of its original conception. As used by most writers, it refers to a set of interdependent variables. It recognizes society as the product, not the sum, of human relationships. What you and I can do together is far more than the addition of what you and I can do separately, and there is an awareness that this involves a different level of inquiry requiring different ways of perceiving and organizing.

The term *emotional system* refers to any group of people who have developed interdependencies to the point where the resulting system through which they are connected (administratively, physically, or emotionally) has evolved its own principles of organization. The structure, or resulting field, therefore tends to influence the functioning of the various members more than any of the components tends to influence the functioning of the system. A family emotional system includes the members' thoughts, feelings, emotions, fantasies, and associations, their past connections individually and together. It includes their physical makeup, genetic heritage, and current metabolic states. It involves their sibling positions and their parents' sibling positions. The essential characteristic of systems thinking is that the functioning of any part of the network is due to its position in the network rather than to its own nature. Nature may determine the range of possible functioning and response, but not what specifically it will express.

One way of trying to understand an emotional system is to apply field theory. A field is an environment of force (for example, gravitational or magnetic) that, upon achieving homeostasis (stability and therefore identity), functions to maintain that balance through inner adjusting compensations. Now here is the conceptual leap: While a field can only come into existence when matter gets close to matter, once it does it has more power to determine the functioning of the constituent parts than any of those parts individually, even though their presence is necessary for maintaining the field.

Systems thinking received its major lift during World War II because of the need to deal with new orders of complexity. It received additional input as computers, created to deal with new orders of complexity, became so complex themselves. In the anti-submarine warfare conducted by the Royal Air Force, one change in strategy epitomizes this thinking. One day, instead of sending planes out in random patterns, the RAF hooked into patterns of German intentions that they were not even aware of themselves. Specifically the RAF began to keep tabs on the "kill ratio" of German U-boats to the patterns of planes being sent out. They kept careful records of which patterns produced the greatest success, and then stuck with them. What that meant, in effect, was that more young German sailors would die that day through no fault of their own, but simply because the RAF was employing systems thinking.

Another example of systems thinking: when it seems that other species function like us, the tendency is to assume that they have learned the behavior from us or to assume that some similar growth process has occurred from experience or the brain. Natural systems theory reverses that assumption. It assumes that when animals do things similar to humans, they are not aping us; rather, it is *we* who are manifesting one aspect of a universal principle that cannot simply be attributed to our larger brains.

◈ THE NATURE OF INSTITUTIONS

Most thinking about institutions in our society is psychodynamically oriented: relationships take their character from the personalities or backgrounds of the people involved rather than from their adaptation to an overall system. Instead, I suggest that individuals function not out of their own personalities or past, but express that part of their nature that is regulated by the emotional processes in the present system. This applies to two factors in particular: their position with relational triangles (see chapter 7) and the forces that have been transmitted from successive generations.

As accurate as the laws of psychodynamics may be in explaining how an individual mind works, this does not hold true on the more complex level of institutions. In a similar way, it is impossible to explain the forces at work in binding atoms into molecules in terms of the forces inside the atoms themselves that give them their discrete identity. Moreover, forces that are the most powerful in one realm are not necessarily the most powerful in another. Gravity, for example, regulates the relationship of the planets; yet within the atoms that constitute those planets, the so-called strong force is ten thousand times more powerful than gravity. Understanding the processes driving any emotional field requires a different level of inquiry. To that end, the term *emotional* is used throughout this work rather than *psychological.*

Consequently, the models I use here differ from traditional social science assumptions in three major ways. First, the models view families and institutions in terms of *emotional processes that are self-organizing and multigenerational* rather than forces that can be reduced to the conventions of psychology or the categories of sociology and anthropology (culture, gender, race, age, and so on). Relationships are not simply the product of the personalities involved, but are constantly evolving structures that take shape from the adaptation of each member to the adaptations others make to them in response.

Whether we are considering families or other types of institutions, therefore, "individuals" do not function simply according to their own personality makeup or background, but according to their position within an institution's multigenerational field. Thus leadership begins with freedom from a given institution's emotional field; leaders neither react to it nor withdraw from it.

Second, these new models differ from traditional social science models in that they view *the past as a continuous process* that goes well beyond the impact of the previous generation. The influence of the past is seen in terms of its presence rather than what has "gone by." As noted above, rather than using a billiard-ball concept to understand the relationship between generations, a more appropriate metaphor would be a collapsing telescope in which each cylinder overlaps, and, to some extent, continually formats the shape of the next.

What is the major ramification for leadership? This continuous view of time enables one to see that the nature of relationships in the present has more to do with emotional processes that have been successively reinforced for many generations than with the logic of their contemporary connection. Institutions, for example, tend to institutionalize the pathology, or the genius, of the founding families. Whether we are considering families, hierarchies, or nations, only a certain type of leadership can alter the inevitability of this "persistence of form."

The third way in which these new models differ is by emphasizing the *unity of life's processes* rather than the distinctions made by the social sciences. The reason for their universality is connected to the view of time outlined above. The emotional processes that shape institutions go back to "creation," or at least to that "Big Bang" when the first eukaryotic cells said, in effect, "I don't have to clone like the rest of you" and initiated the tension between togetherness and self that has been at the root of almost all leadership problems ever since, whenever "protoplasm" tries to colonize.

This emphasis on what is similar rather than what is different has two consequences for leadership. On the one hand, emphasizing similarity means that the principles of leadership extend across the board to all forms of contemporary institutional life. The emotional processes at work in any family of any background are identical, while culture is only the medium through which such processes work their art. Thus the laws which these emotional processes follow apply equally to all forms of human colonization (schools, hospitals, offices, factories, religious institutions, courts, and so forth). The fact that family and other institutional processes run on the same current, so to speak, can enable leaders to improve by gaining a better understanding of how their position in their own extended family's emotional field affects their functioning. I do not mean the way it did in the past, but how the presence of that past affects them now.

The second major consequence for leaders of this shift toward the emotional processes that unify life on this planet and away from conventional social science traditions that emphasize distinctions is that it establishes new criteria for what information is important.

◆ A SUMMARY OF PRINCIPLES *

1. *Society*

◆ The characteristics of a chronically anxious family, organization, or society—reactivity, herding, blaming, a quick-fix
mentality, lack of well-differentiated leadership—will always
be descriptive of a regressed institution.

◆ When any institution, relationship, or society is imaginatively
gridlocked, the underlying causes will always be emotional
rather than cerebral.

◆ All pathogenic (that is, destructive) organisms, forces, and
institutions, whether we are considering viruses, malignant
cells, chronically troubling individuals, or totalitarian nations,
lack self-regulation and are therefore invasive by nature and
cannot be expected to learn from their experience.

◆ For terrorists to have power, whether in a family or in the
family of nations, three conditions must be fulfilled: (1) the
absence of well-defined leadership; (2) a hostage situation to
which leaders are particularly vulnerable; and (3) an unreasonable faith in reasonableness.

◆ A major criterion for judging the anxiety level of any society
is the loss of its capacity to be playful.

◆ A society's culture does not determine its emotional
processes; rather, a society's culture provides the medium
through which a society's emotional processes work their art.

◆ The basic tension that must constantly be re-balanced in any
family, institution, or society is the conflict between the
natural forces of togetherness and self-differentiation.

2. *Relationships*

◆ It is easier to be the least mature member of a highly mature
system than the most mature member of a very immature
system.

◆ Increasing one's pain threshold for others helps them mature.

** This chapter is unfinished. We have included Friedman's outline here as a useful summary
of the past six chapters.—Eds.*

◆ Stress and burnout are relational rather than quantitative, and are due primarily to getting caught in a responsible position for others and their problems.

◆ In any partnership, the more anxious you are to see that something is done, the less motivated your partner will be to take the lead.

◆ In any stuck relationship between an overadequate member and an underadequate other (person or organization), the overfunctioner must change before the underfunctioner can change.

◆ In any relationship anywhere, the partner doing the least amount of thinking about the other is the more attractive one to the other.

◆ When people differ, the nature of their differences does not determine the extent or the intensity of the differing.

3. Self

◆ Trauma lies in the self-organizing quality of the system and the response of the organism rather than in the event. In other words, the trauma is in the experience and the response to it, not in the event itself.

◆ The toxicity of an environment in most cases is proportional to the response of the organism or the institution, rather than to the hostility of the environment.

◆ What is essential are stamina, resolve, remaining connected, the capacity for self-regulation of reactivity, and having horizons beyond what one can actually see.

◆ There is no way out of a chronically painful condition except by being willing to go through a temporarily more acutely painful phase.

◆ People who are cut off from relationship systems, especially their family of origin, do not heal, no matter what their symptom.

◆ Most of the decisions we make in life turn out to be right or wrong not because we were prescient, but because of the way we function *after* we make the decision.

◆ A self is more attractive than a no-self.

4. Leadership

◆ Mature leadership begins with the leader's capacity to take responsibility for his or her own emotional being and destiny.

◆ Clearly defined, non-anxious leadership promotes healthy differentiation throughout a system, while reactive, peace-at-all-costs, anxious leadership does the opposite.

◆ Differentiation in a leader will inevitably trigger sabotage from the least well-differentiated others in the system.

◆ Followers cannot rise above the maturity level of their mentors no matter what their mentor's skill and knowledge-base.

◆ The unmotivated are notoriously invulnerable to insight.

◆ Madness cannot be judged from people's ideas or their values, but rather from (1) the extent to which they interfere in other people's relationships; (2) the degree to which they constantly try to will others to change; and (3) their inability to continue a relationship with people who disagree with them.

◆ People cannot hear you unless they are moving toward you, which means that as long as you are in a pursuing or rescuing position, your message will never catch up, no matter how eloquently or repeatedly you articulate your ideas.

◆ The children who work through the natural difficulties of growing up with the least amount of difficulty are those whose parents made them least important to their own salvation.

You can't rely on your eyes when your imagination is out of focus.
—Mark Twain

Chapter Seven

◈ EMOTIONAL TRIANGLES

For ten days, the Simpsons' adolescent, eldest daughter lay in a hospital bed with a mysterious infection, her body unresponsive to intravenous antibiotics. During this period her parents were having the worst fight of their life over the amount of time Mr. Simpson was spending with a female colleague at work. Throughout, he had steadfastly claimed that he was not romantically involved with her. Finally, he admitted that he was having an affair, and during a visit to the hospital told his daughter the truth. Within forty-eight hours her mysterious infection had mysteriously disappeared.

Mrs. Smith went to see a therapist, troubled over an affair that she had been carrying on since the first year of her five-year-old marriage but that she now wanted to break off. Why, all of a sudden? She could give no clear reason other than that it was becoming increasingly difficult for her to continue it. A history of the marriage revealed that six months after their wedding, the husband entered a four-times-a-week psychoanalysis. Her affair had started shortly after that. Two months before Mrs. Smith came in, troubled about her dalliance, her husband had terminated his relationship with his analyst.

Mr. Brown had worked his way up to the top of a major corporation through his uncommon industry, creativity, and ability to make friends. He was known as someone you could always go to, someone who was always available in time of need, a good mediator, someone who seemed to make a specialty of resolving conflict. As a reward for his long-term loyalty, he was promoted to CEO. Soon after taking over this corporation, which had been like his extended family, he was given explicit orders by the board of trustees to downsize the company by thirty percent within six months. He began to drink heavily, lost his verve and creative edge, eventually became seriously depressed, at times considered suicide, and began to display psychotic symptoms.

What these three stories have in common is the manifestation of an emotional triangle: the manner in which the relationship between any two people, or a given individual and his or her symptoms, can be a function of an often unseen third person, relationship, or issue between them. (Actually, there may be no such thing as a two-person relationship.)

Emotional triangles are the building blocks of any relationship system. They are its molecules. They follow their own universal laws, totally transcending the social science construction of reality, and they seem to be rooted in the nature of protoplasm itself. Triangles function predictably, irrespective of the gender, class, race, culture, background, or psychological profile of the people involved, and also irrespective of the relational context, family or business, the kind of business, or the nature or severity of the problem. They require a different level of inquiry, and they provide different criteria for what information is important.

As will be elaborated below, no matter who the people are or what the context, emotional triangles adhere to the following rules:

- ◆ They form out of the discomfort of people with one another.
- ◆ They function to preserve themselves and, perversely, oppose all intentions to change them.
- ◆ They interlock in a reciprocally self-reinforcing manner.
- ◆ They make it difficult for people to modify their thinking and behavior.
- ◆ They transmit a system's stress to its most responsible or most focused member.

Observing how emotional triangles function is a way of objectifying relationship processes. The triangles make emotional process directly observable. They concretize the field and demonstrate how relationship systems are self-organizing. And they support the major principle of systems thinking that it is *position* rather than nature that is the key to understanding our functioning in any family or work system.

For leaders, the capacity to understand and think in terms of emotional triangles can be the key to their stress, their health, their effectiveness, and their relational binds. Almost every issue of leadership and the difficulties that accompany it can be framed in terms of emotional triangles, including motivation, clarity, decision-making, resistance to change, imaginative gridlock, and a failure of nerve.

Emotional triangles thus have both negative and positive effects on leaders. Their negative aspect is that they perpetuate treadmills, reduce clarity, distort perceptions, inhibit decisiveness, and transmit stress. But their positive aspect is that when a leader can begin to think in terms of emotional triangles and map out in his or her mind (or even better, on paper) diagrams of the family or organization, such analysis can help explain alliances and the difficulties being encountered in motivation or learning. This in turn can help the leader get unstuck by changing emotional processes and becoming more objective about what is happening. Identifying triangles is also useful in evaluating the maturity of family members or coworkers. Indeed, the concept of an emotional triangle is so basic to understanding relationship process and the process of a leader's self-differentiation that this entire book could have been cast in its terms. Triangles are the stuff of emotional process.

That is why the concept of an emotional triangle provides a way out of gridlock, whether one is a parent or a president, and offers a concrete alternative to the substance abuse of data. It also provides a way to regulate our sensitivity so that we do not fall into the trap of empathy. Most important, perhaps, the concept of an emotional triangle describes clearly how self-differentiation can be a more powerful influence on others than any one technique or method for moving them forward.

◆ TYPES OF EMOTIONAL TRIANGLES

As mentioned, an emotional triangle is any three members of any relationship system or any two members plus an issue or symptom. The most common emotional triangles are the following.

1. Family Triangles

Spouse/spouse/any third person	child (natural or adopted), in-law, relative, boss, friend, paramour, therapist, minister, mentor, doctor, etc.
Spouse/spouse/any issue or symptom	either partner's drinking, eating, smoking, distasteful habit, health, job, hobby, credit card, inheritance, etc.
Parent/child/parent	any difference between the parents over leniency, discipline, protectiveness, freedom, individuality, etc.
Parent/child/any third person	sibling, grandparent, other relative, healer, mentor, piano teacher, soccer coach, friend(s), scoutmaster, etc.
Parent/child/habit	laziness, sloppiness, tardiness, cleanliness, carelessness, irresponsibility, lying, cheating, stealing, etc., and the issue that encompasses them all: homework

2. *Workplace Triangles*

Issues at Stake   seniority, fairness, allotment of resources,
                                   space, employee slots, benefits, working
                                   conditions, productivity, hiring and firing
                                   policies, profit-sharing, snafus and goof-
                                   ups, and management practices

Emotional Triangles   CEO/vice president/vice president
                                   CEO/union/board of trustees
                                   CEO/profits/his or her health
                                   CEO/corporate culture/change
                                   Manager (supervisor)/CEO/another
                                       manager
                                   Manager/subordinate/superior
                                   Manager/subordinate/subordinate
                                   Worker/manager/manager
                                   Worker/manager/worker
                                   CEO, manager, or worker/job/family
                                   CEO, manager, or worker/orders from
                                       above/maintaining one's integrity

3. *Healing and Mentoring Triangles*

Issues at Stake   payment, quality of care, expectations,
                                   boundary violations, advice, expertise

Emotional Triangles   Healer/patient (client)/symptom
                                   Healer/patient/patient's recalcitrance
                                   Healer/patient/another healer
                                   Healer/patient/another patient
                                   Healer/patient/patient's relative or friend
                                   Healer/patient/healer's relative or friend
                                   Healer/patient/healer's income
                                   Healer/patient/insurance
                                   Healer/patient/another way they are
                                       connected
                                   Healer/patient/healer's reputation
                                   Patient/healer's expertise/patient's own
                                       intuition
                                   Patient/his or her body/his or her self

◆ THE "LAWS" OF EMOTIONAL TRIANGLES

No matter what the issues (the content) over which two persons differ and no matter who the people are, emotional triangles are regulated by the same "laws." Here is a description of each, with illustrations from family and work systems.

How Emotional Triangles Form

Emotional triangles form because of the inherent instability of two-person relationships. This instability increases because of a lack of differentiation of the partners, the degree of chronic anxiety in the surrounding emotional atmosphere, and the absence of well-defined leadership. They create the illusion of intimacy. How long can any two people talk together without focusing on a third person? It may even be that to the extent the conversations of any two people focus on a third party, there is a flaw in the pseudo-intimacy that has formed. The process involves more than scapegoating or finding a common enemy, however. Triangling a third person (A) *into* a relationship with B and C by agreeing to dislike (or even help) A, or triangling that third person *out* by keeping A in the dark about a secret she or he has every right to know (a mother's suicide, a person's terminal condition, a job transfer, the closing down of a plant) provides stability to B and C, who then organize themselves around the framework of the triangle. The relationship then evolves in a way that makes A, the third party (often unseen), an inherent part of the connection of the other two.

In family life, the most obvious triangle involves an adultery, but the functioning of that triangle has more to do with how the need for secrecy creates an intense emotional bond by triangling out the other partner, A, than with the sex that is the usual focus. And even when A knows, it is the triangled-out position and the way he or she responds to the relationship of the other two (B and C) that stabilizes or destabilizes the extramarital relationship. The relationship of B and C will take on a different tone if A mischievously encourages the affair than if A adopts a pouting, hurt, and suspicious attitude. Indeed, there may be no better proof that triangles are essentially an emotional process than the ways in which the intensity of B's and C's extramarital relationship is governed by the way A responds to it.

The more common family emotional triangle is two parents (B and C) and a child (A). That triangle does not end with a divorce, nor often even with the death of one of the parents. The child so triangled will be chosen by the emotional processes in the family in a way often determined by the timing. An only child is always in a triangled position. Yet the triangled child could also be any child born at a critical time in the parents' marriage when it needs re-balancing—for example, after the loss of a previously triangled child or parent or other relative or therapist who was part of the marriage relationship right from the beginning. And of course this is absolutely true when the mother is already pregnant before her marriage. The process is even more blatant in second marriages where the child to be triangled comes along with the mother (or in some cases the father) and was an integral part of the engagement process. I once did a wedding for a couple where the mother's only child stood right behind the bride and groom during the ceremony. After the final pronouncement, the groom turned to the little girl and gave her a ring also. He knew what he was doing; he married "them."

The child who is part of a marital triangle will tend to go to extremes—be it super achievement or dysfunction (emotionally or physically). When it is the latter, efforts to help the child improve (tutors, Outward Bound programs, therapists, private school) will generally be limited in their success. And if the symptom that develops in the child is physical (allergies, headaches, recurrent fevers and colds, or more pernicious diseases), then the triangle will contribute to perpetuating its chronic state. Whether emotional or physical, the child's symptom will only abate if the marital triangle itself is changed when the parents pay attention to unresolved issues in their own relationship. This always requires that one parent become the leader against the resistance of the other.

The best evidence for the power of such emotional triangles is the extent to which one or both parents seeking help for a troubled child will quit the counselor when they are advised to differentiate more from the child, and this begins to change the marriage itself. I cannot count the number of times that, in an effort to ward this off, I have turned to one partner (usually the husband) and said, "I want to warn you that if your wife succeeds in getting less hooked into your child's shenanigans, it will carry over to your marriage. One cannot differentiate selectively, even if the differentiating efforts are focused on one another person. And you will find her a much more independent partner." The husband would say, "Don't worry about me," or, "That would be wonderful," and then, as his wife does begin to succeed in developing more self-regulation, the husband begins to say things like, "Don't you think you've gone to the counselor enough? We could really use the money for other purposes," or, "Guess what, honey, I've been transferred to Australia."

The concept of an emotional triangle can provide an important variable, a missing link, in understanding why different children growing up in the same family turn out so differently. It helps explain the conundrum well known to educators: Why do difficult or unmotivated or rebellious children often come out of homes where the parents are so nice? The focus on alcoholism, abuse, and divorce completely misses how even in the most stable and loving families children can sometimes suddenly quit school, get recurring illnesses, reject the family's most treasured values, or go over to the railroad tracks after school one day and let a train slash their body in two.

Stepfamilies or blended families, where two partners bring children in from previous marriages, display the triangle more blatantly. They create discomfort to the extent that either partner tries to rearrange the relationships of either partner and their children. The children are not so innocent either, despite the Cinderella fantasy. Many "wicked stepmothers" are simply overly responsible women who are trying to fix an irresponsible child. Cinderella's stepmother might have been an overly responsible woman who had raised her daughters to be orderly, and Cindy might have been a flake. Nothing will break up a second marriage faster than one partner trying to rearrange the relationship of the other partner and his or her child. And the same goes for businesses.

Emotional triangles can also form in society itself. There is an extraordinary similarity between the difficulty of helping children caught in a triangle with their parents and America's race problem. One way to understand this would be that from the beginning the black population of America has served as a displacement focus for the problems of whites with one another, particularly the normal differences between classes. While these differences obviously exist and have political ramifications, they have never taken on the intensity of class struggle that occurs in other nations without a pariah group to focus on. As with families, this is not a conscious process but a self-organizing evolution that results from mutual adaptation patterns.

On the international scene, triangles are cleverly used by smaller nations to create alliances by using their enmity against other larger nations. The Cold War and much of the Vietnam struggle illustrate this. Triangles were at the heart of the beginnings of World War I, the Peloponnesian War between Athens and Sparta, and the continued difficulties between Israel and the Arabs. Much talk about balance of power is also based on a triangle, but that balance of power can exist within the military of one country as well as between the militaries of various countries. When the surface fleets of the United States Navy (battleships, cruisers, destroyers) wanted to arm themselves with cruise missiles, which would make their defense less dependent on submarines and carriers, the other two arms of the Navy put up such a struggle that a compromise had to be worked out assuring them of their rightful hegemony before they would agree to stop fighting the change.

A beautiful example of the way emotional triangles form is the following domestic spillover, which also shows the interlocking nature of triangles. A couple who were divorcing decided to split up their property at a mutually agreeable time. The wife, however, who was distrustful of her husband, asked the local police to provide some protection. When the husband found out about this, he asked for the same. As they began to divvy up their furniture, at one point the wife objected to something the moving men were taking, and her policeman interfered with the moving men, whereupon the other policeman began to interfere with the first policeman's interference. Within the next half-hour the two policemen were almost at the point of fisticuffs and both husband and wife turned into a mediation team in order to keep things calm. One would like to end the story by saying this brought them back together, but that did not happen. As I shall describe shortly, however, stranger alliance shifts can occur because of the functioning of emotional triangles.

Another type of shift involving a physical symptom happened to a divorcing couple who had been married for six years and were separating on good terms. They had no children, although they had never used contraceptive devices. The night before they separated, they decided to have sex one more time "just for the hell of it," and she conceived. Similarly, in a two-sister family if one of the women is having trouble conceiving and the other is having trouble not conceiving, the odds are very high that the one having trouble conceiving is in an emotional triangle of responsibility for their parents.

How Emotional Triangles Operate

Once formed, emotional triangles (1) are self-organizing; (2) are perpetuated by distance; and (3) tend to be perverse.

The *self-organizing* character of emotional triangles is brought out by the second story at the beginning of this chapter, where a marriage (B and C) stabilized when the wife had an affair (B and A), and destabilized when the husband terminated his analysis (C and A). Another aspect of triangles' capacity for self-organization is the management of conflict. In most emotional triangles, one side tends to be more conflictual than the other two sides, and if one can succeed in calming that side the conflict will generally surface in one of the other relationships. Conversely, if conflict begins to erupt in one of the previously calm relationships, the previously disruptive relationship will often calm down.

An example of the former involved a woman having terrific fights with her mother-in-law. The older woman was constantly critical and interfering, and no appeals to her son (the woman's husband) to say something to his mother had any effect. The wife had become so reactive to her mother-in-law's behavior that she could hardly bear to be in the house with her at the same time. After achieving some distance from her mother-in-law by reframing her as a clownish buffoon rather than an interfering bitch, however, the woman reached a point where she could be amused by her antics. On her mother-in-law's next visit she prepared herself for the usual barbs, innuendoes, and criticism by responding ironically, saying, "How did your son have such poor taste as to marry me?" In front of her husband: "Have you thought of moving in with us so you can protect your grandchildren from me?" Within an hour, the mother-in-law had ceased giving any attention to her daughter-in-law and desisted for the rest of the visit; instead she became embroiled in a fight with her son, criticizing him for not getting a better job. By the end of the trip, the two women were exchanging recipes.

Generally speaking, in-law struggles are always false issues, with the mother-in-law displacing problems from her marriage and the daughter-in-law from her relationship with her own mother. In fact, I do not think I have ever seen a daughter-in-law having problems with her mother-in-law who had a playful, open relationship with her own mother. And it is extraordinary to watch the immediate, almost magical effects on a daughter-in-law/mother-in-law relationship that can occur if the daughter will work on her relationship with her own mother instead. The same magical effects hold true if the daughter works on her relationship with her own daughter.

In the second place, *distance* also perpetuates an emotional triangle. Thus secrets and gossip that keep a person in the dark will have an avalanche effect on any community, polarizing those in and out of the secret and inhibiting communication between them. In addition, criticism in the form of "you statements" rather than "I statements" will push people away. And if the person accepts the criticism and becomes defensive, they will become emotionally triangled into the other person's problems. The distance has the effect of creating pseudo-intimacy or alliances and always goes in the opposite direction from openness, directness, and intimacy.

One example is a major Ivy League university that fired its nice but rather ineffectual president and hired a no-frills go-getter to help the school work out its financial problems. He succeeded, but within two years was forced to leave because of the extraordinary enmity he had incurred from the faculty. While the issue at stake was changes in the faculty's benefits and rights, the differences might have been less polarizing if the new president could have eliminated the distance between them. His predecessor, a hail-fellow-well-met sort of guy, could be seen every Sunday, pipe in hand, walking his dog across the main quadrangle. But the successor kept his apartment in Manhattan and retreated there on weekends. If the new president could have closed the distance between himself and the community, moving away from the direction of the cut-off, he would have had a better chance of shifting the triangle or at least making it more fluid.

In this sense, it was the introduction of the hotline during the Cold War that kept the United States and Russia in direct contact and prevented the triangle-forming alliances of other countries and vested interests within each group from creating a triangle that could have had catastrophic consequences.

The third characteristic of triangle functioning is its *perversity*. The harder A works at changing the relationship of B and C, the more likely it is that their relationship will move in the opposite direction. Thus it is not possible for A to change the B-C relationship for longer than a week. And this will hold true no matter what position A occupies in any relationship system and no matter who or what B and C represent in the examples above. This perverse characteristic of emotional triangles is important in understanding some key concepts: the uselessness of willing others to change; how conflicts of will arise and destroy relationships; and why a leader's presence is more powerful than efforts at coercion or therapy.

The general rule is this: One can only change a relationship of which one is directly a part. For example, if a child gets in trouble with teachers or friends because of particular behavior patterns, a parent will not be successful in trying to modify those patterns. The very act of making the attempt creates a stabilizing triangle that makes change impossible. On the other hand, the parent who works on defining self when the "problem" child misbehaves will have greater success at shifting the triangle, hence modifying the pattern.

I have almost never seen one parent respond well to another parent's criticism or advice on child-rearing. Nor are they any more successful in separating their children from their "horrible" fiancées. Worse, such pressure simply makes kids more likely to fall blindly in love with someone about whom they might otherwise have been more objective. The triangle inverts when the aged parents become "the child" and the child tries to move them against their will to sell their apartment, now in the middle of a dangerous ghetto, to move to Florida or to go into a nursing home.

The counterproductivity of trying to change emotional triangles head-on is one of the most frustrating endeavors for leaders. Most leadership training that suggests techniques for this purpose flounders, because this emotional variable is not a part of the social science construction of reality. Leaders are taught how to motivate, and their leaders constantly try to motivate them to be better motivators.

An ironic example of the perverse power of triangles is the following antitherapeutic "cure." A woman found out that her son was the legal father of an illegitimate child when its mother sued for support. Being well-meaning and comfortable financially, she decided to help despite the fact that her husband, her son, and her other children told her to stay out of things. She, however, befriended the mother of her biological grandson, fell in love with the child, and proceeded to plan to put money away for his education. She also tried to help the mother, a ne'er-do-well sort, to find a job and move to a better neighborhood. No amount of effort on the part of her family or her minister helped the well-meaning grandmother to let go, even though on some level she knew she shouldn't be interfering. The oldest of several children who suffered the brunt of her parents' conflictual marriage, as a youngster she would hide under the dining room table and listen to their fights. As she grew older, she became each parent's confidante and to their dying day kept trying to patch up their differences.

Then the young woman's therapist called the grandmother and asked if she and her husband and son would come in to see him. They were surprised, but agreed on the condition that the young woman would be there also. She never showed. At the session, her therapist told a long sob-story of how unfortunate his patient was. He tried to pressure the family into giving financial support for her, appealing to their fortunate circumstances and good will, and adding a little guilt for good measure. By the time the grandmother came out of that session, she was so furious that even if her husband and family had changed their minds there was no way she was going to be involved any longer.

◆ THE INTERLOCKING NATURE OF
EMOTIONAL TRIANGLES

The emotional triangles of any relationship system interlock, and in any family or work system they extend out into far-reaching super-molecules like hydrocarbon. They can extend within the same family or work system or join both; they can involve only relationships in the present; or they can be the key to how the past becomes the present. The side that is shared by two triangles is the key to the transmission of emotional processes from one triangle to another. It is the network of interlocking triangles that accounts for the compensatory homeostatic forces that provide stability, determine communication pathways, and keep things stuck when a leader tries to bring change.

One of the most remarkable interlocking triangles in family life is that between a mother, any habit of the daughter which the mother is trying to change, and the mother's unresolved issues with her own mother. When she is willing to work on this prior relationship, the daughter will often start to improve on her own. (This is true also with fathers, to some extent, although not nearly as automatically or with as much intensity.)

A triangle can also be with the past. Think of hostage situations, which always involve past vulnerability that chains the person in authority, or the terrorist would have no leverage. These triangles form over several generations. A mother might be too seriously involved with a daughter's incipient blooming individuality and take too seriously the child's cursing. Perhaps the mother needs to learn to be less serious and, if possible, to start acting a little outrageously. But suppose her own mother had been out-and-out crazy, making it impossible for her to behave "like her mother" for fear of going over the edge. The same might be true about a father who is failing to discipline his son because his harsh father beat him. The father also is reacting to an old triangle and is unable to distinguish physical abuse and responsible discipline.

It is perhaps in blended families that interlocking triangles are most blatant. So much is this the case that whenever I was engaged in premarital counseling, my standard advice to previously married clients was that blended families are not really different from normal marriages in any respect except one: the guaranteed way to break up the marriage is for either partner to try to rearrange the partner's established relationships with his or her children.

It is my guess that the functioning of baseball managers and football and other sports coaches is often affected by the triangle with the general manager and the owner. I know of one case in which the

functioning of the quarterback—his slumps, interceptions, and failures—were all a function of an interlocking triangle in the team.
One middle linebacker who had been on three different Super Bowl
teams (San Francisco 49ers, Oakland Raiders, and Washington
Redskins), when asked if the teams had anything in common,
answered without hesitation, "The owners. They showed great
interest and support, but never interfered."

One of the most interesting sets of emotional interlocking triangles I ever came across involved a nun who had become prioress of
her order only to become enmeshed in a sisterly squabble over relationships. Her leadership suffered because of an underground
triangle she had never addressed: the woman who had been the head
of her own parochial school when she was young had sexually
molested her over a period of several years.

In a three-physician obstetric practice, one of the physicians
caught up in a severe triangle between his wife and their irresponsible
son began to drink heavily and find excuses for being unable to take
his turn on call. The senior physician kept compensating for his
junior partner by taking the calls and making the deliveries. This of
course left him tired and worn out and unable to serve his own
family. Then his own son began to act irresponsibly, but when his
wife put pressure on him to spend more time at home, he said that
his patients' needs came first and his poor partner needed help to
work through his problems.

One day I had a conversation with Arthur Goldberg, who had
been our ambassador to the United Nations after years as a very
successful labor arbitrator and member of the Supreme Court. I
said, "I imagine all that experience with labor arbitration and constitutional issues stood you in good stead when you had to deal with
similar problems at the U. N." He glanced at me in an "Are-you-
crazy?" manner and said, "There's no comparison with the layers of
vested interest in an international problem. They are way beyond
anything you could imagine when dealing with the relatively
simplistic problems of a union and management."

It is in family business, however, that the concept of interlocking
triangles may be both most enlightening and most helpful. They
show up clearly, help explain struggle, and stress the role of the
family's leader. In corporate life, the interlocking nature of

emotional triangles can cross into family life. In family businesses, all the tensions, alliances, and unresolved feelings that characterize the family leap over into the business and complicate decision-making processes as well as clarity. Consulting firms generally appreciate this and often give advice that will dilute the triangles, such as not having family members report directly to one another or making sure that the board of trustees includes a significant number of non-family members. This is again an administrative solution to an emotional problem and will be limited in its effects.

One of the most important interlocking emotional triangles in the world of business is that between an entrepreneur and his company's problems, on the one hand, and his position as "standard bearer" in his family of origin, on the other. This is true in any business but exponentially so in family businesses. A standard bearer (often male, but not necessarily so) is someone who has been almost catapulted out of his family with a mandate to *achieve*. He is usually an eldest or at least a first-born son, with uncommon drive and energy. Any woman married to such a man should not expect him to have much time for his marriage and family, though he will be a good provider. I believe that when such men experience stress in their business it is exponentially increased because of the importance of their succeeding for past generations. Moreover, when men commit suicide after business failure, it is not only themselves or their immediate family and friends they feel they have failed, but also their ancestors who have been riding along since birth (if not before) on their shoulders.

◈ STRESS IN EMOTIONAL TRIANGLES

A leader's stress and his or her effectiveness are opposite sides of the same coin. This is so not because failure to be effective creates stress, but because the type of leadership which creates the least stress also happens to be the type of leadership that is most effective. The conventional view of stress is that it has to do with overwork. Once again, the thinking processes involved in the social science construction of reality move toward a quantitative formula and solution. For if stress is simply the result of hard work or too much work, then obviously the answer to stress is not to work too hard. This is a totally unrealistic concept given the type of person who tends to wind up in leadership positions. Trying to be creative and imaginative is stressful, being responsible is stressful, maintaining vision is stressful, being on the lookout for and trying to deal with sabotage is stressful. Yet all leaders move in that direction, and not all leaders experience burnout. If the problem is simply quantitative, how do we ever know when too much is enough?

Similarly, if the problem of stress is simply a matter of overwork, then as most rehabilitation programs construct it, the answer is to get away for a while, relax, do favorite things, and when you come back do not work so hard. The concept here, as with sabbaticals, is to recharge one's batteries so one can go back in and run down again.

The concept of emotional triangles suggests a systems view of stress. To the extent that you (A) become enmeshed in the relationship of B and C (either because you have taken on the responsibility for their relationship or because they have focused on you—that is, triangled you out—as a way of achieving togetherness), you will wind up with the stress for their relationship.

Obviously, everyone has limits in how much work they can handle, but the concept of an emotional triangle suggests that the same amount of hard work will be more or less stressful depending on the position from which one approaches or becomes involved with work. It is as with lifting a heavy object: the weight alone does not cause the rupture but the position from which one tries to lift it. Again, there are limits to everyone's strength, but it takes less weight to strain your body if you attempt to lift the object from certain positions.

The stress on leaders (parents, healers, mentors, managers) primarily has to do with the extent to which the leader has been caught in a responsible position for the relationship of two others. They could be two persons (members of the family, any two sides to an argument) or any person or system plus a problem or goal. The way out is to make the two persons responsible for their own relationship, or the other person responsible for his or her problem, *while all still remain connected.* It is that last phrase which differentiates detriangling from simply quitting, resigning, or abdicating. Staying in a triangle without getting triangled oneself gives one far more power than never entering the triangle in the first place. Many slick and charming leaders never get stressed because they intuitively stay out of triangles; but that makes them less effective.

Another way in which the relational view of stress differs from or sheds new light on classical problems is with regard to the emotional and physical sides of illness. The term *psychosomatic* is a false dichotomy because it suggests that two different realms somehow touch each other. Everyone is in a triangle between his or her body and his or her mind; the trick is to put them together through the integrating effects of self-differentiation.

An emotional process view of burnout would work like this: Every individual reacts to stress in his or her own idiosyncratic way. Some of us are more likely to express physical symptoms and others emotional (that is, mental), depending on a variety of factors that include our genes, how our upbringing has "tuned" us, our family's heritage and style, and so on. Thus one person might be more likely to express her stress in her cardiovascular system, another in his endocrine system (gout, cancer), and a third in her muscular-skeletal system (chronic bad back). But the fact that we have a "weakness" in a particular direction or have been tuned by our family of origin to dysfunction, either mental or physical, in that part of our body does not determine *when* we will develop those symptoms. This is similar to the fact that the time when genes express themselves is not a genetic phenomenon but a relational phenomenon—if not of the genes, then of the cells that contain them.

Leaders who are most likely to function poorly physically or emotionally are those who have failed to maintain a well-differentiated position. Either they have accepted the blame owing to the irresponsibility and constant criticism of others, or they have gotten themselves into an overfunctioning position (that is, they tried too hard) and rushed in where angels and fools both fear to tread.

◆ THE TOGETHERNESS POSITION

The position that is most dangerous to a leader's health is what I call the "togetherness position," in which the leader feels responsible for keeping a system together. Such leaders are most likely to suffer burnout, function badly, or suddenly die when forces pulling in opposite directions have stretched their capacity to hold things together to its breaking point. This can be observed in families, in work systems, and especially in the combination of the two, family businesses.

A study dubbed the *Executive Monkey Experiment* serves as a metaphor. It has generally not been considered scientifically valid because it was not repeated, but it is a poignant metaphor. An effort was made to give monkeys ulcers or to promote some other kind of somatic disturbance through frustration. The monkey was taught how to get food and then frustrated when it finally learned. But no amount of frustration seemed to create the desired somatic dysfunction. Then someone got the bright idea to make the monkey responsible for getting food for other monkeys; then, they claimed, they did produce a somatic disturbance. Whether or not the experiment was scientifically valid, it captures an existential reality.

This is precisely what was described in the third introductory story, in which a CEO who had grown up with the company is now put in the position of downsizing it. Similarly, the woman whose headaches go away after she becomes less responsible for her children's homework exemplifies the dangers of the togetherness position.

The togetherness position is one of the most subtle effects of emotional triangles—and one of the most subversive. On more than one occasion, I have seen the stress of togetherness transmitted to secretaries and subordinates who had become too emotionally involved in their bosses' problems. On one dramatic occasion, the staff of a clinic spent a whole day processing their relationships. There was an underlying split due to the fact that a married couple who worked at the clinic had divorced and one of the partners was now having an affair with another member of the staff. Depression and tension had produced a split community. The effort was made, therefore, to open dialogue among everybody. The clinic was also staffed by a very efficient woman who took care of the administrative details. She was so much a part of the system that they let her come to the all-day marathon. Toward the end of the day, when the consultant asked if the intensity of the situation had driven anyone to suicidal thoughts, it was the secretary who raised her hand.

Another example is a professional person whose wife had committed suicide. She had been having an affair after struggling her whole life to separate from her family but never succeeding. Two years later, the father, who had found the suicide note but never told his children about it, decided to show it to them. Coincidentally, his coronary arteries had occluded during that period and he was about to undergo a bypass. After revealing their dead mother's secret, he became relaxed and positive about his operation and soon returned to his work with renewed energy and vision.

I am not trained as a physician and would never try to treat my clients' physical symptoms. But whenever a client of mine has developed physical symptoms of any kind while they were working on relational issues, I have always suspected triangles. I have taught them to think in threes and note where they are located, and I have helped them to de-triangle. In such cases, the symptoms have almost invariably waned if not disappeared altogether. And whenever I develop symptoms, I know I've been lying to myself.

There is a positive side to all this for leaders, who can use their symptoms (headaches, angina, rashes, increased drinking, sexual acting-out, accidents) as early warning signals that they are in an emotional triangle that is pulling, if not tearing, them apart. Too often the tendency of most aggressive leaders when they do begin to develop symptoms is to ignore them, deny them, or try to override them until they get the job done. But somatic disturbances in a leader not only are warning signals but also feedback from the environment. In other words, leaders can use their bodies to help them be more effective leaders. Instead of treating their symptoms as impediments, they can see them as messengers—again, not simply messengers about their own health or tattletales about their functioning and their position in the relationship system they are leading, but messengers about what is going on in that relationship system.

◆ A CROSS-CULTURAL PHENOMENON

The notion that these principles about emotional triangles are white, male, and Western—that Japanese or Kenyan families are different in the way they discipline their children or in their concern for consensus in business matters—is, I believe, one of the great myths of our age. One of my most consistent experiences in this matter has been that while from time to time someone in an audience has risen to say that this does not apply to families in, say, Eastern Europe or western India, or among born-again Christians, I have never had someone from one of those cultures—or for that matter from any other culture—rise and say, "That's not true about my family." In other words, people are always saying it is not true about *other* families. Quite to the contrary, I have had people from Africa, after hearing a presentation, rise and say, "You have described the African family perfectly," or, "Are you sure you've never been to...?" Perhaps my most outstanding experience along this line was with someone who was the son of a king of a small Polynesian kingdom that included several islands. He said, "I never understood all the problems my father has had over the years with his relatives, his subjects, and the different island cultures until your presentation of family process and triangles."

Systems made of protoplasm need leadership to function effectively, and well-differentiated leadership or its absence has the same effect on any relationship system made of people, irrespective of their culture. Focusing on such differences actually inhibits a leader's capacity to be decisive. Moreover, even if one finds outstandingly different characteristics from culture to culture, rarely do more than sixty to seventy percent of the people in a culture conform to those characteristics. For example, a nurse or social worker working in a hospital has to deal with the patient's family and help them deal with loss, failure, and the side effects of the procedure. "I have to know about their background. How do I know who the family leader is in that culture? Maybe they don't like to get together, etc., etc." All of these family process factors are attributed to cultural differences; but within any culture, rarely does one find more than seventy percent or two-thirds of the people following all those traditions. In any system, the norm produces opposites. (Indeed the very term *norm* suggests a range.) Now how is the nurse to know in advance whether this is a Japanese family that does this or that, an Irish family, Catholic, Jewish? All this burden is eliminated when the nurse is mature enough to say, "I am going to get into the anxiety of this family, and its resilience, and keep the problem in them. I'm not going to try to be a savior."

Now if you are a leader, how are you going to know in advance which segment you are dealing with? Focusing on self obviates the need to do all that research and clutter the mind. This focus on cultural differences is a major way in which the emotional processes of American civilization have been co-opted by forces opposed to differentiated leadership.

◆ A SUMMARY STORY

The following case history encapsulates almost every aspect of emotional triangles discussed so far: their interlocking nature, their tendency to preserve themselves, their tendency to prevent change, their distortion of perceptions, their creation of polarization and false alliances, their capacity to funnel stress toward one person. While the names have been changed, the nature of the triangles and the position of the various family and work systems are true. This vignette will serve as a summary of this entire chapter.

Joe Smith was an agricultural specialist working for USAID in Central America. He was good at his job and had worked his way up to a significant position of responsibility, but he had a few personal problems. He was an alcoholic, took drugs, and was engaged in constant homosexual activity, unknown to his wife and family but suspected by his superiors. Then he was caught trying to smuggle some illicit substances from one country to another. The State Department immediately recalled him and took away his security clearance.

Joe went into detox to get a hold on his substance abuse. He then took menial jobs with the State Department until they could decide what to do with him. He and his wife engaged in two years of therapy, during which both dealt with aspects of their own relationship they had never discussed. As a result, his totally adaptive wife became emboldened to strike out for her own development—no longer denying his problems, longstanding difficulties with all four of their children, and important unresolved issues with their respective families of origin.

After showing that he was able to be quite competent at the office, Joe applied for the return of his security clearance. While the application was being processed, the President issued an Executive Order announcing that homosexuality could no longer be used as a basis for denying security clearance. On the basis of his hard work and his obvious efforts at rehabilitation, his clearance was returned, and Joe now began to look for another foreign assignment.

During this period, the State Department went through a huge downsizing and many of his colleagues were "riffed." Joe, however (for reasons that never became clear), was retained. Just as he thought he had finally made a triumphant return, however, a snafu came out of "left field": he had trouble getting a medical clearance. The term "medical" was a euphemism for psychiatric. The psychiatrist he was asked to see said that his own superiors thought he was not ready for a foreign posting. They worried that the stress of living as a married homosexual would be more difficult to handle than the external stress of the job.

The psychiatrist turned out to be a consultant to the State Department, not someone in a position to make decisions. When the psychiatrist was asked, however, how he would decide if Joe was ready, he could give no objective standards or results for him to work for. Joe therefore asked if he could deal directly with the psychiatrist's superiors, but he was discouraged from doing that. In addition, the psychiatrist hinted that maybe Joe would get his clearance back if he divorced his wife. He gave Joe a paper written by another psychiatrist discussing the problems of married homosexual men. The doctor suggested that Joe show the article to his regular counselor (not to his wife). The article, written by a homosexual psychiatrist, stated that married homosexual men could only reduce their conflicts by coming out openly. It seemed to encourage married men with homosexual feelings or desire to move in that direction rather than work to resolve their conflicts over their feelings.

So far, then, we have these triangles:

◆ Joe, the psychiatrist, and the psychiatrist's superiors;
◆ Joe, his family, and his homosexuality;
◆ Joe, his homosexual desire, and the born-again values of his Christian upbringing (an internal emotional triangle);
◆ Joe, his homosexual conflict, and the political forces in the homosexual community;
◆ Joe, the bureaucracy, and the President's position.

Before the Executive Order, homosexuality had been an easy open-or-shut situation for denying clearance; now the bureaucracy, in an effort to circumvent the Executive Order, was focusing on potential emotional conflict and using that as an excuse to retain their power to deny clearance.

But there's more. It turns out that during this period, a long-standing conflict between USAID and the State Department had become exacerbated by the efforts of the State Department to eliminate AID, or at least to have it incorporated into the department and no longer exist as a separate organization. There had been fights in Congress and even among the staff, including an actual physical fight between one of the directors of AID and a high-ranking employee of the State Department. In addition, the State Department was always suspicious of AID employees because the CIA often used AID as a cover, either having their own people infiltrate or recruiting agents from the regular AID staff. Finally, one area where AID and the State Department were not separate was with regard to their physicians: the doctors who were seeing Joe, as well as those who were in a position to make a decision about his clearance, were basically State Department employees rather than members of his own agency.

So we now have the following additional administrative emotional triangles:

- the President, the State Department, and those in the government who want to eliminate AID;
- the State Department, AID, and the CIA;
- the State Department, AID, and Joe;
- the physicians, the State Department, and AID.

When asked what he would do if he could have the situation work out according to his wildest dreams, Joe said he would like a divorce but to remain in a close relationship with his wife, whom he loved. An alternative was suggested: that he talk openly with his wife about his homosexuality (which he had never admitted but of which she was quite aware) and say to her, "I am gay; I am more comfortable with intimacy with men, but I love you and my children and want to stay married. Are you willing to accept this of me?" He at first demurred, saying how scared he was of being that honest with her. When he decided to tell her, he was warned that the great danger of being so open with his wife was that it might encourage intimacy.

In keeping with the principles of de-triangling, Joe was taught first about how triangles operate. Second, he was told to distinguish between seeing therapists for help and seeing therapists who were operating in a power structure. It was suggested that he not be open with the government's therapists about his difficulties but continue to work on the emotional side with his therapist and convey to the government that he was in charge of himself and not likely to violate laws again. He was shown how the anxiety in the system was filtering down and funneling toward him, and that therefore he could not expect any physician in the anxious system to be objective about his needs. Finally, he was encouraged to have his wife join him in therapy sessions, and to tell his children.

The waves have some mercy, at least,
but the rocks have no mercy at all.
—Irish proverb

Chapter Eight

◆ CRISIS AND SABOTAGE:

THE KEYS TO THE KINGDOM

Every experienced boater knows that when one is docking or pulling away from the dock, all efforts to try to overcome wind and current by simply trying harder generally do not work. Mother Nature wins most contests of will unless one has very great amounts of power at hand. Experienced sailors have learned that far better than fighting those natural forces is to position oneself so that they will, in their own natural way, aid rather than frustrate one's intent.

Every experienced physician knows that attempting to overcome disease by trying to eradicate the pathogen head-on is generally a losing battle. Battles of will with viruses, bacteria, and malignant cells are generally wearying and ineffective at best. Even with enormous medicinal or mechanical power at hand, the physician will always have more success if he or she can promote the organism's own natural capacity to win and natural will to survive.

Most parents, managers, and mentors (teachers, therapists, and consultants) have not learned this lesson, however. They still believe that they can teach, motivate, and inculcate values in their charges simply by exerting enough will, without due regard for the natural forces that work against such well-meaning efforts but which, as with the sailor and the physician, can be harnessed to the leader's helm. Four decades of observing clergy, therapists, parents, and managers fighting resistance by trying to overcome it head-on through sheer acts of will has left me astonished at the inability of leaders to recognize what every sailor knows: that techniques designed to change the natural forces of life generally are ineffective and often burn out the "technician."

I wrote above that one outstanding characteristic with families that endure and perhaps even grow from crisis is the presence of a well-differentiated leader. Now I want to add that the factor which is almost always present in relationship systems that are deeply disturbed, if not disintegrating, is a conflict of will.

For example, one will find in almost every family experiencing the severest emotional symptoms (such as suicide, schizophrenia, psychosis, anorexia, abuse) and sometimes the most debilitating physical symptoms (such as multiple sclerosis, coronary conditions, persistent gastrointestinal problems, even cancer) a deep, abiding conflict of will within the family—sometimes blatantly contentious and sometimes subtly masked by charm or passive obstinacy. Similarly, such conflict is always present in the failure of teachers, counselors, clergy, and consultants to make headway against the riptides of resistance that run counter to their intent. It goes without saying that when continued efforts by CEOs, managers, and administrators are producing little or no progress, they are probably swimming against a tide.

How, then, does one go with the flow and still take the lead? Answer: by positioning oneself in such a way that the natural forces of emotional life carry one in the right direction. The key to that positioning is the leader's own self-differentiation, by which I mean his or her capacity to be a non-anxious presence, a challenging presence, a well-defined presence, and a paradoxical presence. Differentiation is not about being coercive, manipulative, reactive, pursuing or invasive, but being *rooted* in the leader's own sense of self rather than focused on that of his or her followers. It is in no way autocratic, narcissistic, or selfish, even though it may be perceived that way by those who are not taking responsibility for their own being. Self-differentiation is not "selfish." Furthermore, the power inherent in a leader's presence does not reside in physical or economic strength but in the nature of his or her own being, so that even when leaders are entitled to great power by dint of their office, it is ultimately the nature of their presence that is the source of their real strength. Leaders function as the immune systems of the institutions they lead—not because they ward off enemies, but because they supply the ingredients for the system's integrity.

Much of what I have said about leadership can be summarized in the following chart:

POORLY DIFFERENTIATED LEADERSHIP	WELL-DIFFERENTIATED LEADERSHIP
◆ focuses on pathology	◆ focuses on strength
◆ is obsessed with technique	◆ is concerned for one's own growth
◆ works with symptomatic people	◆ works with motivated people
◆ betters the condition	◆ matures the system
◆ seeks symptomatic relief	◆ seeks enduring change
◆ is concerned to give insight	◆ is concerned to define self (take stands)
◆ is stuck on treadmill of trying harder	◆ is fed up with the treadmill
◆ diagnoses others	◆ looks at one's own stuckness
◆ is quick to quit difficult situations	◆ is challenged by difficult situations
◆ is made anxious by reactivity	◆ recognizes that reactivity and sabotage are evidence of one's effectiveness
◆ has a reductionist perspective	◆ has a universal perspective
◆ sees problems as the cause of anxiety	◆ sees problems as the focus of preexisting anxiety
◆ adapts toward the weak	◆ adapts toward strength
◆ focuses empathically on helpless victims	◆ has a challenging attitude that encourages responsibility
◆ is more likely to create dependent relationships	◆ is more likely to create intimate relationships

This notion that an entity can modify surrounding relationships through its presence rather than its forcefulness, moreover, is not unknown to science. Catalysts function that way, for example, and we use the term *to catalyze* to mean a reaction that occurs without forcibly rearranging the parts. In such a reaction in a chemical equation, two compounds will exchange molecules on the other side of the equal sign, but the catalyst has not lost its integrity in the transaction. Enzymes in the body function in a similar way. Although it is possible to imagine the work of enzymes as snipping off strands of DNA and putting them in another place, they actually do not function in that manner. In fact, it is not really known how their presence causes DNA to rearrange itself.

But perhaps a transformer in an electrical circuit is the best metaphor for the workings of presence. Transformers can activate or deactivate a circuit that runs through them, depending on the ratio of coils they contain. For example, one side of the transformer has six coils, the other two; this is a three-to-one transformer. If you send the current in from the two to the six it will triple; send it the other way and it will be reduced to a third of its former strength. Household current in the United States is generally 110 volts but it is transported at 11,000 volts because it is cheaper that way. One needs a transformer at a ratio of one hundred to one at either end to step it up or step it down. Reactive leaders function as a step-up transformer. As one education administrator said, "My mother was a step-up transformer, all right. If there was anxiety in the room and she was present, you could count on it escalating. It went into her at 110 and came out at 11,000."

But it is also possible to be a step-down transformer—to function in such a way that you let the current go through you without zapping you or fusing you to the rest of the circuit. This is not easy, and yet it is within the capability of most leaders. It has far more to do with their presence than with their actions. Part of the difficulty in making the conceptual leap from action to presence is that all leaders, parents, or presidents have been trained to *do* something— that is, to *fix it.* This is due to the emphasis on the cognitive aspects of the brain, the resulting emphasis on method and technique, and the anxious atmosphere of contemporary society. To the extent that leaders and consultants can maintain a non-anxious presence in a highly energized anxiety field, they can have the same effects on that field that transformers have in an electrical circuit. Transformers have no moving parts. They reduce the potential in a field by the nature of their own presence and being and the field they, in effect, create. This is not a matter of "breaking a circuit"; it requires staying in touch without getting "zapped." Anyone can remain non-anxious if they also try to be non-present. The trick is to be both non-anxious and present simultaneously.

Leadership that is rooted in a sense of presence can also be misconstrued as a justification for passivity—for avoiding getting your feet wet, for just being "nice so everyone will love or respect you." It can also lead to mistaken notions that data and method are unimportant, that the bottom line does not matter, or that outcome is irrelevant and the approach, therefore, impractical. Leadership through self-differentiation is not easy; learning techniques and imbibing data are far easier. Nor is striving or achieving success as a leader without pain: there is the pain of isolation, the pain of lone-liness, the pain of personal attacks, the pain of losing friends. That's what leadership is all about.

◆ MY CRISIS

In the first few months of 1990, I began to experience two different sets of physical symptoms, each of which suggested the need for surgery. One was severe angina accompanying any intense physical exercise; the other was a recurring tingling and numbness in my left leg and arm. Regarding the angina, tests conducted on blood flow to my heart indicated the need for angioplasty to unclog one of my coronary arteries, lest I experience a heart attack. Regarding the numbness, tests of my right carotid artery (in the neck) showed a very high degree of occlusion there and indicated the need to unclog that artery lest I experience a stroke. The problem was which opera-tion to undergo first, since either procedure would jeopardize the other organ, bringing about exactly what the other procedure was designed to prevent.

What I came to realize after I had worked my way through this crisis was that my experience was a metaphor for the handling of any crisis anywhere, and that major principles could be drawn from my own personal experience for helping any leader, no matter how the "ball bounced" or the "cookie crumbled." It is also fair to say, however, that since I was already developing the ideas that eventually went into this book, the experience was also for me a test of my own hypotheses.

It was probably this personal experience of the need to be the leader in my own life at that moment (despite the myriad of experts who surrounded me) that helped me understand what I have said above: that all leadership begins with the management of one's own health. For there is little question in my mind that my capacity to navigate the narrow passage left open to my future existence has affected my leadership capacity in all other endeavors ever since. While this may not mean that the best form of leadership training is experiencing a major health crisis, it does sharpen the importance of self-differentiation and the response of the organism, rather than methodology and data, as the essential basis for all leadership endeavors.

What follows is a description of how I worked my way through this dilemma and the leadership principles for enduring crisis that I abstracted from, or used to guide me through, that experience. As will be seen, the story will touch on every issue of leadership discussed so far: the management of information, the management of relationships, the management of anxiety, and the management of self.

The Ball Bounces

One November some time ago I underwent coronary bypass surgery on all three arteries. My first anginal pains had occurred nine months previously and I had been able to calibrate the rate of progression of my disease by the number of city blocks I could walk without experiencing pain. It had gone from ten in June to one in September. Part of the problem had been that at-rest cardiograms showed no problems. I had never had a heart attack, and for one reason or another the physicians I was going to at the time did not think to give me a stress test, diagnosing the problem as gastrointestinal rather than coronary. By October, things had become so severe that they gave me a stress test, saw the dire results, and sent me for an angiogram. And then the truth showed.

The operation was completely successful and I remained angina-free for the next eight or nine years, able to walk, run, chop wood, carry heavy objects, and engage in strenuous activity without any symptoms. Then the angina began to reappear, slowly at first and then more rapidly. Medical technology had made advances. The first balloon techniques would only work on a natural artery, not a graft; but now I was told they had balloons big enough to work on the normally larger grafts. In addition, vascular surgeons were also experimenting with stents that could be inserted to keep the arteries from closing up, although there was also evidence that the very presence of the stent could create some kind of reaction in the artery that made it close up again faster.

While I was pondering when to have the procedure and whether or not to accept the stent, a second set of symptoms began to appear. I began to experience tingling and numbness in my left leg. I had had a major TIA (transient ischemic attack) five years previously, from which I had completely recovered although left with residual inability. So I recognized its recurrence in the midst of a speaking engagement. It then went away but kept returning. Since this could have indicated another kind of arterial problem, this time in the major artery to the brain, I again underwent tests to determine the health of my carotid arteries, the major blood supply to my brain. These tests showed a very high degree of occlusion in the right carotid artery. Since as is well known the brain crosses over so that the right side controls the left side of the body and vice versa, this was strong evidence that the symptoms on my left side could be related to the occlusion in the right carotid artery.

The neurologists did not recommend surgery, however, saying the mortality rate for this kind of operation was even higher than bypass surgery. During the operation, blood has to be stopped from flowing to the brain for about two minutes while a temporary shunt is inserted to take the place of the artery, which is opened, cleaned, and sewed back together. Two aspirin a day, which would thin the blood and reduce clotting possibilities, were recommended instead.

Then suddenly in the midst of my considering when to have the angioplasty, a bulletin was sent to all physicians and published in the newspaper saying that research had shown that there was clear evidence that anyone having a greater than seventy percent occlusion in either artery and experiencing symptoms on the other side of their body should not wait to have surgery; the combination of these two factors was so likely to produce a stroke that the procedure, despite its mortality rate, should be undergone as soon as possible. In fact, the information was considered so vital that it was released immediately by the medical journal to which it was submitted, without waiting for publication.

Now the dilemma engulfed me: which procedure to undergo first. For the carotid artery surgery could increase the likelihood of a heart attack, while the angioplasty could increase the likelihood of a stroke. I had also been told that with either procedure, it was going to be hard to find a physician willing to go first. What complicated matters was that the percentage of carotid occlusion was on the borderline, and the tingling and numbness did not appear to many of the physicians to be typical TIA symptoms. Thus I was faced first with the dilemma of verifying exactly what was going on and how critical a stage I had reached, and then of having to make a decision about which procedure to undergo first.

I was helped out of my dilemma about which way to go first by another longtime friend and colleague who said to me, "You know, Ed, you wouldn't be worth much without your brain. Clearly you have to jeopardize your life to save your brain. There's just no point in jeopardizing your brain in order to save your life." Somehow everything fell into place after that comment.

Getting a solid information base did not turn out to be so easy, partly because of the state of technology and partly because of the relationships of my physicians. After the Doppler test on my carotid arteries had shown a close to seventy percent occlusion, I was told that a more accurate test could be obtained from a carotid arteriogram done in a hospital, where dye could be injected directly into my arteries and traced through X-rays. This procedure, however, had some danger to it and was invasive. On the other hand, said my neurologists, a new, more powerful MRI machine could also give a more accurate reading. That made sense, and I agreed to that. The MRI equipment turned out to be down for a week or two, however, and so I was rescheduled. This response both scared and encouraged me. It couldn't be so bad if they were willing to wait; still, I wondered if I was a potential walking time bomb. Why wait two weeks? Shouldn't I be sent elsewhere, even out of town? Meanwhile, a newspaper story that week said Congress was going to look into the practice of physicians owning their own diagnostic equipment.

The MRI did indeed show an occlusion of greater than seventy percent. But there was still the matter of the atypical symptoms. If the symptoms had another cause, seventy percent occlusion would be less serious and the procedure could be delayed. Deciding that the problem might be orthopedic, I asked the MRI people to also do an image of my neck. That report showed that there was some flattening of the spinal cord that also could have been producing the numbness.

Finding myself in a quandary between the various specialists, I went to my internist, whom I considered a good diagnostician and reasonable fellow, and said, "I want you to listen to my thinking processes. I don't need you to do anything; just listen and tell me if I sound right in my thinking." He agreed with my reasoning, but without my asking began to anxiously overfunction and on his own called a different vascular surgeon and suggested I meet with him. I did so, and this surgeon said that while neurologists may be satisfied with MRIs, for vascular surgeons the gold standard is the invasive arteriogram.

What also made things difficult was that I had a very heavy schedule of speaking engagements, seminars, and consultations, and I kept aiming for a period when things could let up if I rearranged or canceled previous commitments.

I could see clearly that I ought to do the arteriogram in the next week or so. At this point, the vascular surgeon said he could arrange for me to have it in two days; if the results were as expected, he could operate two days later. It fit my schedule and his, so I agreed to the arteriogram.

As I was being wheeled from the procedure room following the procedure, the vascular surgeon informed me that the results showed eighty percent occlusion and that we could schedule the procedure for the following week. I balked to agreeing so readily, however, in part because I experienced him as too eager. He reminded me of certain types of entrepreneurial physicians I had grown up with in New York. And there was another problem: my cardiologist had said that if I were to have the carotid surgery first, I should make sure it was in a hospital with good cardiac backup and thus equipped to do bypass surgery immediately if that became necessary. There was no such backup at the hospital this vascular surgeon worked at.

So, still a little woozy from the arteriogram and trying to keep my bearings, I mentioned that fact. The surgeon said, "Well, I can't say." I added that maybe I should go to the other vascular surgeon where that backup existed and that I would see if his schedule had room. The vascular surgeon surprised me by saying somewhat sardonically, "I'm sure he'll have room." That put-down jolted me a little but also helped me decide that I was not going to go with him. I trusted my cardiologist implicitly, and if he had recommended the other one, that was good enough for me.

I still wanted to check out the orthopedic possibility, so I called an orthopedic surgeon whom I knew personally and told him my dilemma. He said, "Come on over to my house and bring your X-rays," which I did. He looked them over and said it could be orthopedic, but that was not likely. He explained how when MRIs first came out, orthopedic surgeons were discovering all kinds of abnormalities in all their patients' bones and finally realized that if they took a random sampling of people from the street, they would find a myriad of abnormalities there too, even though these people were not symptomatic. In other words, what showed up in the tests was not always enough to explain the symptoms.

At one point in our conversations I said, "I just experienced the tingling and numbness," and he said, "But Ed, you didn't move your head." Within twenty minutes, I was on the phone to the vascular surgeon recommended by my cardiologist. It was a Saturday afternoon and I had gotten him between procedures, but he said, "Come right over, bring your X-rays, and meet me at the hospital."

There he put the photographs on a backlit wall and carefully measured what he saw. (He was the first person I had seen do this.) Then he turned to me and said, "I can't be positive about your symptoms, but I am positive about what shows up here. Frankly, if it were up to me, I'd put you in the hospital tomorrow."

I was struck by several aspects of his approach: his reasoning, his willingness to admit where he was unsure, his stating his opinion clearly, and yet his not trying to pressure me into a decision. I explained that I had a speaking engagement on Tuesday and another one in North Carolina the following weekend, and I really didn't want to cancel them both. We made a bargain: I would go to the Tuesday engagement and then show up at the hospital, canceling the longer-range one.

At the last moment, as I entered the room for the procedure, the cardiac surgeon said, "We are not going to use the balloon but a new procedure. In fact, the inventor is here along with some other surgeons who want to learn more about it, so they will be watching also." At first this annoyed me and scared me with the lack of privacy, but then I decided it would make him all the more careful to do it right. And indeed, the procedure (a carotid endarterectomy) went well. I was out of the hospital in two days, flew to the West Coast for a speaking tour, and returned for the cardiac angioplasty two weeks later.

All during this period, I was helped immensely by two close friends, both in the medical field, who were able to funnel additional information to me about both procedures. They also helped with their humor, and with reminders of the addictiveness of information and the fallaciousness of expertise. I found they had just the right distance.

◆ LEADERSHIP THROUGH SELF-DIFFERENTIATION

In leading myself through this crisis, I tried to employ several principles. I was less aware that they were principles at the time; instead, my functioning seemed to come from what I believed about response of the organism, non-anxious presence, and so on.

Management of Information
As I have said, having information and expertise does not take the place of making decisions. One wants to make informed decisions; but being informed, if that takes over, can be overrated. Moreover, in gathering information it seemed to me that at some point, reliance on expertise can complicate matters. This is because the experts are not clear with you about what is a fact, what is a hypothesis, and what is a finding.

Findings, by definition, are based on a particular research method; the assumption is that other research methods might produce other or even contrary results. For example, it seemed important to me to have the information provided by the Doppler, the MRI, and the arteriogram. What was never explained to me until after the procedure, however, was that they had taken their pictures from different angles with different axes of symmetry, and what shows up as seventy percent on one could be eighty percent on another. I learned to be wary of those who were too sure.

Similarly, it was important to know if the prognoses were based on my condition or on statistical averages. I had learned this ten years previously, before my bypass surgery. A cardiac surgeon had come in to my room after my angiogram showed that I definitely needed a bypass and said, "I can pretty much assure you of ten good years." I remember thinking this was absurd, and I asked him, "Why not eleven?" (My roommate, whose physicians were at the other end of the room behind a curtain, later told me they said to one another, "This guy is asking pretty good questions.") What I knew to be true then was that this surgeon was a valve man, not a bypass man, and he had just come to this hospital and was probably looking for more experience. I later found out that he had gotten his estimate from a then-recent study (the procedure was only about ten years old at the time), showing that most people were living ten years.

The biggest issue regarding the management of information, though, is this: When should you decide you have had enough, and not let the fact that experts know more than you rob you of your responsibility for being decisive? I learned to handle the first part of this issue by the rule that whenever the same question asked several times in a row to various experts brought no new information, it was time to stop gathering facts.

The second lesson also came out of the bypass experience. At that time I was also in a quandary about how long to wait, having heard several opinions. It was a presidential election year with the election only a few weeks off, and suddenly I saw the way out. I would treat my physicians as my cabinet in a kind of "bypass confer-ence" with the Secretary of this, Secretary of that, and Secretary of the other. Each of them knew far more than I could possibly ever know about their bailiwick, but I was the one elected to be responsible for my territory.

Management of the Relationship System

I had had enough experience working with physicians and their families as well as consulting for medical practices and hospitals to know that as competent as any physician might be, everyone has ups and downs, prejudices, relational binds, Achilles' heels, and vulnerabilities. They also have other relationships with each other: joint business ventures; residences in the same neighborhood; memberships in the same club, church, or synagogue; children in the same class or on opposing soccer teams. I had observed in certain malpractice cases that where physicians had done poorly or handled relationships with their patients poorly, something usually was at work elsewhere in their life. (This has proved true of other professionals, also.) It has always seemed important to me, therefore, to pay attention to the relational networks of my physicians and me, including their relationships with one another. Not only might this contribute to the desired outcome, but it also would keep me de-triangled and would affect my own clarity.

I therefore practiced much of what was described in chapter 7 regarding emotional triangles. A diagram of the interlocking triangles would include all of these elements, and more:

◆ neurologist;
◆ cardiologist;
◆ vascular surgeon #1;
◆ cardiac surgeon;
◆ arteriogram person;
◆ internist;
◆ vascular surgeon #2;
◆ orthopedic surgeon.

The most obvious triangle (me, my heart, my brain) was the initial one with which I navigated my way through cardiology and neurology, all the differences in the specialties, the information-gathering, and so on. A second triangle involved the cardiac surgeon and the vascular surgeon; a third, the two vascular surgeons; a fourth, my internist and cardiologist, who had recommended different vascular surgeons; and a potential fifth involved the orthopedist and any of the above. Still another was with two different MRI testing places. In every case, I was in the "A" position—the apex—of the triangle.

Management of Anxiety

In one sense, this entire story is about the management of anxiety and, as I will show, overlaps with the management of one's self. The principles illustrated here have to do, among other things, with injecting humor and keeping things loose. The looser your presence is, the looser everyone's relationships will be with you and one another.

Two examples. First, a close relative had become very anxious about my condition and phoned me daily to find out the latest results. No matter what I did to assure her that things were under control, that I was managing fine, and that the information was accurate, she kept coming up with other possibilities that I had not thought of and urging me to take more tests, slow down, and so on and so on. Finally one day I decided to try and loosen things up by reversing the flow of anxiety. When she called that evening, even though I had reassuring information, I decided to get on the other side and said, "You know, I've been telling you that you are unnecessarily anxious and trying to reassure you all the time; but it turns out you were right after all. In fact, it's worse than you could possibly imagine." Whereupon I proceeded to exaggerate all my symptoms and give a horrendously gory idea of what the future entailed. There was a complete silence for a moment and then, with lilt in her voice, she said, "C'mon, what did you really find out?" From that point on, she stopped being pessimistic and I no longer had her haunting doubts to contend with.

Second, an example from medicine. The instrument used in angioplasty, whether it is a surgical instrument or a balloon, is not inserted directly into the artery but into a tube that is first inserted in the artery. After the procedure, the tube is not taken out immediately because the anti-clotting medicine (usually heparin) that is given during the procedure makes it more difficult for the insertion wound to heal. So the tube is taken out a few hours later after you have returned to your room.

That evening, two nurses, one male and one female, both black, obviously good friends, came into my room to remove the tube. As the male nurse who was going to perform the procedure began to explain it to me, it became immediately obvious from her responses to some of my questions that the female nurse was quite jittery about this. The male nurse leaned over me, one knee on the bed as he reached down to take the tube out, and it seemed to me that he was having a little trouble getting hold of it. I could gauge this by the female nurse's increased anxiety. Seeing that this was not going to help him, or me either, I said in a jocular tone, "Did you ever lose one of these?" (Bingo! I'd hit her fantasy.) The female nurse almost too quickly reacted with reassurance, "Oh no, Mr. Friedman, nothing like that has ever happened."

But the male nurse, now withdrawing the tube, responded, "Well, actually we did. At the beginning we didn't know to put a knob at the end so it wouldn't go down too far, and it slipped all the way down."

"What did you do?" I went on.

"Well, we had to do a bypass and replace the whole artery; we couldn't let him go round with the damn thing in there."

"Who paid for that?" I continued.

"Oh, the manufacturer. They were really scared."

As the triangle shifted, the female nurse now left the room, saying she had other duties to perform, while the male nurse and I went on in this vein until she had to call him out.

Management of Self

In a sense, everything I have described to this point could be listed under the title of "Management of Self": the effort to remain clear, the management of my own anxiety, the effort to remain de-triangled, the determination to be responsible and decisive. But there is another dimension which has simply to do with me and myself—perhaps another triangle.

On one occasion, I almost lost it. The anxiety in my family and the numerous questions being asked about whether I was sure I was doing the right thing began to get to me. I began to wonder if I had put in too much effort, or if I had missed something, and began to regress into precisely the attitudes that I had so proudly avoided.

Then one evening while at my beach house, I awoke at four in the morning ruminating about the danger, the loss of the future. I left the house and went down to the ocean. Standing on the beach beneath the stars, with the waves licking my sandals, I remembered how Columbus looked across the sea in the direction he had come from, and I got back in touch with that essence of adventure I had been writing about.

A second method of self-regulation I practiced was deep breathing. Biofeedback specialists have found that like meditation or prayer, deep breathing can keep you focused on yourself, and it has the additional advantage of oxygenating the blood. (I even tried it on the operating tables before going under.)

Here again, I had had some experience. When I was first told about the need for a bypass, the cardiologist at the time thrust a vial of nitroglycerin into my hand and said, "Every time you begin to feel those pains, take one quickly." I thought his response was a bit over-anxious, however—as subsequent events showed to be the case—and said to myself, "If I keep popping those nitros every time I feel a twinge, I will lose touch with my body. I will not know the true state of my arterial flow." So I made a bargain with myself that whenever the pains came on—and they could suddenly appear while just walking from my office to the elevator—I would go motionless for thirty seconds and try to regulate my reactivity. If the pain was still there after thirty seconds, I would take a nitro. In the month between the time I was given the nitro and the time I was wheeled into the operating room, I never had to take one.

I kept in mind two principles of healing to guide me. One was that the way one responds to processes starting up in one's body, either mental or physiological, could have an effect on how far they advance. The second was related to the immunity-integrity notion. It has long been my perception that there is a relationship between side effects and complications in medicine and a lack of integrity in the organism. Medicine usually explains aberrations as due to the partic-ular physiology of that person, including their genes. But if healing is a natural process that cannot be willed, and if an organization functions best when all parts are unified toward a goal, so it is with the human body. I therefore began to imagine that the complications that could occur from these surgeries—a heart attack or a stroke—

could be visualized as sabotage. The key was to have an integrated team.

I therefore sat down one evening and, as I would write one of my fables, I imagined a dialogue between my heart and my brain in which I discussed with them the importance of our working as a team and neither part screwing up the effort to help the other. As so often happens in writing stories or plays, the characters take over and tell the writer what to write. (The carotid artery is, after all, the pathway between the heart and the brain.) At some point, instead of writing down what I wanted them to say, they dictated to me, in unison: "We're doing fine; just take care of yourself!" It was probably at that moment that for the first time in my life I ceased equating myself with my brain.

To summarize these principles in time of crisis:

◆ Keep up your functioning; don't let crisis become the axis around which your world revolves.
◆ Develop a support system outside of the work system, such as professional helpers, family, and friends.
◆ Stay focused on long-term goals.
◆ Practice deep breathing, prayer, or meditation.
◆ Listen to your body.
◆ Watch the triangles.
◆ Work out the balance between being responsible for self and being labeled obstreperous.
◆ Keep the system loose through humor.
◆ It's time to make decisions when the same question brings no new information.
◆ Accept the possibility that your own functioning brought it on, which means that you may be able to influence your recuperation.

The table below further illustrates the tensions that leaders face in managing themselves during periods of crisis. There is no "right" answer to the question of how to find the correct balance between these opposing stances; all one can say is that to the extent that the leader has been continually working at self-differentiation, he or she is more likely to avoid the extremes. The key to self-regulation in crisis is (I) understanding that it is appropriate to go in different directions at different times; and (2) being able to go in one direction or the other without triggering a counterbalancing reaction.

TENSIONS IN LEADERSHIP DURING CRISIS

Lean on others	⟷	Stay accountable
Get information	⟷	Be decisive
Keep distance	⟷	Stay connected
Do not avoid	⟷	Do not try to solve
Keep up functioning	⟷	Refrain from avoiding or denying
Maintain commitment to see it through	⟷	Do not let it become the axis of life
Be willing to risk, take chances	⟷	Regulate reactivity
Work at being objective	⟷	Honor perversity
Appreciate loneliness	⟷	Do not cut off
Stay in triangles	⟷	Do not get triangled

◈ THE QUESTION OF SABOTAGE

Leaders endure two different kinds of crises. One has little to do with their own functioning—for example, a health crisis or a problem that bursts upon the scene, as if randomly, from the environment, as I have described above. The second type of crisis, however, is precipitated by the leader's own leadership—it is not due to failure or incompetence but to his or her success at self-differentiation. While this type of crisis has much in common with those described in the previous section, and while all the principles described there apply in this case as well, there is something special about this type of crisis that makes it worthy of note. It is the "second half" of the story of leadership and crisis.

As I said earlier, it is simply not possible to succeed at the effort of leadership through self-differentiation without triggering reactivity. This is a systemic phenomenon and a highly subtle problem that is generally not accounted for in leadership theory. Yet the capacity of a leader to be prepared for, to be aware of, and to learn how to skillfully deal with this type of crisis (sabotage) may be the most important aspect of leadership. It is literally the key to the kingdom.

So much is this the case that dealing with sabotage should be seen not as a way of handling reactions to well-differentiated leadership, but as part and parcel of the leadership process itself. Some of the principles to be enumerated in the first part of this chapter will carry over, of course; but the second type of crisis experienced by all leaders has its own typology of symptoms and its own prescriptions for survival.

As the saying goes, no good deed goes unpunished. Having spelled out throughout this book the value of self-differentiation, a caveat must now be added. Self-differentiation always triggers sabotage. This is the aspect of leadership that is not emphasized enough, if at all, by most leadership theories that focus on vision, team-building, and so forth. It differs from other kinds of crisis in that it is systemic in nature. The tendency of any leader when faced with this kind of crisis is to cease doing all that which had gone into differentiation. This is the moment when the adaptation pattern is likely to reverse itself and go in the direction of the most dependent and scared. This is the moment when a leader is most likely to have a failure of nerve and experience a strong temptation to seek a quick fix.

If there is a moment of truth in leadership, it is amid this type of crisis. The important thing to remember about the phenomenon of sabotage is that it is a *systemic* part of leadership—part and parcel of the leadership process. Another way of putting this is that a leader can never assume success because he or she has brought about a change. It is only after having first brought about a change and then subsequently endured the resultant sabotage that the leader can feel truly successful. While a military analogy might seem too aggressive for some, the fact of the matter is that an army has won a battle, not after it has invaded and captured, but only after it has successfully withstood counterattacks. Lest this sound too hostile, however, what needs to be added is that most sabotaging initiatives are mindless. Some of course are intentional, and thus a Category One crisis.

It is in the ability to deal with this systemic phenomenon that all principles addressed here about emotional process and differentiation culminate.

*Just because a page is torn off the calendar
does not mean that unit of time has ceased to exist.*

Epilogue

◆ THE PRESENCE
OF THE PAST

I grew up in the stickball streets of New York City, where car fenders served as the bases we touched as we ran by and trees were something that got in the way of a line drive. It was not until several decades later, as I was clearing saplings to make room for my own children's suburban playground, that I learned the truth about trees.

The first one, a skinny twelve-foot dogwood, came out so easily. All I had to do, it seemed, was bend it back and forth and watch it pull itself out of the ground by its own roots. Dogwoods rarely live more than a century. The second, however, hardly half that size, was a beech. To my shock, no amount of bending seemed to work. Finally I began to dig around its base, found its nourishing filigree network below the surface, and then to my surprise located its tap root, almost as thick as its trunk, which would not have surrendered to any force I exerted up above. Beeches can easily live six centuries or more, defying all manner of storms. The next tree was an oak, barely one or two generations of leaf old, maybe a foot above the ground. "This one will be the easiest," I thought, as I reached down with both hands to yank it from the soil. I lost the tug of war

248

completely. The well-known "sturdiness" of the oak begins at the beginning.

What made such a deep impression on this city-slicker that autumn afternoon was that the strength and fruitfulness that trees exhibit above the ground is connected in the most direct and natural manner to that part of the tree we rarely see. Indeed, a tree's root system not only formats its kind; it is the repository if not the presence of its past, as it grows through the generation-to-generation process of its limbs and branches. Most efforts to understand relationship systems recognize the impact of the past, but most often they only consider the immediately previous generation. As discussed above, the connection between generations is generally understood in billiard-ball terms: one generation has an impact on the next because it bumps up against it.

Borrowing Rupert Sheldrake's phrase, "the presence of the past," I want to suggest that just because a page is torn off the calendar does not mean that that unit of time has ceased to exist. What trees teach us is that the connection between generations of living things is more like an infinitely long collapsing telescope in which each generation to some extent overlaps the next, thereby contributing in a significant way to its form and shape. The resulting "persistence of form" has extraordinary importance for leaders. They must understand that what they are up against goes beyond the way things are organized. The nature of connections in the present can have more to do with what has been transmitted successively for many generations than with the logic of their contemporary relationship. This perspective also has revolutionary implications for the way consultants (whether to families or organizations) tend to operate, since they are constantly trying to fix problems through administrative, technological, or managerial changes—which is what most "advice" consists of. Unless these structural changes are accompanied by changes in an institution's multigenerational emotional processes, they will almost always regress eventually.

The presence of the past is equally evident in families, in organizations, in sports teams, and in entire nations. It is a process that transcends gender, class, or culture. In institutions, the presence of the past can be seen both in their ability to survive crisis and in their inability to change. This understanding differs from conventions in the social sciences, starting with the arbitrary convention regarding the way the previous generation is viewed. The problem with parents, after all, is that they had parents. This explains a lot. For example: Why do certain sports teams build dynasties? Why do some corporations recover and not others? What is it about American history that preserves democracy? Why is it not possible to plant the American Constitution in another land? Why is it so rare for family businesses to last more than three generations?

For leaders, the task in face of this reality is not merely a matter of understanding. Leadership is what mobilizes a system's multigenerational process; it can also throw the more pernicious processes off track. Furthermore, nothing in this chapter will be truer of one culture than another, one gender than another, one class than another. Well-differentiated leadership will have the same effects in any group. The presence of the past is the best argument for the ecumenicity of humankind.

This analysis has several benefits for leaders. First, it puts them in touch with the nature and power of emotional process. Second, it delineates both difficulties and capacities, offering a way of understanding how their own past supports the power of presence (differentiation). Third, it enables them to understand why relationships and institutions do not change. Finally and most important, it gives them an angle of entry into their own past, their differentiation, and their presence as leaders.

Here is an example of the presence of the past in the life of institutions. If you take any religious hierarchy in America, you will find that some institutions (churches or synagogues) have the reputation for being "plums" and some for being "pills." And all the clergy of that denomination know which is which. The plums generally have three or four clergy in a century, while the pills spit them out after a few years. I know of no hierarchical executive (bishop, district supervisor, executive, placement coordinator) who has ever succeeded in changing a pill into a plum. While religious institutions are often seen as esoteric, they are marvelous institutions for observing family process. They are on the border between families and workplaces, and are often family businesses.

The leadership lesson for a new clergyperson or executive is that without well-differentiated leadership, the past dysfunctions of a "pill" congregation can make a newly arrived leader ineffective as well. By contrast, a modest leader arriving in a highly differentiated "plum" congregation can appear to be an effective leader, pushed along by the effective functioning of the congregation.

On the third day of Creation, just before all forms of life were about to multiply, the Holy One said to his creatures:

> I see that what some of you treasure most is survival, while what others yearn for most is adventure. So I will give you each a choice. If what you want most is stability, then I will give you the power to regenerate any part you lose, but you must stay rooted where you grow. If, on the other hand, you prefer mobility, you also may have your wish, but you will be more at risk. For then I will not give you the ability to regain your previous form.

Those that chose stability we call trees, and those that chose opportunity became animals.

◆ INDEX